CRIME in Britain Today

CRIME
in Britain Today

**Clive Borrell and
Brian Cashinella**

Routledge & Kegan Paul
London

First published in 1975
by Routledge & Kegan Paul Ltd
Broadway House, 68-74 Carter Lane,
London EC4V 5EL
Set in Press Roman Medium by Autoset
and printed in Great Britain by
W & J Mackay Ltd Chatham
ISBN 0 7100 8232 0

Contents

To Pat and Julia

chapter one

Introduction

Crime costs Britain's taxpayers more than £500 million a year and yet seven out of ten of all crimes committed remain unsolved. It is a high price to pay for what seems so little achievement in return. There is ample evidence to show that the cost will continue to rise annually; but there cannot be such a sure forecast that the detection rate will rise as dramatically. A favourite pastime of the British is to cast around, seeking someone to blame. Are our police as wonderful as every visitor to Britain would have us believe? Are our law makers men of wisdom and foresight? Do our judges and magistrates help to deter law-breakers? Are the probation officers and the so-called 'do-gooders' too soft? Surely some—or even all to a degree—could be said to be responsible for the flourishing crime industry. Few, however, when they stare aghast at the frightening crime statistics, think to blame crime on the criminal. There is a growing, and perhaps dangerous, section of the community which feels that the criminal is more deserving of help and understanding than his victim. The reasons for committing crime seem to receive a higher priority than the fact of the crime itself, except, that is, from the police whose every action is microscopically examined for fault or error in an increasing atmosphere of mistrust.

One of the most disturbing aspects of human behaviour in the last decade has been the lack of leadership and example from our politicians—the law makers. Some have been proved to be corrupt and immoral and some just faded out of public view before the proof could be established. Whatever course they decided to take, their contempt for the very laws they made and the people they represented quickly rubbed off, leaving the attitude: 'If they can get away with it so can we.' As a result Britain is regarded by many abroad as a nation of 'fiddlers', with getting caught the greatest crime of all. Shop-lifting alone costs the country's storekeepers £1 million a week, much of it stolen by women aged between forty and seventy and children between seven and fifteen. Very few of those caught could honestly be said to be in need of the goods they stole. In fact, nine out of ten could have afforded to pay.

Fraud, not surprisingly in this climate, has flourished, too, running up an annual bill of tens of millions of pounds. Many detectives, however, are convinced that this is only the tip of the iceberg. By its very nature fraud is complicated and often cleverly perpetrated over long periods, making the task of unravelling its ramifications protracted, costly and sometimes practically pointless. Finding a jury intelligent enough to understand the complex details of a fraud case is no easy matter and is hardly fair to them, the defendant or, for that matter, the prosecution. It is in this sphere of crime that plea bargaining has come into its own, and, what is more, come into disrepute. This is where the defence agrees to plead guilty to some charges if the prosecution do not proceed on other charges to which the defendant pleads not guilty. If the two sides can strike a bargain it dispenses with the need for a jury. It is a poor sort of justice but it is a practical way out of what could at times be an almost impossible situation.

While fraud and theft have continued to increase steadily over the years violence and terrorism have become an everyday feature of life in Britain. Weapons, especially sawn-off shotguns, are frequently carried by thieves and used with little hesitation. The police, too, are being armed far more regularly, especially in London, where gangs have no compunction to exchange shots when cornered or chased. The troubles in Northern Ireland have undoubtedly influenced many in other parts of the United Kingdom with graphic reports on television and in the newspapers of bombings and shootings too vivid to ignore and lurid enough to impress. Film and live reports of small children hurling rocks and stones at policemen and soldiers in Belfast inevitably influence children elsewhere. One manifestation of this contempt for authority was noticed by the Fire Protection Association when they discovered that children were responsible for nearly one hundred school fires during 1973 costing just under £6 million in damage. In 1969, the year that the Ulster violence flared up, there were only thirty-seven school fires throughout the whole of Britain. Imitators and sympathisers of the IRA have also copied many of their techniques in attacks in England, Scotland and Wales. Car bombs, incendiaries hidden in empty packets of cigarettes, letter bombs, in fact, most of the terror tactics listed in the IRA manual have been tried in varying degrees. Scotland Yard was forced to set up a new squad—the Bomb Squad—with at times, as many as one hundred men to combat the urban guerrilla.

Without doubt the greatest aid to the criminal is the man-power shortage suffered by police forces throughout the United Kingdom. In London alone the force is about 5,000 below strength. On average there are three or four men to every square mile of the capital. Just a casual glance at the statistics for 1921 and 1973 illustrates the problem facing the commissioner, Sir Robert Mark. In 1921 the force was 21,020 strong. In 1973 this figure had dropped to 20,320. In 1921 crimes recorded in London totalled 17,404 of which 29 were homicides, 56 robberies, and 3,723 breaking offences of differing kinds. Crime recorded in London in 1973 amounted to 355,248 of which 110 were homicides, 2,680 were robberies and 72,750 were breaking offences. In just over fifty years crime increased twenty-fold and there were 700 fewer officers to combat it. The Chief Constable of Glasgow, Mr David McNee, whose force of just over 3,000 is short of 300 men analysed the reasons given by the men leaving. In the end he wrote to his police committee: 'I am persuaded that the main causes are unsocial hours, the consequent disruption to family life and the inadequacy of the pay offered to young men embarking on a career in the police force.'

The theorists who for years have exercised their minds enquiring into the causes of crime still have not been able to improve on the old fashioned sicknesses of greed, lust, hate, envy, jealousy and downright wickedness. In fact in some company it is considered heresy even to suggest that evil men, and women, actually exist or that some people have a natural 'bent' towards criminality. Yet, there is hardly a policeman in Britain who could not reel off the names of at least a dozen men and women he knows personally who have never done a day's work in their lives, have no intention of doing so and have what they have through crime. It seems a great pity that the so-called experts don't more often consult the real experts—the men on the beat—before they introduce new legislation or make profound statements which have little relevance in reality. In fact, the 'expert' that took the local Bobby off his bicycle and put him in a Panda car performed a disservice to both the police and the public. The policeman, instead of being part of the community, became more and more remote. Many chief constables quickly realised that what was gained in mobility was in no way comparable to the loss of contact with the local people. A few chief constables even had to rebuke some of the Panda car drivers for putting on weight—they were spending too much time sitting down and not getting enough exercise!

It has been widely accepted for many years that crime in Britain, or anywhere for that matter, will never be completely eradicated but at least, in certain circumstances, it can be contained or even cut. The greatest deterrent to some forms of crime is the certainty of detection and conviction, but with an under strength police force the odds on escape are still a good bet for the criminal. The future, however, is not wholly depressing. When one considers that there are about a million people living in Britain today with a criminal record who have not been convicted of another crime in the last ten years or longer, it does seem that the shock of being caught is all that is required by the amateur criminal to make him or her 'go straight' in the future.

To many of these people, most of whom have only ever committed that one crime, the shame of having a record and the fear that it will become known to people whose respect they have gained, is a punishment far greater than any judge could inflict. A committee set up by three eminent organisations, the Howard League for Penal Reform, Justice, and the National Association for the Care and Resettlement of Offenders, recommended that those who have spurned crime should be allowed to wipe the slate clean. Their records would still be retained by the police but only used if they were convicted again for a serious offence. The committee also suggested that anyone disclosing the previous record of a rehabilitated offender should be severely punished.

In an atmosphere of frank public accountability there is little about the police, their work or their views which is not generally known. Their work, especially when it results in a court case or some other dramatic conclusion, is widely reported in the press, radio and television. The views of chief constables and senior officers often get blanket coverage, as do those of the 90,000 strong Police Federation, the policeman's 'union'. On the other hand, Britain's 'secret' police, the Special Branch, is shrouded in mystery to the majority. Most of what has been written about it has been fiction. The function of the Branch is simple: State security, a delicate assignment requiring chameleon-like qualities. Since the end of the 1960s their task has been increasingly one of infiltrating extremist organisations which have flourished in London and some of the larger provincial cities.

One of their notable successes has been the way they have helped to capture IRA terrorists by paying informants, many of them Irishmen, to spy on their activities. Public concern was aroused, however, in 1974 when a young Irishman, Kenneth Lennon, was found shot in the head (a traditional method of assassination used by the IRA) lying in a ditch at Chipstead, Surrey. When his identity became known the National Council for Civil Liberties revealed that only three days earlier Lennon had made a seventeen page statement to one of their legal officials in which he claimed he had been blackmailed by the Special Branch to become a £20-a-month spy. What was more alarming were his final words as he left the Council's London offices: 'If they find me lying in a ditch you will know that what I have been telling you is true. I am afraid the Special Branch will murder me and make it look like an Irish job.' The Home Secretary ordered a full investigation by the Metropolitan Police. Two weeks later the report of their inquiry was on his desk—no blame was to be attached to any member of the force. Of necessity officers of the department operate in a cloak and dagger manner on occasions and sometimes have to bend the rules. If their assignment is concluded successfully such an action is forgotten. If, however, it goes wrong the public outcry that follows is deafening, especially from the direction of Westminster where some MPs, greedy for a headline, demand to have their cake—having already eaten it. They would probably choke on the crumbs if they knew how many politicians, at one time or another, were being discreetly watched by the police.

chapter two

Police

Manpower problem   Civilianisation and the clue seekers   Struggle for the
Commissioner's baton   CID in revolt   New complaints department   Special
Patrol Group   Armed police open fire   PC 'Piggy-in-the-middle'   Special
Branch manipulation   Regional Crime Squads   Dangerous informants

The greatest single problem confronting Britain's police today is a shortage of
manpower. With very few exceptions forces are well below establishment
strength and expensive recruiting campaigns have failed to attract enough
suitable candidates to plug the gaps which senior officers and the Home
Office fear will get even wider. Today's well educated young men, it seems,
do not see the police as a career which offers suitable rewards for their
talents. They feel that neither pay nor conditions can equal the opportunities
available in commercial or business life.

Not surprisingly, the problem is highlighted in London where the
Metropolitan Police, by far the largest single force in Britain, is nearly 5,000
men and women below strength. This can be more readily understood by a
simple comparison: If every policeman and policewoman in the whole of
Wales was moved overnight to London there would still be a considerable
number of vacancies in the Metropolitan force.

Even costly television and newspaper advertising campaigns—the last one
undertaken by Scotland Yard cost over £100,000—have failed to make any
significant inroads into the chronic shortage of manpower. But the situation
is being increasingly worsened by what is described as 'wastage', mainly early
retirements and resignations. Many forces in Britain are so alarmed at this
situation that they have begun to conduct their own surveys in a belated
attempt to discover why hundreds of first class officers, often with many
years invaluable experience, suddenly decide to resign—or, in their own
jargon, 'put their papers in'. Again, the Metropolitan police are taking the
situation perhaps more earnestly than others by employing their own full
time psychologist to interview disillusioned officers as they hand in their

uniforms.

Sir Robert Mark, in his first annual report as Commissioner of the Metropolitan Police, voiced his concern and listed the 'severe shortage of operational manpower aggravated by a continual loss of men to industry and other forces' as the first of five main problems he found on taking office in April 1972.

The Metropolitan Police, without any doubt, one of the most technically advanced and best respected forces in the world, had an establishment of 26,049 men and women and yet, at the time he submitted his worrying report to the Home Secretary, he was short of 4,589 officers. Sir Robert explained:

> While recruitment of men, women and cadets has shown an improvement as compared with 1971, the exceptionally large number of men leaving the force has outstripped the intake. This has occurred in spite of a vigorous recruitment drive backed by the most extensive police publicity campaign ever launched in London, using all the mass media including press, television, cinema and posters, and the announcement in the Autumn of a substantial pay increase. The slow build-up in manpower, evident in the early months, was later eroded by a sharp rise in premature retirements, which has resulted in the heaviest net reduction of strength in any one year since 1958. In the last six months of the year the overall wastage of 688 men exceeded recruitment by 172 and it is ominous that during the first three months of 1973, the quarter during which wastage is usually at its lowest, the overall net loss of men was at an even higher rate, totalling 116.

That, statistically speaking, is what makes Sir Robert's lot an unhappy one. Senior civil servants at the Home Office, not normally noted for their readiness to sanction expensive advertising campaigns, were perturbed by their apparent lack of success. It seemed the problem was insoluble. What little return they received for their money in terms of new recruits was instantly nullified by experienced officers deciding to quit for more lucrative employment elsewhere or moving to other, smaller forces where their talents would ensure speedier promotion. Sir Robert tried to rationalise the situation:

> The check in manpower growth suffered in 1972 and the serious outlook for the future has, I feel sure, developed from the special and mounting problems we are facing in the Metropolis. The situation underlines the urgent need for greater public awareness and more material recognition of the vital service the men and the women in the Force give to the community, often in unpleasant, difficult and dangerous circumstances. The demands on police in London are exceptional in two respects. In the first place, living and travelling conditions are less congenial and yet housing and transport are more expensive than elsewhere, and, although these are drawbacks common to all workers in the capital, the travelling difficulties of police officers are accentuated because of the requirement

for shift duties. Secondly, service in the Metropolitan Police brings burdens that are different in kind or scale from those met in provincial forces. In 1972 there were 470 demonstrations and processions in Central London, most of them at week-ends, many making heavy demands on police manpower.

This, in effect, is perhaps the heart of the problem. Any young married officer in the Metropolitan police literally cannot afford, on his salary, to live anywhere near central London. Housing is simply too expensive, even with a not over-generous rent allowance to help him pay the mortgage. For policemen with families the situation is just that much worse. It is not uncommon for a man to travel twenty or thirty miles between home and his police station and this often at times when public transport is virtually non-existent. Further, he is often required to do the same thing on his 'rest day' and at week-ends, in order that some embassy, whose politicians have incurred the wrath of one group or another, be protected from damage, invasion or worse. Sir Robert showed in the report that he was only too aware of the domestic difficulties that these situations could bring to family life:

All these and other tasks create a demand, often at short notice, for
stoppage of leave, for overtime and, more particularly, for weekend
working. Many wives of police officers go out to work and the demands for
weekend and overtime working intrude considerably into the times during
which police officers and their wives can be together with their families.
The uncertainty of whether it will be possible to spend any weekend
together can be particularly irksome. To this is added the anxiety of wives
of policemen that their husbands may be injured while engaged on
demonstrations or protection duties.

All these problems are not unique to the Metropolitan force. They are shared, in varying degrees, by every force in Britain. Like the army, most police forces have attempted to overcome manpower shortages by employing civilians in as many jobs as possible, clerical and administrative work, telephonists, drivers and so on; in fact, in every sphere where specialised and expert police knowledge is not an essential requirement. For example, only twenty years ago it would have been considered heresy even to suggest that civilians should assist officers investigating crime. Now, however, it is becoming a general rule that civilians are attached to crime investigation teams as 'scenes of crime officers'. Their expertise at finding clues has proved of great value to the police in the wave of bomb outrages in London and provincial cities.

Traffic wardens, that much maligned body of men and women who seem to have few friends, deserve special mention and commendation, too. Without their help, hardly a force in Britain could cope with the thousand-and-one problems that beset them daily. Ironically, the police were among the first and most vociferous critics of the introduction of traffic wardens. These 'yellow-perils' as they were unkindly nicknamed, would usurp the authority of the police, it was claimed. Experience has shown, in fact, that if anything, they have enhanced the standing of the police in the eyes of the public.

Other forces are examining the possibilities of employing retired policemen to carry out certain jobs. One of these, Hampshire, already has a sub-committee investigating whether the plan is feasible. Sir Douglas Osmond, chief constable of the county force, considers that about 200 jobs could be done by 'pension policemen'. In effect, this is a further move towards the 'civilianisation' of the police, leaving uniformed and CID staffs free to devote more time to investigate crime and protect the community.

Although speaking for his own Metropolitan force, Sir Robert Mark echoed the fears of all chief constables when he said: 'The danger of the present unsatisfactory and steadily worsening situation lies in the continually increasing demands decreasing police resources at a time when personal standards and respect for law and order in many parts of society are declining.'

In a nutshell, what Sir Robert was telling the Home Secretary was simply: I need more men but unless you substantially increase their pay and improve their conditions I can see little prospect of attracting them. The ball is in your court, what are you going to do about it? This broadside, coming from a man who, when he was appointed, was heralded by both Press and politicians as the 'liberal academic', seemed surprisingly out of character and more the words of a tough hard-liner that few expected he would be.

But the Commissioner, who had already been written off as a 'softie' by many policemen, including some of his own senior colleagues, had more surprises in store. In many ways he is typical of a new breed of chief police officer which is rapidly ousting the old fashioned 'Blimps in Blue', for decades on golf club terms with their local councillors but barely on nodding terms with their ratepayers. If ever there was a wind of change whistling around the corridors of Britain's town halls today, it is one that emanates from the chief constable's office. This is not to say that they do not have any respect for their political paymasters, but, at long last, the 1970s have thrown up a corps of intelligent, independent-minded men who refuse to be bludgeoned into submission by the Lord Mayor's chain.

Ironically, Robert Mark, soft-spoken, university educated, whose polite and gentle manner belies a tough and sometimes uncompromising attitude, had to struggle for respect. When appointed, he faced considerable opposition from some influential members of his own force, especially from senior and middle rank detectives who feared he was a 'weakling' who would take a soft line with criminals and rowdy demonstrators. There had been two men in the race for the Commissioner's baton once Sir John Waldron announced his impending retirement. One was Mr Mark, as he then was, who occupied the post of Deputy Commissioner. The other was Mr Peter Brodie, the Assistant Commissioner in charge of the criminal investigation department at Scotland Yard and head of 3,200 detectives who had tremendous admiration for his tough, traditional attitude to the business of dealing with criminals.

While little was known outside the confines of Scotland Yard, Fleet Street and Whitehall, of the power battle that was raging within the multi-storey office block in Victoria Street, the lower ranks of London's policemen were openly nailing their colours to one mast or the other. Their superiors, however, were playing a more diplomatic game. Although willing to express their preference privately, few would commit themselves openly for fear of it becoming known later that they had supported the loser. There is little doubt that the CID, almost to a man, favoured Mr Brodie for the job. Equally, most of the uniformed branch was behind Mr Mark. In the event, Mr Mark won and Mr Brodie quickly retired. Once the appointment was known, one senior detective at the Yard muttered philosophically: 'The King is dead, long live the King.' But this was one of the more generous remarks from the worried men of the CID who were still convinced the wrong man had been selected. Mark, they reasoned, was going to be anti-CID and their worst fears seemed to be justified when one of his first moves was to place divisional detectives under the authority of uniformed commanders. No longer would they be able to claim they were answerable only to 'The Governor'—as Mr Brodie was known throughout the CID. This and other immediate changes, did much to boost the morale of the uniformed men who had always lived in the shadow of their apparently more glamorous colleagues. While the changes cheered the man on the beat and gave his job a prestige it had lacked in the past, many detectives feared their role was being devalued in the eyes of the public. One disgruntled group took the unprecedented step of circulating a clandestine pamphlet which summed up their feelings about the change at the top. It read:

1 As from 24 April, 1972, the Criminal Investigation Department will cease to function as an effective crime fighting unit.
2 Senior CID officers will lose any responsibility which they thought they might have had.
3 In future TDCs (Temporary Detective Constables) will be recognised when on duty by the wearing of an armlet which instead of being white and blue as in the case of uniformed officers, will be blue and white.
4 The Flying Squad will be staffed by officers experienced in the art of 'flying' i.e. Central Traffic Division (Holier than thou).
5 Officers destined for intermediate and senior ranks will be so informed after a period of not more than two weeks service and will thereinafter not be required to perform mediocre tasks such as night duty, late turn, and tea boy.
6 CID officers will be recruited from the ranks of such august bodies as the Church Commissioners, Salvation Army, National Council for Civil Liberties and Black Power Movements.
7 The Fraud Squad will be disbanded and a new and more efficient Fraud Squad will be brought into being, staffed by the Juvenile Bureau.
8 Officers selected by secret ballot to be CID officers will be required to take a nine week residential course in animal husbandry, midwifery and the Mary Whitehouse (Clean up TV) course.

9 Detective inspectors will not be considered for promotion if they have more than one year overall service.

10 Current CID officers who have had Naval training in their previous calling will be considered for selection to Thames Division.

11 Any current CID officer who is living in a house which is valued in excess of £7,000 will be required to appear before a Board formed by journalists from *The Times* and *Sunday People* newspapers. Usual legal representation will not be allowed.

Amusing as it may have seemed to some, it was a fairly accurate barometer of CID feelings at the time, particularly since Mr Mark had appointed as his new head of detectives Mr Colin Woods, previously in charge of traffic police and a man with no recent experience in crime detection. Persistent rumours that the Yard's famous Flying Squad was to be disbanded (the rumours were totally wrong) did nothing to reduce the high temperature in CID offices. The reference to *The Times* and the *Sunday People* dated back to cases when both newspapers 'exposed' crooked detectives who were found guilty of accepting bribes and were sent to prison.

What many of the malcontents failed to realise at the time was that Mr Mark was trying to weld both branches into one efficient unit so that each would help and complement the other. Initially the new commissioner spent much time and energy explaining his policies to all ranks and made two points perfectly clear: first, he was going to administer London's police force his way and, second, those who refused to accept it could either keep quiet or move on. Some who felt they could not reconcile their own views with those of Mr Mark did leave the force and among them were several senior officers whose experience and expertise was difficult to replace. Some others were transferred into uniform and yet more were given stern lectures by their seniors who eventually saw the wisdom of what Mr Mark was attempting to do.

Not surprisingly the grumbling did not stop immediately. A small but persistently noisy lobby openly forecast that at the end of the Commissioner's first year in office crime figures would prove him to be a failure. In fact, some of the more militant detectives openly threatened, not in Mr Mark's hearing, of course, to 'cook' the statistics by juggling the figures which showed reported and detected crimes. Whether or not this threat was ever carried out is not known. What the figures eventually did show was that the number of indictable crimes reported to the police did increase—but so did the detection rate. In fact, Mr Mark must have been quietly pleased that of the 354,445 indictable crimes reported in his first year in London (an increase of 4.1 per cent on the previous year), 107,484 were cleared up (30.3 per cent). This clearly indicates that even if a few disgruntled detectives were not pulling their weight and refusing to give the new Commissioner their total support, the majority in the department were. The prophets of doom were proved wrong and Mr Mark's far-reaching changes were beginning to pay off. The figures also showed that every detective in the Metropolitan area had, on average, marginally over one hundred serious crimes to solve in that year with an encouraging success rate of about one in three.

While some of the introverted members of the Metropolitan police force were selfishly worrying about the implications of Mr Mark's revolutionary changes, newspapers, politicians and the public were expressing increasing concern about the frequency of reports of police corruption and behaviour. It was quickly recognised that the cancer of the 'bent copper' was nationwide and not confined solely to London, although, by the very nature of its size, the Metropolitan force came in for the most criticism. Mr Mark, like his fellow chief constables in other forces, recognised that a serious problem existed and unless checked was likely to get worse. The depth of the problem was, and still is, unknown. How can anyone, for instance, say with any certainty how many policemen out of one hundred would either accept a bribe or commit any other criminal offence? The opportunities for temptation in London are far greater than elsewhere in Britain. Most detectives have, at one time or another, been offered money to ignore a crime. It is fair to say that most detectives, underpaid though they are, react swiftly and angrily by immediately charging those who offer the bribe. Inevitably some, either through weak character, financial circumstances, or simply because they are criminally inclined, accept. It is a well-known and established fact and can probably never be totally eradicated, but it can be contained.

It has long been held by senior police officers that the most dangerous criminal is a popoliceman 'gone wrong'. Having accepted one bribe he is immediately vulnerable to blackmail which can, unless checked, completely undermine the whole structure of a police force. Mr Mark was quick to realise this and one of his first moves was to establish a special complaints department in Scotland Yard to investigate all allegations made against members of his force. It was given the code name A10 and staffed by forty CID men and twenty uniformed officers operating a round-the-clock shift system under Commander Raymon Anning. A large number of men recruited to the special squad is indicative of how seriously the Commissioner viewed the situation on his appointment. This was further emphasised when, within four months, the strength of the department was increased to eighty-four. Prior to this, the situation at Scotland Yard was getting out of hand with senior detectives, in increasing numbers, being taken off crime detection duties for 'rubber heeling', police jargon for investigating complaints against their own men. Of all the unpleasant tasks policemen have to perform, none is more distasteful than having to treat colleagues as suspected criminals. Furthermore, it was denuding the CID of valuable detectives who were desperately needed for major crime investigations elsewhere. The majority of complaints against the police, not only in London but throughout the country, come from two main groups; the criminal fraternity who have nothing to lose and take great delight in attempting to blacken an officer's reputation and subject him to the embarrassment of a formal internal inquiry; and minority pressure groups who are well versed in legal procedures. Others, of course, come from ordinary members of the public whose sense of justice and fair play has been offended. In its first six months, the new branch investigated 451 complaints. This was an indication of how necessary its establishment was and it quickly won itself the title of 'Gestapo' within the force, despite Mr Mark's warning that frivolous or malicious complaints would be reported to the Director of Public Prosecutions. After the initial wave of complaints this threat, which was subsequently carried out in several cases, did much to stem the flow.

Although the new department attracted considerable attention, both inside the police and from the public, another unusual unit was also receiving extensive coverage of its activities—the Yard's Special Patrol Group. Again, because of the unique problems of policing an area the size of greater London, it was the Metropolitan force which first experimented with such a squad. For example, all the foreign embassies are, naturally, situated there, the centre of the nation's political activity and, therefore it acts as a magnet for all forms of dissent, protest and demonstration. Furthermore, its very cosmopolitan nature creates difficulties and problems for the police which are not to be found elsewhere in the country.

Taking care of foreign diplomats, dealing delicately but firmly with yelling mobs of demonstrators, conducting intensive searches for missing children or murder victims, all placed an impossible burden on the already overstretched resources of the Metropolitan police. It was clearly advantageous to have a 'force within a force', a squad specially trained and equipped to handle these and other problems which were outside the normal day-to-day duties of policing London. So, in 1965, the Special Patrol Group was born. Originally it consisted of four units, each with one inspector, three sergeants and twenty constables. Two women officers were also attached to the group whose transport then consisted of small vans, equipped with two-way radios. Its role and strength has since been expanded—and is likely to increase further—as more and more demands are being made on police time.

Now it has an overall strength of 204 men, divided into six units, each stationed at strategic points around London. Besides its greater strength, the Special Patrol Group has won itself a considerable reputation as a 'corps d'élite' of the uniformed branch with more than half its members trained marksmen. They proudly claim that within an hour the whole group could be marshalled together, at any time of the day or night, for deployment anywhere in greater London. All members of the Group are volunteers and a vital quality insisted upon by the Yard is that each man must be well balanced and able to cope well under stress. There is no room for the headstrong type, or those liable to over-react to any difficult situation. Furthermore, each member is officially told before he joins:

General suitability to remain in the Group is not dependent on the number of arrests you make. It is determined by your application to any task that the Group might be given and whether you have the adaptability to deal with the public properly under any circumstances.

The work of the SPG is varied and often members are called upon to saturate an area plagued with house-breaking, vandalism or mugging. Such is their experience and expertise that some are assigned to assist in CID work, notably helping with the capture of the Kray and Richardson gangs. In recent years some of the Group, working in plain clothes, have been used for day and night surveillance on foreign embassies.

The SPG hit the newspaper headlines one spring morning in 1973 while one of its vehicles was on routine patrol in central London. Suddenly, over the radio, came a message: 'Three armed men are holding up staff at the Indian High Commission in the Aldwych.' Within a minute of receiving the call the vehicle was on the spot. Out jumped Police Constable Stanley Conley and his colleague, Police Constable George Burrows. Both were in uniform and each was armed with a police revolver. They raced to the foyer inside the High Commission building where they saw members of the staff being held at gunpoint by three young men, all Pakistanis. Eleven shots later two of the gang lay dead, both shot through the head. The third surrendered, uninjured. By this time thirty-five officers of the SPG had arrived in the Aldwych. Only then was the tragedy discovered—the young Pakistanis had been carrying toy guns.

Only three months earlier, another London Policeman had used his gun to kill. Police Constable Peter Slimon, then aged twenty-seven, had just been issued with a Webley revolver at Kensington police station having been assigned to guard the sensitive Israeli Embassy in Kensington Palace Gardens. He set off down Kensington High Street, busy with early morning shoppers. As he neared the National Westminster Bank a passer-by shouted: 'The bank is being held up by armed men.' The young officer drew his revolver, which had been concealed in the pocket of the raincoat he was wearing over his uniform, and went inside. As he walked through the glass doors a man inside swivelled round and pointed a double barrelled shotgun at him. What happened after that was explained by Judge Edward Clark who later tried two men at the Central Criminal Court for their part in the robbery:

It might seem amazing to people in other countries that Police Constable Slimon stood in the middle of the bank and shouted 'I am a police officer. I am armed,' giving the potential murderers the opportunity of blowing his head off. In other countries police officers would have probably shot them without warning. You, in accordance with our fairness, gave these criminals an opportunity, which they did not take to surrender. Instead at that moment when they were trying to kill you, you shot one of them. Your conduct was of the highest possible standard and the most outstanding example I have ever come across, of an officer behaving in devotion to duty and with extreme bravery.

The young constable, himself wounded in the chest and arms by the blast from the shotgun, killed one of the bandits and injured another as he lay bleeding on the pavement outside the bank. He was hailed as a hero and, after the trial, photographers clicked their shutters. 'Let's have a smile,' they chorused as the stern-faced Police Constable Slimon walked outside. 'I don't want to look happy. A man has been shot dead,' he told them.

Public reaction to this shooting was predictable. No praise was too high for the brave young constable. He had, after all, been severely wounded himself and had taken on a gang of bank robbers single-handed in the best British tradition. On the other hand, the two officers involved in the Aldwych shooting were heavily criticised for their action, mainly, perhaps, because it was later discovered the three coloured men's guns were only imitations.

This, according to many critics, was unfair. Policemen were not supposed to go around shooting men who were, in fact, unarmed. But both situations were in many ways parallel. Constables Conley and Burrows had no means of knowing that the men they faced could not shoot back. They were, after all, hiding behind pillars for most of the time and refused to throw down their 'arms' despite repeated warnings from two officers wearing uniform. For Conley and Burrows, the dilemma was frightening: to shoot or not to shoot—that was the very real question they faced. As far as they were aware, innocent members of the High Commission staff were in danger of being murdered in cold blood. Many of the early shots fired by the two officers were specifically intended to encourage the hold-up men to drop their 'arms' and surrender. Even if language was a barrier, the three men could have been left in no doubt that their lives were in imminent danger. Without seeking to libel the majority of the British public, the general reaction was that the police were right to shoot the two men in those circumstances. There was, of course, the usual outcry from those who seem to be permanently perched on the end of a microphone, ready to criticise the police in the most vociferous terms to anyone prepared to listen. Some suggested the two officers, instead of opening fire with their revolvers, should have used tear gas to deal with the 'gunmen'. Others considered they should have fired wooden bullets, unaware perhaps of the fact that these have been prohibited—even in war—for more than fifty years by the Geneva Convention because of their devastating capacity to cause horrifying injuries. Why not use rubber bullets, like they use in Northern Ireland, others asked. The answer is simple. Rubber bullets are specifically used for crowd control and are hopelessly inaccurate when fired at a target.

When the dust had settled on this episode, the majority of people still genuinely believed the British police were not armed and still had to rely on their truncheons and the sporting good nature of criminals. The number of occasions when arms are issued to police is increasing annually. If terrorism in Britain's major cities continues to escalate it is certain that guns will become a regular feature of police equipment. Sadly, it now seems certain that the days of the ruddy-faced 'bobby' cycling round his beat with nothing more lethal than his truncheon and whistle are gone forever. Without doubt, the abolition of capital punishment has meant that more and more criminals are prepared to use guns. Equally, it is certain that the police will be forced into a position whereby they have no alternative but to carry arms themselves, whether they like it or not. It is unlikely, however, that we shall see all policemen carrying guns as part of their uniform, at least in the foreseeable future. Gun law will have to reach virtually epidemic proportions in Britain before that situation is likely to arise. Rather, the likelihood is that it will soon be commonplace for an officer to request permission to carry a revolver while on duties he considers potentially dangerous to himself or the public.

However, recent figures show that the number of occasions on which policemen carried guns is increasing dramatically in Britain. These came in a Parliamentary reply to a question from Mr Michael Meacher, Labour MP for Oldham West, at a time when there was nationwide concern at the number of shooting incidents in which policemen exchanged fire with armed criminals. The most sensational Parliamentary news often has a habit of coming out almost casually and this was no exception. For Mr Meacher released the text of the Home Secretary's reply, which said that the number of occasions in England and Wales on which one or more firearms were issued in connection with a particular incident involving criminals or other persons known or believed to be armed and dangerous were: 1970 - 1,072; 1971 - 1,935; 1972 - 2,237.

The figures startled many, including some with close police connections, for they meant that officers were issued, on average, with firearms every four hours. Mr Robert Carr, then the Home Secretary explained: 'The police officers concerned retained the fire arms only for the duration of each particular incident.' He then attempted to allay any public fears by stressing that the issued guns were rarely fired. In fact, they had been used only three times 'against criminals or other persons'. He listed the three events: the first, in Hertfordshire in 1971 when a man who was wanted for stealing firearms and the attempted murder of a policeman fired at officers attempting to arrest him. Four shots were fired at the man, one of them wounding him in the shoulder; the second, occurred in London the following year when a man who entered the country illegally was shot in the foot by a policeman who believed him to be armed; the third, was the Kensington Bank raid when Police Constable Slimon shot two of the robbers including the one who died.

Mr Carr spoke of a common policy adopted by chief police officers in England and Wales which was simply: Firearms were issued to policemen only in circumstances when they might have to face a person who was armed and dangerous or attempting to arrest such a person. Two main points emerged from this reply. The first was that although policemen in Britain still, as a rule, carried out their duties unarmed the line of the graph was unmistakably upwards which could only mean one thing: an increasing number of criminals were relying on the use of weapons, or at least the threat implicit in carrying one, to achieve their object. The second was as the Home Secretary particularly emphasised, official marksmen. No officer without such qualifications would be allowed to handle a gun. What Mr Carr may not have known was the effect such a rule has on policemen and their families. Among the men themselves, those who fail to qualify feel that somehow their 'potency' has been called into question. Some policemen say that trained marksmen are regarded within the force to have a slight edge on their colleagues who fail the stiff arms course. Ironically, wives and families of the 'failures' are usually delighted. For they know that their sons and husbands will not be allowed to carry a pistol, revolver or rifle, and are therefore less likely to become involved in a pitched battle with bullets flying between the police and violent criminals.

But there is one police force in Britain which is at the moment permanently armed—The Royal Ulster Constabulary. Their circumstances are, however, somewhat different from those in the rest of the United Kingdom. Whereas a policeman on the mainland would be unfortunate to come face to face with a gunman even once during a long career, men of the RUC are likely to look down the wrong end of a gun barrel virtually every week as a target for an IRA or other extremist gunman. To meet this situation RUC officers are intimately familiar with the regular use of not only side arms but sub-machine guns and even light machine guns. They have to be, for their stations, heavily fortified, are likely to come under attack at any time. Even off duty they need to be armed to protect their homes and their families who have also become frequent targets for terrorist attacks. One senior RUC officer explained:

> We have had a long history of being armed and every man in the force—and woman for that matter—has been trained to use their weapons efficiently and meaningfully. We lost our arms for a while when Sir Arthur Young was appointed from the City of London Police to take over the RUC on a temporary basis. During his time here there was considerable reorganisation and a drastic re-thinking of the role we had to play in the Province because many people saw us as an arm of the Government, a sort of para-military organisation. We do not see ourselves in this way at all. We regard ourselves as ordinary bobbies doing the same job that policemen do in the rest of Britain. While there were conflicting views about the rights and wrongs of the re-organisation that Sir Arthur instigated one thing that did win approval was the disarming of the police. Now the IRA and later, extremists from the Protestant side, have made it impossible for us to walk around without some form of firearm protection. Even with guns a large number of our men have been murdered, many of them senselessly and mercilessly shot in the back. You cannot legislate or protect yourself from a gunman who resorts to these methods. But make no mistake, as soon as this trouble is over we want to return to being an unarmed force. We are looking forward to the day that we can put away our guns and resume a civilised way of life.

Traditionally the British policeman has loathed weapons of any sort and moves to arm him on a permanent basis would be fiercely resisted at all levels. This in itself is an indicator to the character of the average policeman in this country. To arm the force would certainly have two immediate effects; mass resignations of those quite unprepared to become legalised gunmen;

recruitment of 'cowboys' who see some form of glamour and glory in displaying a gun on the hip. The obvious repercussion from such a move would clearly be an open invitation to criminals in even greater numbers to match gun for gun. For in the final analysis the maintenance of law and order can be honed down to the constant struggle between the forces of justice protecting society from the ambitions of the criminal classes. One has only to look across the Atlantic to the USA which (while admittedly its social order and historic background is so different from ours) is reaping the rewards of arming police with staggering numbers of violent deaths, which are increasing every year.

In the end, the choice rests with the British public. Any society given the right to choose gets the police force it deserves. Do we want gun-toting trigger happy 'cops' or our traditionally friendly neighbourhood constables who are happier helping than shooting?

However, there is another aspect of the policeman's role which is causing increasing concern among many senior officers in Britain. It is simply: how far should policemen become involved in situations which have politics as their base root? We have seen the growth of political demonstration, particularly in London, and in some respects it has become an acceptable part of every day police duty. But the presence of police at industrial disputes, at pit heads, engineering firms and dock gates is a comparatively new and some say unhealthy phenomenon. In these cases it usually falls to the policeman to ensure that picket lines operate in an orderly fashion, that 'blackleg' labour is allowed to enter premises involved in any dispute unharmed and unhindered. They have found themselves facing angry workers who feel they have a legitimate grievance against the management and want to close factories and pits completely. Strictly speaking, the dispute is rarely one in which law and order is a question. But police, called in to maintain the public peace and safety, find themselves the butt of workers' fury and frustration. More frequently these days, 'visiting' speakers, often little more than rabble rousers with a certain penchant for oratory, whip up ill-feeling towards the police where it previously did not exist. It must be hard for any young constable to have to stand and listen to himself being publicly denounced as a 'pig' and 'a tool of the Capitalists'. Few stop to think that, in many of these situations, his weekly take-home pay could easily be half that of the strikers. Occasionally the officers on such duties are not only abused. There have been several instances of them being attacked by an assortment of weapons, including bricks, iron bars, bill hooks and—in at least one case—meat cleavers and car jacks.

The question is: should the policeman be there at all, particularly in disputes which centre around the rights and wrongs of a purely industrial squabble? For example, during the furore over the Industrial Relations Bill, which later became law, we had on the one hand the trades unionists, bitterly opposed to the legislation, and doing everything in their power to stop it working effectively. On the other, industrialists and the Conservative Party saw it as an essential ingredient in curing the nation's economic ills. Inevitably, the two were at loggerheads and the unfortunate policeman was again in the middle of a potentially explosive situation which was basically political and which was more likely to result in injury, or worse, to the 'neutral' officer than either of the opponents. The policeman himself may have had very strong views about the Act. But then, as now, he must not express these in public and, anyway, he is prohibited by law from taking industrial action on his own behalf and cannot use the ultimate strike weapon.

Often, but usually unnoticed at these affairs, are members of the Special Branch, men whose job it is to protect the security of the State against all forms of subversion, whether from internal political strife, or determined foreigners anxious to undermine the well-being of the nation by a variety of methods. In many ways, the title of the Special Branch is a misnomer because the men who make up the strength of the department are no more 'special' than any other serving officer. The only difference between them and any other police department is the nature of the work they undertake.

For example, while detectives are more likely to spend their time chasing and hopefully, capturing robbers, burglars, murderers, rapists and fraudsmen, and so on, members of the Special Branch endeavour to maintain the political 'status quo'. In other words, anarchists, revolutionaries, spies and anyone else who wishes to change the British way of life by means other than by the established democratic process, will become their responsibility. So while other detectives will have informers among what might be classified as 'ordinary' criminals, the Special Branch men are keener to discover, for example, the intentions of some extremist organisations. For this reason they are avid readers of the 'underground Press', attenders of obscure political meetings, frequenters of coffee bars where the revolutionary 'intelligentsia' hold court, and diplomatic cocktail parties where a loose word over a dry martini could mean a vital piece in an international jigsaw puzzle and the discovery of a dangerous spy network. But there is a general feeling among many people that the Special Branch has some magical quality, a charisma which automatically makes a member of the department a master detective.

In fact, the SB—as they are called—have one of the most boring and least exciting tasks in crime prevention and detection. Contrary to their television image, which appears to give the distinct impression to the general and unknowing public, that each man has direct and personal access to the Prime Minister at least, many of these detectives would readily claim that standing in the pouring rain at a union meeting, or one sponsored by a political organisation, is so unattractive that pounding the 'beat' in uniform would be a welcome and more exciting relief.

For example, most forces throughout the country have their own Special Branch officers, not always an employment to be envied within the established structure of the police force. Can there be, for instance, anything apparently more mundane than being a member of the Special Branch in

Walsall, Watford or Warrington? Or Barnsley, Bolton and Brighton? All have SB men within their forces, for it should be remembered that not all plots against the State are formulated behind closed doors in Camden Town, Kilburn or even Westminster. Many are concocted elsewhere and it is the SB man's job to know, politically speaking, what is happening in his own particular area. It is the jigsaw within the national pattern that is important. A plot to blow up London's underground may originate in Liverpool just as easily as in, say, Chelsea.

To give a specific case: it is now known that Special Branch detectives, many disguised to fit suitably into their surroundings, infiltrated anarchist and other extremist cells in 1968 when plans were being actively pursued to disrupt a major portion of central London by direct sabotage. Although much cold water has been poured on what could well have been a disastrous situation for the capital—many groups, for example denied that any such plans were afoot—it was established beyond doubt that some extremist organisations as far apart as Liverpool, Scotland and South Wales, were actively engaged in a scheme to plant bombs in Westminster and the City of London. Further, there was direct evidence that their plans could have more serious consequences for, although it may have seemed far-fetched at the time, serious plotting was taking place on how to take over, on military lines, such institutions as the Bank of England, Lloyd's, the Stock Exchange, Ministry of Defence major communication centres and even Scotland Yard itself.

All this was discovered by Special Branch officers who had infiltrated a number of organisations—in the early summer of 1968. The timing is significant because it bears directly on the period of the student riots in Paris which disrupted the French capital during May of that year. It was the era of 'Danny the Red' the German-born leader of the French students and 'Red Rudi' another German with political aspirations who was later shot and seriously injured. There is little doubt that these and other people were convinced the same situation of confusion, disorder, even almost anarchy could be brought to prevail in London. The coup, for that is exactly what it would have been, was set for 28 October, the day of a planned major anti-Vietnam war demonstration to the United States Embassy in Grosvenor Square in London's Mayfair. In fact, apart from the usual crop of injuries, many of them policemen, and arrests there was no attempt to sabotage or disrupt London, or anywhere else. Why? There are two possible explanations. The first, and the one propounded by the extremist groups themselves is that there never was a plot. They have, even to this day, consistently laughed off the suggestion as 'Special Branch nonsense and rumours'. The march, they insist, was nothing more than that—a show of solidarity by people who objected to 'American aggression' in Vietnam. The second—and the one which we, frankly, are most disposed to believe—is that such a plot did exist but was thwarted by the advance publicity it received. Significantly, perhaps, we are in a unique position to know, for we broke the story jointly in *The*

Times once the Special Branch was certain that it had concrete evidence of what was being planned. After our story had appeared and was taken up by the rest of Fleet Street, Mr James Callaghan, the Home Secretary in the then Labour Government, called a secret meeting of newspaper editors and proprietors.

At this gathering in the Home Office he privately voiced his fears that 'something' could well happen on 28 October. As a result a 'hot line' was opened between his private office and Sir John Waldron, then the Scotland Yard Commissioner. Furthermore, it can now be disclosed, scores of police were given hurried special firearms training to meet any eventuality and police leave was cancelled over a wide area in the south of England. Equally significantly, immigration restrictions were placed on known trouble makers from the Continent – particularly Danny the Red and Red Rudi and their followers who had disrupted Paris. Mr Callaghan made it quite clear that he would take no chances if these people tried to cause trouble at a time when anti-Vietnam War feeling was running high among the student population in this country. At the same time, Sir John Waldron called a meeting at Scotland Yard of senior Fleet Street editorial executives and spoke freely, but privately, of his fears. There was no doubt that both he and Mr Callaghan took the situation seriously and considered the Special Branch information warranted every possible precaution being taken. In the end little or nothing on that day happened. Certainly nothing as catastrophic as was feared. Again, why? Because the Special Branch, having informed the Home Secretary via the Commissioner of the threat, had still not fully completed its role in the affair. It was essential, politically, that an 'anti-demonstration feeling' should be fired in the public imagination. It was felt necessary that public opinion should be against the demonstration, with all its hidden threats, without alarming people generally that London was about to suffer like many other Continental capitals.

The Special Branch then hatched up their own plot. They decided to 'leak' their fears to the press and allow the situation to snowball. Public antipathy would do the rest, they reasoned. Certain Fleet Street journalists, including ourselves were quite independently appraised of the situation through the 'old boy' network. It was a story no one could refuse, coming from such an immaculate source. It was a story no newspaper could ignore, and as article followed article, public reaction against the march quickly grew. It was a clear case of the media being manipulated by the Special Branch to serve their own ends. But in our view it was totally justifiable, because the consequences otherwise could have been devastating. What might have happened had the Special Branch not been aware of the threats? Would life that day in London have been so comparatively peaceful? No one can know, but it serves to illustrate the function and the techniques employed by the Special Branch within the context of the British police organisation.

Inevitably, at a time in which the law is constantly being challenged and questioned, the Special Branch is not without its critics. There are occasions, of course, when, like any other group of human beings, they make mistakes. In a debate on the police in the House of Commons in December 1974 Mr Roy Jenkins, the Home Secretary, spelled out the problems facing the Branch. The Branch, he said, knew that it had to operate within 'proper limits' but one of the difficulties with all police work was that if they failed to give adequate protection to the public they were bitterly criticised. If on the other hand, he commented, they stepped an inch over the line, they were just as bitterly criticised. This was part of the challenge of police work, Mr Jenkins told the House, to strike the right balance—'and a very difficult balance it was'.

Mr John Prescott, MP for Hull, was not, however, altogether convinced by the Home Secretary's remarks. On the question of confidence in the police, Mr Prescott agreed, that they were moving into more delicate social areas, such as race relations, trade union disputes and civil liberties—all highly sensitive areas which were liable to misinterpretation and lack of confidence in those enforcing the law. He said that the Branch was originally set up to deal with Irish terrorists and to combat a potential threat to the State but, whereas the Home Secretary had said that the Branch operated within proper limits, it was beginning to become clear from a number of incidents that 'the Branch is involved in matters which certainly do not constitute a potential threat to the State'. He certainly doubted whether the Special Branch had a role in industrial relations, for example. As a former seaman he said he had seen Special Branch activities with his own eyes and had evidence that they had been involved in seamen's disputes.

Mr Prescott said that the manager of one company engaged in a dispute had admitted that he was the contact man for the Special Branch and that he had fed information to the Branch about workers because one of them belonged to the International Socialist Group. He cited another example; that of the admission by the Chief Constable of Kent that a Special Branch man had been present at a nurses' demonstration with a camera (which contained no film). Mr Prescott was anxious to know who it was that decided which groups of industrial workers should be brought to the attention of the Special Branch.

In many ways it is heartening to know that while Britain has a democratic parliament the 'S' in SB will stand for Special and not Secret. On the other hand, by the very nature of their task, much of what the Special Branch does has to remain secret.

Unlike many other police officers, it is often difficult to 'spot' a man from the Special Branch. Quite often his appearance is far from that of the screen image of a detective. More likely, he is the complete antithesis—sometimes long haired, possibly unshaven, clothed in ragged denims but always very much part of the environment in which he has been assigned to operate. The Special Branch detective, a chameleon-like character, is able to slot into surroundings so as to become unobtrusive. A docker in Bermondsey looks like a docker; a miner in Yorkshire looks like a miner; a Special Branch man must be able to adopt both roles when the need arises.

In this sense he is by no means unique. Detectives in all branches in specialist departments need to play the chameleon at some time or other. Because of the very nature of things London has more heavily manned and specialised squads than any other police force in Britain. It is imperative that detectives assigned to deal with crime in a particular field look the part. Even the slightest hint that a stranger might be 'Old Bill' (a policeman) he would be immediately rumbled, thereby placing himself in danger and possibly ruining an important investigation.

On the other hand, it would be wrong to give the impression that detectives walk around in wigs and false beards every day. These extreme lengths are only on special assignments. Generally, detectives are reasonably well dressed and as such can venture without embarrassment into any surroundings, rich or poor. As a rule they need to be well dressed. Many have experienced the psychological disadvantage of being faced with an opponent wardrobed by Savile Row while being clad in a cheap 'off the peg' suit. Another simple, but totally relevant, reason for the usually smart appearance of most detectives is that—apart from their own personal pride—the majority of criminals with any claim to professionalism are 'snappy' dressers. Members of the Fraud Squad for example, spend countless hours in company offices surrounded by highly paid executives. Their job, as the inquisitors in Britain's biggest illegal growth industry is to pick out the genuine businessman from the one attempting to make a fortune the easy way.

Most criminals have the same objective. Some try robbing banks, others deal only in stolen works of art, some rely on their arrogance and personality to cash books of 'dud' cheques and a few even manufacture their own money by forging currency and travellers' cheques. Scotland Yard, again only because the problem is most prevalent in London, has expert squads or specialist detectives hounding them all. In fact, there is not one sphere of criminal activity that has not received special attention from one group or another within the confines of the Yard's Victoria Street headquarters.

There is, however, one group of policemen who together operate on a nation-wide basis—the Regional Crime Squads. The men of the RCS—the 'Scarlet Pimpernels' as they are known by their colleagues—are linked through the National Co-ordinator, Mr Leonard 'Nipper' Read at Tintagel House, a multi-storey office block on the south bank of the Thames facing the Houses of Parliament. Mr Read, the man responsible for bringing the notorious Kray twins to justice, is in day-to-day control of the squads throughout the country on a regional basis. The nine squads, covering England and Wales—there is a further one responsible for the whole of Scotland—deal solely with long term serious crime. The very nature of their inquiries allows them to cross traditional county police boundaries and often squad officers, based in Cornwall, for example, turn up quite unexpectedly on the trail of a wanted criminal in a rural area of Yorkshire where only the chief officer of that force knows of their presence. Conversely, inquiries by officers of the RCS in Wales, for instance, are sometimes finalised hundreds of miles away from their own headquarters. As one of the former co-ordinators of the Squad, Mr Ian Forbes, explained: 'We are called the Scarlet Pimpernels because of our motto—"We seek them here, we seek them there, we seek those crafty bastards everywhere." ' Their motto best describes the way they operate. Men of the RCS, like the famous Scotland Yard Flying Squad, have a reputation, a justifiable one, for being one of the new élite squads of detectives in Britain.

Their record is already impressive, although they have been established only since 1965. If ever a team of detectives, which numbers just under 1,000 men and women, could be described as the nation's 'Ghost Squad' it is the Regional Crime Squad. For, although they often unravel complicated crime in one area, they usually hand over the end of the inquiry to the local force which then instigates prosecutions. Then they are off elsewhere to solve a serious criminal problem in another area.

As with all specialist crime investigation squads, the RCS depends largely on tip-offs from informants. These are often members of the criminal fraternity themselves and can, sometimes, be dangerous men. More often than not, they flit around the fringes of the criminal world, picking up snippets of information at bars, betting shops, anywhere that villains might be found. As any detective will be happy to confirm, these 'snouts', as they are known, seem to have an uncanny knack of treading a razor's edge, often coming within a hair's breadth of being arrested for criminal activity. At the most, these informants earn only a few pounds for passing on the latest tip to the police. It is hardly a lucrative activity and often not worth the risks they run should they be discovered by the criminals they 'shop' to detectives.

But, whilst being a danger to their own kind, they can also cause considerable problems for the police who attempt to steer them clear of trouble. For example, by protecting his informant—and most officers regard this as part of the unofficial 'deal'—a policeman may unwittingly lay himself open to allegations of assisting a criminal act. It is a thin dividing line, as some Metropolitan police officers have discovered to their cost. For, by seeming to show undue favour towards his informant, the over-zealous officer can find himself in a position where he lays himself open to blackmail and threats of 'exposure'.

To protect his officers from falling into this dangerous trap, Sir Robert Mark issued an order in 1972 to all his detectives that, under no circumstances, should junior ranks—constables and sergeants—keep secret rendezvous with underworld tipsters without formal permission of a senior colleague, or unless accompanied by one. It was a major internal policy decision and one which the Yard even denied, for a time, existed. Its effect, detectives feared, would be catastrophic; the flow of regular information would dry up. Without it, no detective force could function effectively. On the other hand, criminals regarded it as a bonus for their activities for it meant they could, unless caught almost by accident, go about their business with even greater confidence. Working detectives were in a quandary. What should they do, they argued, quoting the well-worn, but fairly accurate CID adage: 'A detective is only as good as his informants'. In the end, a large number ignored the edict and, with the risk of disciplinary action always hovering about them, they continued with the meetings. There was little else they could do. An officer, being pressed to clear up a string of crimes in his area had no alternative but to go where the information which might lead to arrests could be found. It was an absurd situation, rather like asking a boxer to fight with one arm tied behind his back.

The ruling, however, did have one good side effect—it enhanced the reputation and increased the value of the Criminal Intelligence Bureau, a department used for collecting, collating and disseminating information about known criminals throughout the country. Further, it added status to the role of the collator, an officer permanently employed at every police station to keep a comprehensive filing system on local criminals. By meticulously cross referencing every scrap of information about known criminals, a collator was in a position greatly to assist the CID. To any collator no detail is too trivial. The fact that a criminal wears only brown shoes, prefers pastel-coloured shirts, drinks left-handed, has some distinctive mannerism or other, all goes towards building a complete picture of the man. He is helped constantly by uniformed officers on the 'beat' as well as detectives. One constable might report seeing so-and-so sipping tea in a local cafe with strangers to the area. To the casual observer it would mean nothing. To the collator, in the light of other information he had received about the man, it might prove enough to warrant special round-the-clock watches being kept on the individual and his friends.

But there are other files on all known criminals, apart from those kept at a local level. These are housed in the Criminal Records Office at New Scotland Yard and constitute the most comprehensive and highly detailed account of a criminal's career. In all about four million files are kept and more than two million sets of fingerprints. Anyone who has a court conviction, no matter how trivial, can be checked within seconds by the highly efficient records staff who receive hundreds of telephone calls each day from officers throughout the country. They are, of course, officially confidential and classified and not openly available to anyone but the police.

Although many sources of information are available to the police, detectives, especially, still have to rely to a large extent on the public for help and assistance in many of their inquiries. But there seems to be a new morality creeping into the British way of life, possibly caused by economic pressures, whereby the public readily condone certain types of crime, particularly those euphemistically described as 'fair perks'.

In these circumstances, and the others already described, the role of the police is becoming even more difficult and, to some extent, more hazardous. While public assistance towards them may, in certain circumstances, be waning, and a new sense of 'my rights' is certainly becoming part of the British way of life, can we really expect our law enforcement authority to be any more efficient? Their job is difficult and often dangerous; their hours long, domestically anti-social and unpredictable; their pay is comparatively poor and job prospects are not all they might be; their responsibilities are onerous with little margin for human error. The vocational spirit has been widely canvassed on behalf of other public service jobs, particularly doctors, nurses and the like. Perhaps a similar case could be made out for the police.

chapter three

Violence

Mindless violence a national sickness Stiff sentences cure mugging
Hanging—the people and the politicians Women in violence Murder and
violent gangs Ten top criminals

One of the clearest indications that a particular type of crime has become
commonplace is when it no longer receives major coverage in our newspapers.
Hooliganism at football matches, gang fights, stabbings and 'muggings', now
rarely rate more than a passing mention in the daily Press. Remarkably, perhaps,
only the more macabre and sensational murders qualify for banner headlines
while many others are dismissed with a brief paragraph or fail to be mentioned
at all.

Violence has become such a feature of our everyday existence, particularly
since the beginning of the 1970s, it is now accepted as part of our normal way of
life, especially in the poorer areas of our major industrial cities and new overspill
housing estates. But even these traditional breeding grounds for thugs and
criminals can no longer claim the monopoly they have held for so long. It is no
longer unusual for once peaceful suburbs, even rustic country areas, to suddenly
erupt into a battleground. This mindless violence and motiveless aggression is
fast becoming the sickness which is undermining the social health of Britain. In
the words of Sir John Hill, the Chief Inspector of Constabulary for England and
Wales: 'We face the fact that conflict and violence are deeply rooted in human
nature.' In one of his reports in the early 1970s he added:

It is manifested in a variety of forms—battered babies, hooliganism, assault,
vandalism and mugging. The causes are as varied as the type and the most
disturbing manifestation is, perhaps, aggression towards property or persons
with no apparent motive other than possibly a general grudge and antagonism
against society as a whole. . . . . . There exists for everyone a duty as parents,
teachers, etc.—and above all as responsible citizens to seek to reduce the
amount of violence. Those who control the potent means of communication
bear a responsibility to ensure they do not present excessive violence or extol

its virtues.

Sir John, formerly one of Scotland Yard's most distinguished officers, made his comments after studying crime figures for the whole of England and Wales, which showed an enormous increase in violence. He is by no means alone in taking this view and most of Britain's leading policemen and criminologists adopt a similar attitude. One of them, Mr James Haughton, Chief Constable of the Liverpool and Bootle Police, also noted that, despite slight decreases in some forms of crime, violence continues to escalate, 'in spite of every effort being made to bring about a reduction'.

In the autumn of 1973 Mr Haughton was one of the main speakers at a three-day Study Conference on 'Crime—Cause and Cure' at Liverpool during which he left his audience in no doubt about his feelings. We were, he said, living in a 'mediocre and violent' society and he went on to give the packed conference hall a refreshingly realistic insight into the mind of one of the country's most experienced policemen.

He described gang violence, for example, as 'infantile, senseless, deplorable and disgraceful'. Despite every effort, the police and courts seemed almost powerless to contain it. Parents, educationalists, clergy and sociologists had been equally unsuccessful. Meanwhile, the public, heartily sick of this kind of behaviour, were demanding drastic action.

> There is an increasing lobby for corporal punishment for the more serious crimes where death results, such as armed robbery and terrorism, the cry for capital punishment is gaining momentum. I have heard it argued that it is difficult to understand the logic of nuclear bombs to prevent wars and no death sentence for vicious premeditated murders.

Although some perhaps, might be less forthright than Liverpool's police chief, most of his colleagues in other forces broadly agree with his sentiments. Several surveys have shown that the vast majority of Britain's chief constables—indeed, most policemen of all ranks—are in favour of re-introducing hanging for certain types of murder. One even suggested that if the rope was socially unacceptable, then murderers should be given a dose of hemlock in their food. There is a strong Parliamentary lobby at Westminster, almost exclusively among right wing MPs, in support of the police attitude, though few would back Mr Jonathan Guinness who, during a by-election campaign, advocated that razor blades should be discreetly left in the cells of convicted murderers who could then save the hangman a job by committing suicide.

Despite the periodic clamour for the return of capital punishment, it is highly unlikely to return to the Statute Book this century—unless violent deaths reach proportions where they would be equally unacceptable to the abolitionists. It has long been agreed that the majority of the population would favour the re-introduction of hanging, but politicians in 'free' House of Commons votes have chosen to ignore the consensus view. If violent crime continues to escalate at its present rate of over 11 per cent a year, they may be forced to re-assess their own personal attitudes by 1980. At the moment there seems to be no effective deterrent to violent crime. Murderers, for example, are sentenced to 'life' imprisonment. For many this means no more than nine years or so behind bars before the Home Secretary of the day chooses to set them free. Obviously many convicted murderers serve much longer sentences and a few in prison at the moment will never be released. But these are the exceptions. Therefore, given that 'life' means nine or ten years, violent men who are prepared to commit any act short of murder are, on average, likely to serve shorter terms. If murderers were made to pay the ultimate penalty, it is not inconceivable that convictions for other crimes of violence might quite justifiably attract longer sentences than is the practice at the moment.

However, the violent criminal remains with us, and because no solution readily presents itself, is likely to remain a malignant part of contemporary life, eroding principles which have been valued in Britain for generations.

Moreover, it should be remembered, people whose make-up, possibly as a result of environment or deprivation, contains a violent streak, are equally likely to cause trouble and commit further acts of violence even in prison. This has been evident in recent years by the increasing number of prison riots, namely at Parkhurst, Albany, Leicester, Peterhead, Brixton and Camp Hill. What reasonable hope is there then, that a man under close supervision in prison who cannot resist attacking a warder, fellow prisoners or both, can be rehabilitated to the point where he could become a valuable, or at least acceptable, member of society? But why is it that violence, especially among the young, has emerged with such a devastating impact only in the last few years?

Since the Second World War Britons have often been criticised for their behaviour as well as their dress. There was the 'Teddy Boy' era with lurid stories of gang fights, razor slashings, and old ladies being robbed of their pension books and handbags. Following them were the 'Mods' and 'Rockers'. Again, similar hair-raising stories abounded of groups clashing at sea-side resorts in set-piece battles. Now there are the 'Hell's Angels' with their studded leather uniforms, motor-cycles and 'gang bangs' (group sex) and the 'Bovver Boys' with their lethal steel capped hob-nailed boots.

Statistics indicate that the present breed of young hooligans is a different proposition from his predecessors. Whereas, for example, the average 'Teddy Boy' would beat a diplomatic retreat when faced with the police, the new contingent, with far less respect for the law, seem more than anxious—and, indeed, sometimes seek—a direct confrontation with authority.

When considering crimes of violence, there is a natural public tendency, perhaps because of the very nature of the crime, to think only in terms of men; that actually resorting to thuggery is something beyond the physical and mental make-up of a woman. But one of the most alarming statistics to be published since the beginning of the 1970s shows that increasingly more women are turning to criminal aggression. While the advent of the 1970s brought an increase of just over 11 per cent in violent crime committed by men, the comparative figure for similar offences committed by women showed a startling rise of 16 per cent. This figure, however, is really only the tip of the iceberg and indicates the number of women actually convicted. It does not take into account hundreds of others who are formally cautioned but never changed by the police. Contrary to popular belief, the official caution is not merely a 'ticking-off' but a formal interview conducted by an officer of at least Superintendent rank, who is often loath to bring a young woman before the magistrates. In many cases this interview serves its purpose, creating such fear not only to the female offender, but also to her parents who would usually be present on such an occasion, that the offence is unlikely to be repeated. This, in normal circumstances, means that no further police action is taken but the caution is recorded. Similar leniency is unlikely to be shown again. Analysis of these figures, compiled by the Home Office, indicate that girls are much more likely to be dealt with in this way than men. In fact, it is estimated that three times as many females receive the official caution as those actually convicted.

The emergence of women into the tough world of violence is a comparatively recent phenomenon. With only one in seven of known indictable offences committed by females, it was generally considered that these hinged on shoplifting and perhaps handling stolen goods. The changing picture is even now only slowly beginning to take shape, but it is already clear that women are becoming expert in, not only crimes of violence, but other activities, especially fraud. Many theories have been expressed about the upsurge of aggression amongst females, particularly among the young. One psychiatrist who is a consultant at a girls' Remand Home believes that one of the major factors is the broadening emancipation in society, and another points out that the last time there was a similar escalation was during the Second World War when more women worked full-time, often in arduous jobs formerly occupied by men. Strangely, perhaps, the trend is particularly visible among girls in the 14 to 17 years age group, although those between 17 and 21 also seem to be showing more aggressive tendencies than their elders. Again, theories abound, but the medical expert with wide experience in the field believes that West Indian girls may have influenced the situation. He argues that they are sexually mature at an earlier age and bigger physically than their white school friends, and further, the theory goes, they are much rougher fighters because home discipline for them often tends to be physically orientated. Another doctor is convinced that lesbian girls may often show dramatic violent tendencies and more of them now seem to be sent to Remand Homes than in previous years.

One thing is certain: they can be as tough as any man and quite prepared to commit unashamedly the most ruthless of crimes. Some psychiatrists confidently forecast that by the mid-1980s gangs of violent women will be a familiar feature of the British criminal pattern. For example, most courts have heard lurid stories of gangs of teenage female 'muggers' who even employ men to drive stolen cars round lonely urban shopping centres at night as they search for elderly victims, both male and female. These have become known as the 'Granny bashers' who often, after a session on cheap drugs and alcohol, attack the innocent and defenceless in search of excitement and pocket money. When asked why she took part in such an escapade, one teenage girl simply shrugged her shoulders and said: 'I was bored. Fed up and short of cash.' Had she no remorse or even any feeling for the old lady she had helped rob and injure? 'Why should I feel sorry? She's all right now. I am sorry because I got caught. I have been punished,' she explained after serving eight months in a Borstal institution. Then there was the similar case of two young girls who attacked another elderly woman, stole her bag and battered her on the head with a hammer. Again, they felt no guilt, only anger at their capture. But this is only the primitive type of crime in which women are becoming specialists. Their activities now cover a much wider and more dangerous area. Greater freedom and an acceptance of equality, fostered no doubt to some extent at least by the success and propaganda of the Women's Liberation movement, has drawn female political activists into extremist groups prepared to achieve their ambitions, no matter what the cost.

Leila Khaled, for example, became an overnight heroine in the Palestine Liberation movement for her part in the hi-jacking of at least two aeroplanes, a role she shared equally with her male companions. Further, the IRA bomb squad which attacked London in March 1973 was led by Dolours Price and her younger sister, Marian, both now serving life sentences for their part in the escapade. If they sought equality they certainly received it from Mr Justice Sebag Shaw, who sentenced several men who had been operating under their command to similar terms. Even sophisticated and well planned robberies are not beyond the female criminal nowadays. One gang of housewives from South London scoured their local newspapers for advertisements, looking for possible victims to rob. They found a likely candidate in a 71-year-old pensioner who was anxious to sell some furniture and family valuables. The three young wives, wearing stocking masks, answered the advertisement with a personal call at the old woman's home. As she answered the door she was bundled inside and immediately bound and gagged. Within minutes, the gang carried her advertised furniture which included some antiques and silverware into their waiting van, stealing £2.50 from her handbag on their way. By chance a neighbour noted the vehicle's registration number and told the police. At the Old Bailey later, the leader of the three was sent to prison for three years after the court had been told she had twenty-one previous convictions. Her two partners in crime each received eighteen months in gaol.

Three teenage girls who attacked a school mistress and robbed her of 10p while she was waiting for a bus were sent to Borstal by Judge Edward Sutcliffe QC who told them:

These crimes of robbery in the street are so serious and are increasing at such a pace that it is necessary to pass sentences which are right outside those which

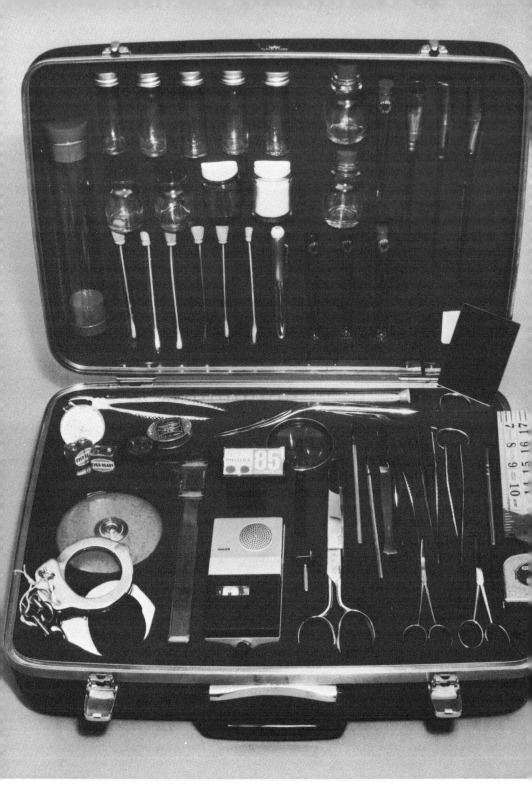

The Murder Bag

Fingerprinting

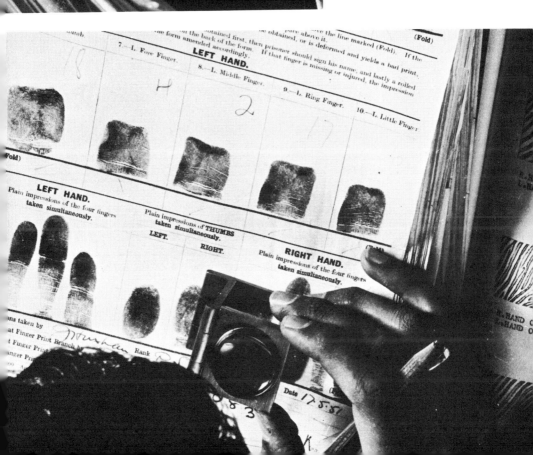

would normally be passed. I have to make it clear that it is not worthwhile for other people to follow your example. If you had been men there would have been a prison sentence.

The Judge's anger was understandable. The court had heard how the girls had attempted to wrench the teacher's rings from her fingers. In the process, she had been knocked to the ground and kicked.

But 'muggings' and other crimes of violence are by no means confined to women. During 1972, for example, there was a frightening spate of attacks by both men and women on unsuspecting people, especially the aged and infirm. Violent crimes were taking place nationwide at the alarming rate of 1,000 a week, with London, not surprisingly, being the worst affected with a reported four 'muggings' every day. With the strength of the police force depleted, it was impossible to expect them to contain a situation which was rapidly reaching epidemic proportions. The obvious solution lay with the courts and the judges handed out such punitive sentences that this cowardly hit-and-run form of robbery quickly ceased to be profitable.

Mr Justice Croom-Johnson, sitting at Birmingham Crown Court in March 1973, shocked the nation with his severity but set the pattern for other judges throughout the country. He sentenced a 16-year-old boy to be detained for twenty years and two of his companions, both aged 15 to ten years each for 'mugging' so vicious that it was classified as attempted murder. The victim had been accosted by the three youths who demanded five cigarettes from him. They dragged him to waste ground and, while two of them kicked their victim, the third battered him about the head with a brick. At the Old Bailey a 14-year-old youth was sentenced to be detained for five years after admitting 'mugging' two women and attempting to rob two others. At Norwich, a 19-year-old received four years in gaol for attacking a 76-year-old widow. In London, two teenage youths were sent to prison for life after they attacked and killed a 79-year-old man at Wallington, Surrey. London's underground was a favourite venue for gangs of young hooligans who terrorised passengers, especially late at night. Passing prison sentences of three years, Judge Alexander Carmel QC commented:

Mugging is becoming more and more prevalent, certainly in London. We are told that in America people are even afraid to walk in the streets late at night for fear of mugging. This is an offence for which deterrent sentences should be passed. Little did you know that the man you attacked, struck and kicked, was a detective sergeant of the British Transport Police in plain clothes and that in the adjoining carriages were two other officers who were part of a patrol formed because of what had been going on, on the Northern Line.

Another, Judge Hines QC told three young muggers before sending them to prison for three years apiece: 'This kind of offence is so serious that the courts are taking the view that the overwhelming need is to put a stop to it. Although the course I feel bound to take may not be best for you individually, it is one I feel driven to take in the public interest.' It was these kind of sentences that many liberal reform groups considered to be savage and unwarranted. Even some of the national and leading provincial newspapers, in addition to weekly journals, were shocked at the heavy hand of the law. But they certainly had the desired effect and were undoubtedly instrumental in stemming what could easily have become a floodtide of senseless violence in which the only sufferers would have been the innocent unable to defend themselves adequately. For, apart from the few exceptions, like mistakenly attempting to rob a detective, most of those attacked were old people hardly capable of putting up much of a struggle against young, strong thugs. The sentences may have been harsh, too harsh perhaps in some cases, but the streets of Britain became safer because of them.

Beating up a person or 'mugging' them is one thing—murder is quite another. Even the heaviest of prison sentences, perhaps even the death penalty itself, is unlikely to deter anyone determined to kill. Basically, murders could be categorised into three types: those which are premeditated and carefully planned; the 'crime passionel'; and panic murders. There is, of course, a fourth and quite separate category—killings by the insane who cannot be held totally responsible for their actions.

It has long been argued, with some justification, that there can be no deterrent sentence against premeditated murder because the person responsible, through what he believes is careful planning and meticulous attention to detail, believes either the death can be concealed forever or his 'cast iron' alibi will stand even the most rigorous police attention. Which authority can legislate against the 'crime passionel'? The French have long recognised this and included it in a special category where either the person responsible is freed completely or given a light sentence, depending on the particular circumstances. Thwarted husbands, wives or lovers, when killing in this way, give no thought to the possible consequences. They do not care what happens afterwards. On the other hand a thief or burglar who kills, say, a householder who catches him red-handed attempting to steal almost certainly does it from sheer fright in a blind panic to make good his escape. In those circumstances he is unlikely, at that particular moment, to consider the results of his action. Finally, there are those who kill through their own sense of responsibility being diminished because of either temporary or permanent insanity. Categorising deaths caused in these circumstances is always most difficult. Even eminent psychiatrists, after long and careful examination of the killer, have been known to reach totally opposite conclusions about his mental condition. Lawyers have long realised this and, where all else would be likely to fail, have entered a plea of temporary insanity on their client's behalf. There is little doubt that this legal 'ploy' before the abolition of the death penalty saved many a sane murderer from the rope.

Significantly, public attitudes towards murder vary enormously and even hardened long term prisoners in top security establishments react in different ways depending on who was killed and how the death took place. For example, moor's murderer Ian Brady was given such a rough time by fellow inmates that he requested permission to be placed in solitary confinement. The prison authorities fearing for his life, granted this unusual request immediately. Even the toughest criminals have no stomach for child killers and prison warders are well aware of the terrible beatings that such men can suffer from other prisoners. Naturally there was a vast public outcry over the moors' murders case, the Cannock Chase killings and the violent deaths of three young children from the same family in Worcester in 1973. But few people cry for justice, vengeance or retribution when a group of gangsters kill one of their own kind. Public reaction to these deaths is simple: 'So what? They are killing each other.' The shooting and disappearance of 'Ginger' Marks, the East London car dealer aroused considerable public curiosity. Newspapers at the time were full of articles theorising about, initially, whether he was dead or still alive and perhaps in hiding. And, later, when it was generally accepted that Marks was, in fact, dead there was much speculation about the circumstances. Had he for example been buried in a 'concrete coffin' in the River Thames? Or were his remains embedded in an M4 bridge support? But on 9 January 1975, police arrested and charged three men with his murder. It was almost ten years to the day he vanished. Furthermore, few shed tears of sympathy over the brutal death of John 'Scotch' Buggy, a small-time hoodlum whose body was found riddled with bullets, bound and weighted with concrete slabs in the sea near Shoreham, Sussex. It was believed at the time that he was acting as a 'treasurer' for some of the £2,500,000 Great Train robbery money and refused to part with it to a London gang who demanded a share.

But police investigate every suspicious death and will seek a murderer unceasingly for years, even when his victim may have been a vicious member of a gang or part of the seamy underworld with whom they could feel no sympathy at all. The procedure is always the same—the establishment of a murder room, a squad of detectives assigned to the case, a hard and often tedious search for witnesses, meticulous sifting of all available evidence. In most cases this set pattern produces results and, with few exceptions, the officers eventually come up with the right answer. There are instances, of course, where they know a killer's identity but lack sufficient proof to bring him before the courts. These occurrences, in Britain, are comparatively rare. However, the solving of a murder can often take a long time and necessitate re-checking old ground twice or even three times. The murder of attractive Nicola Brazier, aged twenty, whose body trussed with wire and shot in the back of the head, was found in woods at Broxbourne, Hertfordshire on 17 September 1970, was a classic example. Nicola had the previous day driven her red mini car from her home in High Street, Whitchurch, Buckinghamshire, to the Broxbourne area in the course of her work as a company representative. A few days later police recovered her cheque book and other belongings and a pistol, with a number 40084 engraved on it, from a locker at Euston railway station. About the same time a young man threw himself under a train near Hoddesdon, in Hertfordshire, not far from the murder scene.

As a matter of formality, police took the dead man's fingerprints. There was no reason at that time to connect his death with the murder of Nicola Brazier. It was only some time later, towards the end of December that year, that police, apparently baffled by the murder case, decided to re-check every possible factor once again. This time they discovered that fingerprints found on the pistol recovered from Euston station matched those taken from the dead man. Here was the answer. A check of the man's background—he has still not been publicly named—revealed him as the obvious murderer. Further checks clinched the case against him. Though by no means unique this does tend to serve as a perfect example of the total thoroughness and painstaking methods adopted by the police, particularly when it is realised that literally thousands of fingerprints had been taken during the inquiry, hundreds of people separately interviewed and the origin of the pistol traced to countries as distant as Canada and South Africa via a lonely merchant seaman who had once been its owner. It was the seaman, in fact, who sold it quite legitimately to the man who later committed suicide.

It is not generally realised that murders in Britain run at the rate of about three or four a week. Often, as has been explained, they hardly arouse public interest at any level. But one which caused considerable alarm was the case of Graham Frederick Young, aged twenty-four, who was gaoled for life at St Albans Crown Court on 29 June 1972. The man in the street had every right to be angry over the Young case. This assistant storeman was a psychopath and a poisoner, the perpetrator of probably the most wicked of all types of murder, if such a crime can ever be categorised by degree. Even the all-male jury was moved to add a recommendation after their verdicts in which they found Young guilty on six charges of poisoning two of which resulted in death. They told Mr Justice Eveleigh:

We consider it to be our duty to draw the attention of the authorities to the present system whereby poisons can be sold to the general public. We strongly recommend that the present procedures be reviewed so that the public may be more safely safe-guarded.

This came at the end of a nine-day trial during which they had been told that Young had poisoned his victims, all workmates, by dosing their tea and coffee with either antimony or thallium in order to gain speedier promotion within the company. It was only after they had reached their conclusions that the jury was told that Young had, in fact, appeared at the Old Bailey ten years earlier and was then committed to Broadmoor for poisoning his father, sister and a school friend, with a recommendation to the Home Secretary from the trial judge, Mr Justice Stephenson, that he not be released for fifteen years. In fact, the recommendation was ignored by the authorities and Young was released in February 1971 when he began his job as a storeman, still under the supervision of a probation officer. Pleading with the judge to send Young to prison and not Broadmoor, Sir Arthur Irvine QC, his defence counsel, said: 'This result may appear in the light of these events to be a serious error of judgment on the part of the authorities who have a duty to protect Young from himself as well as to protect the public.' The judge accepted the plea and sent Young to prison for life without further comment.

This psychopath might have escaped detection entirely but for the suspicions of a local pathologist who had been investigating what was locally described as the Bovingdon Bug, an apparently mysterious virus which had affected many people in the area. It was not until the death of two of Young's victims that the pathologist remembered reading Agatha Christie's mystery novel *The Pale Horse*, in which thallium was used by the murderer. After making further tests, his suspicions were so aroused that he reported them to the police.

But the police are rarely told, at least by the means of a formal complaint, about the threats, punchings, stabbings and acid throwing incidents which are a regular occurrence in the sinister world of gangland. Although mob violence was once a familiar part of life in Glasgow, particularly after the Second World War, it has seldom spread far outside London. Whilst it is true that gangs on varying scales of professionalism have been active in provincial cities like Manchester, Liverpool, Birmingham and other big towns, they have never had the aura, or glamour or success of the 'Big Teams' of the capital. Although the Krays and the Richardsons can now boast from their prison cells that they once held sway, they were by no means the only groups to be reckoned with. Strangely enough, most gangs have a family background, not in the euphemistic sense of the Mafia, but in real live, blood relative terms. This was not strictly the case until the beginning of the 1960s, but it has certainly been true since then. Some of the families whose livelihood comes almost exclusively from crime, usually by running a 'protection' business are still at large. Their activities compared with those of the murderers, Kray, and the torturers, Richardson, are on a much smaller scale. They may not resort to murder but they can and do make sure that people who fail to pay their 'fees' spend considerable time in a hospital bed or are bankrupted by extortionate demands for money.

Traditionally most of these gangs are still ruled by the elders of criminal families, usually the father or uncle who himself has considerable experience of violence and of prison life. Their sons and nephews—even sometimes daughters and nieces—make trusted lieutenants, all able and more than willing to inherit the family 'business'. Thanks mainly to the fastidious and courageous efforts of the Metropolitan Police Serious Crime Squad—the Gang Busters, as they are known in the underworld—the activities of these mobs have been considerably curtailed. So much so, in fact, that some of them attempted to shake off their unwelcome watchdogs by moving to the provinces in an effort to offer the same 'protection' and other 'services' to club and restaurant owners in Britain's other major cities. It was a move that was largely unsuccessful. For provincial police forces, especially regional crime squads, had been alerted and the gangs or their representatives were told in no uncertain manner to beat a hasty retreat back to the Metropolis.

There was one case where a well-known London gang decided that Manchester could well be the centre for some easy pickings. Initially, they sent two emissaries to reconnoitre the city's lively and prosperous clubland. The two men, now both safely in jail for long terms, were followed day and night by local detectives who not only noted but photographed their every meeting. Blissfully unaware of what was happening the two decided to summon their bosses. But no sooner had they arrived than they were met by a group of detectives who told them: 'There is the train for London—get on it.' One of the gang leaders replied: 'What for? You have got nothing on us.' One officer, with just a hint of a sense of humour, pointed to a van load of television sets waiting for collection at the railway station and said: 'That lot is nicked. If you do not get on the train it's all down to you.' The gang immediately bought their tickets and less than three hours later were back among friends in London.

Although not played strictly according to the police rule book, the action of the detectives was a form of crime prevention. It certainly stopped a dangerous group of London gangsters getting their grips on one of Britain's most prosperous cities. A similar attempt to cash in on the fortunes of Blackpool's Golden Mile again ended in disaster when a London gang was given a sound physical thrashing, told not to come back, and sent on the painful return journey to London. This time the police were not involved, only some tough local businessmen ably assisted by a few 'heavy-weights' with some considerable experience in the law of the criminal jungle.

Probably the most frightening aspect of violent crime is the speed at which it can strike. One minute all is peace and serenity—the next, all hell breaks loose. This was the situation Princess Anne and her husband Captain Mark Phillips found themselves in one evening in March 1974. They had spent a pleasant, happy evening as guests at a function in the City of London and were being driven back to Buckingham Palace along The Mall. Suddenly a car overtook theirs and cut in front forcing them to stop. The driver of the other car, a Ford Escort, was Ian Ball, aged twenty-six, who planned to kidnap the princess and demand £3 million ransom money from the Queen for her safe return. The plot was outrageous—but it nearly succeeded. As Ball left his car Inspector James Beaton, the princess's bodyguard, jumped out of the front passenger seat of the royal car, and went to meet him, not realising Ball had a pistol in his hand.

As they walked towards each other Ball fired a .38 bullet into the inspector's chest. It passed through his lung and lodged in his back. Inspector Beaton tried to return the fire with his own revolver but his injury distorted his aim, missing Ball and thudding into the Royal car. He tried a second shot but the gun jammed. Ball lunged towards the car and, holding a door open, said to the princess, 'Please get out of the car.' Captain Phillips was holding on to the princess as Ball was trying to pull her out. Then turning to Inspector Beaton, Ball said, 'Put your gun down or I will shoot her.' The officer did as he was told and then placed himself between the Princess and Ball. Captain Phillips managed to slam the door shut and Ball prepared to aim into the back of the car. With incredible courage Inspector Beaton placed his hand at the window in direct line of fire and absorbed the impact of the bullet. Furious, Ball wrenched open the car door and at almost point blank range fired a .22 bullet from a second gun into the officer's stomach. Inspector Beaton fell unconscious at the gunman's feet.

Mr Alex Callender, the princess's chauffeur, tried to get out of the car to help but Ball held a gun to his head. Within seconds he found his chance and grabbed Ball's arm in an attempt to take his gun. Despite threats that he would be shot unless he freed his grip Mr Callender hung on. Ball shot him in the chest. A witness to the incident was Mr Brian McConnell, a journalist who was passing the spot in a taxi. He immediately leapt from the cab, and quickly appreciating the danger of the situation, tried to calm Ball. 'Please don't shoot these people, they are friends of mine,' said Mr McConnell, using just a little journalistic licence. He held out his hand and pleaded with Ball to hand the gun over—Ball shot him in the chest.

Police Constable Michael Hill, on duty in The Mall, was dimly able to see a scuffle beside the car and went over to investigate. As he discovered Ball was armed so he was also shot. With four men lying injured Ball began to panic. A passing motorist rammed his car in front of Ball's Escort to prevent his escape as another passer-by, Mr Ronald Russell decided to 'have-a-go' and clouted Ball on the back of the head. Ball spun round, fired but missed. Ball then went back to the car and tried to pull Princess Anne out. Again, Mr Russell crept up behind him and hit him with his fists. As the area was attracting considerable attention, Ball decided to escape. He began to run through St James's park when he was brought down by Police Constable Peter Edmunds, a keen Rugby player.

The seven men who risked their lives to save the princess were thanked personally by the Queen at a Buckingham Palace reception and between them received one George Cross, two George Medals, three Queen's Gallantry Medals and one Queen's Commendation for Brave Conduct. At the Central Criminal Court, the Lord Chief Justice, Lord Widgery, sent Ball to the top security Rampton Hospital 'without limit of time' under the Mental Health Act.

Finally, while still on the subject, proof, if any were needed, that violent crime is on the increase, came in official statistics issued by the Criminal Injuries Compensation Board at the end of 1974. In fact, the exact total for the year 1973-4 was £4,077,125 compared with £3,457,519 for the previous year. During 1973-4 the Board received 12,215 claims and confidently forecast the figure would rise to over 14,000 by the end of 1975. The CICB is also concerned that only what they call 'relatively few' ever apply to them for compensation. They believe that many victims of violence may be unaware of the existence of the scheme. The latest figures showed that twenty-six awards were made to members of the public who received injuries while assisting the the police and 1,557 police officers were compensated for injuries sustained while on duty. One officer, aged thirty-seven, was awarded £200 for a fractured ankle received while arresting a young hooligan at a football match. The youth was fined £50.

Two other examples, taken at random, make lurid reading. The first involved a blind and deaf woman of seventy-seven who was alone at home when she was attacked by four boys. They saw her purse in the pocket of her apron and tried to snatch it. After a fierce struggle the old lady was knocked to the floor, bruised, cut and suffering from shock. The boys were convicted and their victim was awarded £254 with £4 out-of-pocket expenses.

The second case involved a man of forty-one, who went to the assistance of his girl friend and her sister who were attacked by a man wielding an iron bar. The victim sustained a fractured forearm keeping him away from work for two months. He was awarded £641 including £241 loss of earnings.

In its report the Board pointed out that it was able to pay compensation to the dependants of a person who had died as a result of his injuries but only for the actual financial loss suffered. Where a person was approaching the end of his working life, for example, and was in poor health an award to his dependants would probably be fairly small, while the parents of a child victim were unlikely to receive any compensation at all.

Violence, it must now be abundantly clear, takes many forms and there may be many permutations of which form is the worst. Who, for instance, would rate as Britain's ten most violent men within the last decade? On the following pages we offer our own list but readily agree that other people may come to entirely different conclusions. However, there can be little doubt that all would be considered dangerous in any society. Their eventual release if at all, rests with the Home Secretary of the day. Which one would be brave enough—or foolhardy enough—ever to order their release?

Ian Brady
The sadist of the moors

Police are always immediately anxious when young children disappear. Most times, fortunately, they turn up safe and well after a few hours, their 'disappearance' involving nothing more sinister than a family row or a juvenile prank with their friends. But it is a different matter when they vanish from the face of the earth and are never seen again. Without witnesses or clues, there is little police can do except wait and hope.

When pretty Lesley Anne Downey went missing from her home in Manchester and young John Kilbride vanished from nearby Ashton-under-Lyne a massive police search failed to uncover even one clue as to where they might be. In both cases there was no question of family difficulties and neither had run off with friends for a lark. 'Missing' posters with the children's photographs were displayed all over the North West but months went by without even the smallest piece of information reaching the police. It was a complete mystery which baffled everyone. Police were certain of only one thing: something terrible had happened to them.

When, by a stroke of luck, they actually did discover the truth, it was so shocking and horrifying that tough, experienced detectives who thought they had seen and heard everything sat down and wept. Some were physically sick and others seriously considered leaving the force for jobs which would shield them from such sadism and savagery.

The telephone rang at the police station at Hyde, Cheshire, a small market town considerably enlarged by a Manchester overspill council estate at Hattersley. It was from a public call box there that a small, shaky and obviously frightened voice told astounded officers: 'I want to report a murder.' It was 5am on a cold wintery morning in October 1965 and young David Smith and his frail little wife Maureen huddled together in the phone box as they told police of a body, wrapped in a large polythene bag, at 16 Wardle Brook Avenue, Hattersley. Police were on the scene within minutes and found Smith clutching a sharp bread knife which he said he was carrying in case he was attacked by his sister-in-law and the man with whom she was living—Myra Hindley and Ian Brady. Smith and his wife—Hindley's younger sister—were taken to the police station and senior detectives were called from their beds to listen to a remarkable story.

Smith told them that the previous night, Brady had picked up a young man named Edward Evans in a Manchester city centre bar and taken him to Wardle Brook Avenue. There, after drinking cheap sherry, Brady had produced an axe and, with Smith and Hindley looking on, began hacking at the luckless Evans who ran round and round the room, screaming in terror. But there was no escape from the axe-wielding maniac and eventually Evans, who had been subjected to other perverse and sadistic practices, fell dead, his skull split open and his body terribly disfigured. His remains were then bundled into the polythene bag and placed upstairs in an empty bedroom next to where Mrs Eileen Maybury, Hindley's sick and feeble grandmother, slept, totally unaware of the happenings downstairs.

Then, according to Smith, he was forced to help Brady and his mistress clean up the gory mess before he was allowed to return home to Maureen at their small council flat a short distance away. Later, frightened for his own life in case he was next on Brady's death list, he had decided to tell the police.

At dawn, police surrounded the house in Wardle Brook Avenue and within minutes found Evans's body, despite appeals from Brady and Hindley that it was all a lie and that Smith had been telling fairy stories. The hawk-faced Brady, then twenty-seven, and his twenty-three year old mistress, were taken into custody as police made a thorough search of the house and what they found made them quickly realise they were not dealing with just another murderer. For, among other things, they found Nazi literature, a Nazi uniform which Brady used to wear, stomping through the house, German martial music and records of Nazi leaders' speeches, the works of the Marquis de Sade and pornographic photographs he had taken of Hindley. And, in a prayer book belonging to the once-religious Hindley, they found their most important piece of evidence, a ticket for two suitcases which had been left in a Manchester

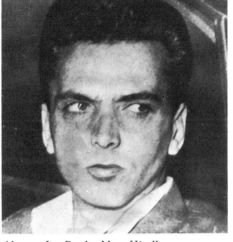

Above: Ian Brady, Myra Hindley
Centre: The Richardson Brothers. Charles (left) and Edward
Below: The Brothers Hosein. Arthur (left) and Nizamodeen

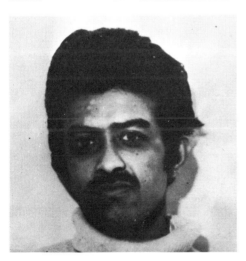
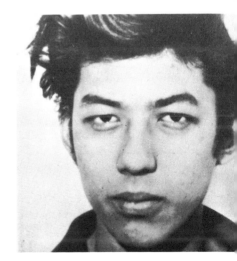

Above: The Kray Twins. Ronnie (left) and Reg
Centre: Harry Roberts, Raymond Morris, Frederick Joseph Sewell
Below: The Beast of Jersey, Edward John Paisnel

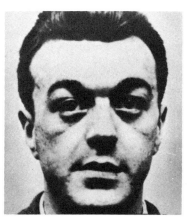  

 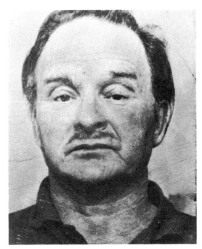

railway station. When officers collected the cases and opened them they discovered the most horrifying evidence which completely damned Brady and showed Hindley as his more than willing partner. There were photographs of pretty little Lesley Anne strapped to a bed in lewd and obscene positions, tape recordings of her voice pleading to be allowed to 'go home to Mummy' and photographs of Hindley, not only in her pornographic poses, but standing on the windswept moorland, only a few miles outside Hyde on the Lancashire-Yorkshire-Cheshire boundary.

Having established that little Lesley Anne had actually been in the house, it did not take police long to guess the truth about the pictures on the Moors . . . that Hindley had been standing on the spot which was the unmarked grave of the unfortunate little girl. Other pictures—of both Brady and Hindley—on another moorland stretch led them to a further accurate conclusion: there was probably another body up there. Because Brady and Hindley had been picked up in Cheshire, the case, technically, was one for the Cheshire police to handle and Det. Chief Superintendent Arthur Benfield, head of the county CID, led the inquiry. But Lesley Anne and John Kilbride both vanished from the Lancashire police's area and a squad of their senior officers was closely involved with events, especially Mr Joe Mounsey, then a detective chief inspector and now head of the Lancashire CID, who was responsible for much of the questioning of the arrested young couple. Mr Mounsey is a big, tough and hardened policeman who once walked round Cyprus with a price on his head after arresting terrorist Nicky Sampson—the man who, briefly, replaced President Makarios after the archbishop fled during the 1974 clashes on the island. But even he and his colleagues were appalled when they listened to the pathetic tape recordings and looked, through tear-filled eyes, at the pictures of Lesley Anne.

Meanwhile, hundreds of policemen scoured the miles of boggy moorland, attempting to identify the exact places where Hindley and Brady had posed for the pictures. Only those who know such bleak and featureless places would fully realise the enormity of the task. One bit of moorland looks very much like the next, with not even so much as a tree to aid navigation. But, virtually against all the odds, they found what they were looking for—the grave of Lesley Anne Downey. It was a shallow affair and her young body had been buried not more than a few inches below the squelchy surface. Shortly afterwards another grave was discovered not far away, that of John Kilbride. And it was into this isolated, private and macabre graveyard that the body of Edward Evans was to have been placed, almost certainly the night after his death.

For Brady and Hindley, the murderers of the moors, the Jekyll and Hyde days were over: the lovers who worked normally in an office by day and, behind the locked doors of their council home, practised their perversions, sadism and murder by night were well and truly damned. The evidence against them was watertight and there was plenty of it.

The public conscience was stirred by the horror of the couple's crimes and one outraged relative of Lesley Anne Downey's publicly threatened to shoot the pair once they got into court. This threat—and others—were treated seriously by the police. When Brady and Hindley stepped into the dock at Chester Castle in April 1966 they found the entire structure had been shielded by bullet-proof glass. Everyone was searched for weapons as they went into court and even the Press had to show specially-issued passes. Not surprisingly, the case aroused wide interest as journalists from all over the world congregated at Chester; lawyers came from as far as California, and writers, intent on recording the events in books, all came to see these two murderous freaks.

Hindley, wearing a black and white check suit, spent the court days passing notes to her lawyers, but Brady, arrogant, superior and aloof to the end, spent his time sketching the judge, lawyers and journalists, occasionally pausing to chat to his girl friend from whom he would soon be parted forever.

But who were they, these unlikely pair of criminals who shocked the world with their terrifying activities? Brady, the illegitimate son of Glasgow tea-room waitress, Margaret Stewart, was a product of the tough Gorbals district. Even as a baby, his foster parents, Mr and Mrs Sloan, with whom he lived at Camden Street, Hutchesontown, could not deal with his frenzied tantrums, his habit of banging his head against the wall when he failed to get his way. It was not long before his sadistic tendencies began to manifest themselves and his first victims for torture were cats. Once he threw a cat out of an upstairs window and on another occasion buried one alive under a gravestone because he 'wanted to see just how long it would live'. At school, he took little interest in lessons and spent all his spare time and pocket money going to see horror films, some of them over and over again. His preoccupation with this sort of violence soon earned him the nickname 'Dracula' among the other local children. Mr and Mrs Sloan moved from their cramped tenement flat into a spacious new house on an estate at Pollock. Brady is remembered there by neighbours as a quiet boy who did not attract attention. But the police had noticed him and he first appeared in court at Glasgow in 1951 for housebreaking and attempted theft.

He was given two years probation. The following year he was admonished on housebreaking and theft charges from Govan court. Then came nine separate counts of housebreaking and theft. Again the court treated him lightly and once again he was put on probation—a condition being that he moved to Manchester to live with his mother who by now had married a Mr Patrick Brady. He was still only fifteen. He moved in with his mother and stepfather into a house in Cuttell Street, Gorton, Manchester, but was soon in trouble with the police again. In 1955 he was sent to Borstal for theft and, when he came out in 1958, returned to his mother and her husband who now lived in Westmorland Street, Longsight, Manchester. After a short term working for a brewery, he finally obtained a job with Millwards Merchandise, a small chemical distributing firm where, in 1961, he met Myra Hindley.

Hindley, a war-time baby from a Manchester slum, spent a reasonably normal childhood which suddenly changed when she saw a young boy drown. This had a profound effect on her. She organised a street collection for a wreath for the child and began attending Mass at a local Roman Catholic church. In fact, she became a Catholic and, for her first Holy Communion, was given the prayer book in which the tickets for the infamous suitcases were found. After having several boyfriends as a teenager and an unsuccessful engagement, Hindley developed an interest in Germany and obtained an application form to join the NAAFI staff there. But the idea was quickly abandoned when she moved to Millwards in 1961 and there, for the first time saw Ian Brady.

The slim-featured young Scot was already far from the most popular person in the office with his arrogance and his conviction in his own superiority. Moreover, his outbursts of 'Hitler was right . . . Britain is decadent' were hardly like to win him friends. He was anti-British, anti-religion and opposed most of the social conventions. He even voiced his unstinting admiration for some of the German war leaders.

For a whole year, much to Hindley's frustration, he all but ignored her. Eventually they had their first 'date' and, from then on, they were hardly ever out of each other's sight. They spent their holidays together in Scotland, travelled to work together and, when Hindley's grandmother moved to Hattersley, the couple moved in with her. His influence on the impressionable young woman was enormous but there is little doubt she was more than a willing tool for his twisted and perverted ambitions. He called her his 'Myra Hess' and she adopted the infamous Irma Grese, the female 'Beast of Belsen' as her own personal heroine and even carried a picture of Grese in her handbag.

Then came the pornography, their long discussions about the philosophical 'ideals' of the Marquis de Sade and nights listening to the rantings of Hitler and his henchmen on their records, with Brady sometimes marching round the house in his jackboots and Nazi uniform. But it must have been a million-to-one chance that brought them together, the demonic Brady who was convinced he could control Fate and the once apparently normal young woman who became a sadist and took pleasure watching an innocent child being subjected to vile and inhuman practices before being brutally murdered. What Brady did not know was that he was a figure of fun for two sisters who lived at Longsight and often saw him walking in his long black overcoat which almost reached his ankles. With ironic foresight they had dubbed him 'The Undertaker'.

Charles Richardson
Torture gang boss

Charles Richardson was the undisputed 'King' of crime south of the River Thames. His reign of terror spanned a little over five years and came to an abrupt end at the Central Criminal Court in June 1967 when he was sent to prison for a total of fifty-eight years. Some of the sentences for assault, causing grievous bodily harm, robbery with violence and demanding money with menaces, were ordered to run concurrently, so in effect he was led away to the cells to serve a total of twenty-five years. At the end of the forty-five day trial, Mr Justice Lawton, as he then was, said:

On the evidence I have heard I am satisfied that over a period of years you were the leader of a large, disciplined, well led, well organised gang and that for purposes of your own material interests, and on occasions for purposes of your criminal desires, you terrorised those who crossed your path and you terrorised them in such a way that was vicious, sadistic, and a disgrace to society.

The judge, considered by many to be one of the boldest on the Bench—his father was a prison governor—could barely hide his revulsion of some of the evil and bestial acts for which the jury had found Richardson responsible. He was, he said, 'ashamed to think that one lives in a society that contained men like you.'

Charles Richardson, then aged thirty-three, had two overwhelming passions; wealth and power. He amassed a considerable personal fortune, estimated to be about £250,000, with business interests in his native London suburb of Camberwell, the West End, Greece and South Africa. But fair-trading had no place in his business philosophy. Awkward competitors were driven out of business by threats of violence. Those foolhardy enough to ignore the warning would be 'invited' or shanghaied to one of Richardson's seemingly respectable offices either in South London or the West End for a 'conference'. On one side of the 'conference' table sat Charles Richardson twiddling a stiletto. Occasionally a loaded revolver lay on the desk blotter in front of him. Half a dozen of his henchmen, including his brother, Edward, two years his junior, were ranged round the thick leather chair occupied by the 'Boss'. This was the setting for one of the many 'sick trials' at which Richardson presided as judge and jury. There was never any need for the 'charge' to be read; the 'accused' had simply upset Richardson or refused to part with information the gang leader needed to expand his empire. An almost imperceptible flicker of an eyelid was the cue for the 'trial' to begin. The victim was coshed from behind, either with an iron bar, a golf club, a chair leg or more often a length of twisted and knotted barbed wire. Dazed, bleeding and slumped on a rickety wooden chair the hapless 'guest' was then interrogated.

No response or the wrong reply was swiftly dealt with. The victim was stripped naked and pummelled and beaten to the brink of unconsciousness. Few were in a condition by this stage to offer further resistance but the torture continued. For often the 'trials' were witnessed by other business associates Richardson was anxious to impress.

They were left in no doubt that they would suffer the same brutality unless they fell into line. Those who felt that perhaps they could stand up to the torture they had already seen were then treated to a series of horrifying demonstrations of depravity. The victim was then forced to stand upright against a wall to act as a target as members of the gang threw kitchen knives at him. When this began to pall an electric generator was ceremoniously carried into the office and placed on the desk. Electric leads from the machine were then attached to parts of the man's body, often including his genitals, while one of the gang cranked the handle. The electric shock was often so severe that some victims were seen literally to jump three feet into the air. On occasions water was poured over the crumpled body to ensure a better 'earth' for the electric current. The methods of torture tended to vary after the shock treatment. Some victims were then burned as members of the gang stubbed out their cigarettes on his bare flesh; others were scorched by an electric fire held only a fraction of an inch from their bodies; a few were given the 'dental' treatment, that is, their teeth were pulled out by a gang member using a pair of electrical pliers. One victim had his feet nailed to the wooden floor to keep him still. The final degradation came when Richardson ordered his victims to mop up their own blood from the office floor and walls with their own clothes.

At the end of such terrifying experiences many men were in urgent need of medical attention, being literally half-dead. The gang took care of this, too. On their pay-roll was a struck-off doctor employed to render first aid, not out of compassion, but to keep victims away from hospitals and legitimate doctors who would doubtless ask awkward questions and probably contact the police. Hence the underworld code of silence was maintained. Those who for a second considered going to the police were warned that not only would they receive a second and tougher 'dose' but their families would suffer a similar fate, too.

Richardson, who boasted that 'he knew half the coppers in London', genuinely believed he was untouchable by the police. He reasoned that after experiencing a session in his 'torture chamber' no one would be brave enough, or foolhardy enough, to make a complaint to the police for fear of the consequences. But as with all criminals he made one mistake; he overlooked the bravery of one of his 'business associates' who had suffered at the hands of the gang, most of whom laughed and jeered as his contorted body was sent into gruesome spasms of pain. Secretly, James Taggart made a statement to the police. The then commissioner, Sir Joseph Simpson, had at last penetrated Richardson's armour. He assigned Detective Chief Superintendent Gerald McArthur to smash the gang.

'Uncle Mac', as he became known to both criminals and his men alike, carefully picked five top detectives and within a week they formed a hundred-strong 'Richardson Squad' to keep a twenty-four-hour watch on every move made by the gang. Mr Taggart was immediately given an armed guard and moved to a safe hiding place. Slowly the underworld realised that at last they could rid themselves of the evil yoke which had crushed them for years. Legitimate businessmen, who had been threatened and intimidated by the gang, as well as members of the criminal fraternity, began to pluck up courage and meet detectives secretly to make statements. Even men serving sentences who had information about Richardson were given special protection in prison to ensure their safety. After twelve months the police had built up the dossier they needed to bring the gang to trial.

Even as they stood shoulder to shoulder in the dock of the famous No. 2 Court at the Old Bailey the gang still wielded considerable influence outside. Three times attempts were made to 'nobble' the jury of one woman and eleven men which were guarded night and day by eighty armed policemen. Fears for their safety were such that the judge ordered that each one of them should have a special 'hot line' telephone installed in their homes so that they could contact the police in the event of threats. All twelve were kept under constant surveillance for several months after the trial in case other members of the gang who were not captured tried to avenge their 'boss'. As he left the dock to begin his sentence Charles Richardson snarled at the jury: 'Thank you—very much.' As he glared at the weary jurors many averted their eyes. If it was through fear they could not be blamed. Many others who had gazed into those menacing pale blue eyes still bear the scars to remind them of the bestial torture they were forced to endure.

The Brothers Hosein
The kidnappers of Rook's Farm

Kidnapping is a crime so rare in Britain that when police were told that wealthy Mrs Muriel McKay had disappeared from her luxurious home in Wimbledon, London, they were at first reluctant to accept that she could have been abducted. The house had been ransacked, the front door forced and her car was still in the garage. Even after a telephone call demanding £1 million ransom for her safe return, senior Scotland Yard officers, almost totally inexperienced in this type of investigation, were still sceptical. A number of other possibilities were first examined: had she walked out on her husband, Mr Alick McKay, deputy head of the *News of the World* newspaper organisation, deliberately leaving a false trail? Did her husband know more about her disappearance than he was saying. Could the house have been entered by thieves in Mrs McKay's absence? Had she fought an intruder, been hurt and was now lying injured nearby? Inquiries quickly eliminated all these possibilities. The couple were devoted and a thorough search of the district revealed nothing. It was only then that detectives faced the realisation that Mrs McKay had been kidnapped, the first case of its kind this century.

What happened in the next five weeks before Arthur and Nizamodeen Hosein, Trinidadian-born brothers who lived on the remote fifteen acre Rook's

Farm near the tiny hamlet of Stocking Pelham in Hertfordshire, were arrested for her kidnapping and murder, has become a textbook classic in wickedness and crime detection. Even now, as they serve life sentences in separate prisons, the brothers are the only two who know where, when and how Mrs McKay met her tragic death. But they have flatly refused to say.

Why she died is probably the one question that Scotland Yard detectives can answer with some certainty. She was kidnapped by mistake. The brothers, in fact, intended and probably thought at the time, that they had abducted her close friend, Mrs Anne Murdoch, wife of the *News of the World* proprietor, Mr Rupert Murdoch. Their awful error happened when they saw Mr McKay climbing into the back of Mr Murdoch's chauffeur-driven blue Rolls Royce outside his newspaper office just off Fleet Street. Having seen Mr Murdoch only once, and then on a television programme, they thought the man in the car was the one they wanted. In fact, the Murdochs were at that time celebrating Christmas 12,000 miles away at their other home in Australia and Mr McKay was using his car.

On 3 October 1969, Arthur Hosein, a successful East London tailor who often boasted that one day he would become a millionaire, was watching television at the £17,000 farm he had bought on a mortgage a short time before. Sitting beside him was Nizamodeen, his surly and penniless younger brother who was shortly due to return to Trinidad when his visitor's permit expired. David Frost was interviewing Mr Murdoch who talked at some length about his newspapers, his wealth and his beautiful wife, Anne. Arthur whose burning ambition was to become a country gentleman and be accepted as an equal by the local gentry, suddenly saw a way of obtaining the money he thought was necessary to reach his social status: kidnapping Mrs Murdoch and demanding a £1 million ransom.

He told his brother and together they began planning their intended coup. But it was their greed and amateurism which eventually led to their downfall. First, they kidnapped not the vivacious young wife they were after, but a 55-year-old homely mother who needed regular medical attention. Second, their astronomic demand convinced police that they were dealing, not with professional criminals, but with amateurs whose ignorance made them even more dangerous.

The day after Mrs McKay disappeared two telephone calls were made to the McKay home which signalled the start of one of the biggest and strangest police investigations ever undertaken in Britain. The first was a two word message 'Grey Hillman' thought to come from Mrs McKay herself. The second was a demand for the £1 million from a telephone box at Epping. Police received their first clue the next day when a letter, posted in North London and written by Mrs McKay's hand, arrived addressed to her husband. It said: 'I am blindfolded and cold. Only blankets. Please do something to get me home. Please co-operate or I can't keep going.' Such a pathetic and plaintive note, so obviously written by a woman in considerable distress, angered Detective Chief Superintendent Bill Smith, who took charge of the investigation. He decided he needed experienced expert help and he immediately cabled every known fact and even suspicions to the Federal Bureau of Investigation in Washington, a force with considerable expertise in handling kidnapping cases. Within twenty-four hours, the FBI wired back: 'On the evidence you have given us, we feel that Mrs McKay is already dead.' This was only three days after her disappearance.

Then came the first of a series of telephone calls to the McKay home, all of which were carefully tape recorded. Each time the caller introduced himself by saying: 'This is M3 of the Mafia'. As members of the McKay family kept him talking while police attempted to trace where the calls were being made, the brothers lost control and threatened to kill Mrs McKay immediately unless the money was paid. Rendezvous were arranged, always at night and in the Epping Forest area, for suitcases of money to be dropped at pre-arranged spots. The brothers warned the family not to trick them because their gang, they said, would have them covered constantly by marksmen carrying machine guns and rifles with telescopic sights.

At this stage, the police had every reason to believe that what had been threatened might be carried out and several brave detectives, including a woman officer, impersonated members of the McKay family as they kept the appointments. On one occasion, one million pounds of specially printed notes was dumped on a grass verge in a country lane to await collection by the kidnappers. Hidden behind trees and bushes in the vicinity was a small squad of selected armed police, waiting to pounce once the cases were picked up. For two hours nothing happened so the officers, wet, tired and shivering the in cold night air, decided to recover the suitcases and return to London.

But their miserable vigil had not been wasted. One of the detectives had noted the number of a Volvo saloon seen hesitating as it passed the pick-up point. He paid particular attention because the same vehicle travelled the route three times. A simple check with records revealed it belonged to Arthur Hosein and before dawn that morning the quiet little Rook's Farm was completely surrounded by police. The house was searched and police found the tell-tale paper flowers that 'M3' had said would be planted to indicate where the money should be left. The brothers were taken to Kingston-upon-Thames police headquarters for questioning. They were later charged with kidnapping and murdering Mrs McKay and the following summer sentenced at the Old Bailey by Mr Justice Sebag Shaw to life imprisonment.

Until there is hard evidence to show exactly how and where Mrs McKay died, her file at Scotland Yard will never be closed. There are many theories but the most likely explanation is that she died, possibly from hunger, exposure, shock, lack of medical attention or wilful neglect at the hands of her captors. Many police officers involved in the case believe the final gruesome act was that the Hoseins dismembered her body and fed it to the eight farrowing pigs kept on the farm. They also believe her bones were crushed and left for collection at the farm with others from dead animals.

Harry Roberts
Police killer extraordinary

When tough Harry Roberts stood erect and straight-backed in the Old Bailey dock, he heard the judge tell him: 'You have been justly convicted of what is perhaps the most heinous crime to have been committed in this country for a generation or more.' And significantly, Mr Justice Glyn-Jones added: 'I think it likely that no Home Secretary in the future, regarding the enormity of your crime, will ever think fit to show mercy by releasing you on licence.' With that he sentenced Roberts, and his two small-time cohorts, John Duddy and John Witney, to life imprisonment with the recommendation that they not be released for at least thirty years. And since former trained jungle fighter Roberts was then only thirty years of age, in the prime of life, when he began his long sentence at the end of 1966, he is likely to be a pensioner before he tastes the sweet smell of fresh, free air again.

It was just four months earlier that Britain awoke to the shock news that three London policemen had been brutally gunned down and murdered while on duty in Braybrooks Street, Shepherd's Bush. They had been patrolling the area in a Scotland Yard Q-car when they saw three men driving a battered old saloon, its exhaust hanging off, making a terrible noise because its silencer was virtually non-existent.

The officers stopped the car and Detective Sergeant Christopher Head, aged thirty and Detective Constable David Wombwell, aged twenty six, walked forward to question the three occupants. They began talking to Witney, who had bought the car—registration number PGT 726—for just £20 some time earlier. Within minutes the officers discovered it had no current road fund tax disc and that Witney's insurance had run out three hours earlier.

Then, Roberts, leader of the three-man gang, who was sitting in the front passenger seat, pulled out a Luger and shot the young detective constable through the head. Mr Head raced back towards the police car to escape, but Roberts followed him and shot him through the back. Duddy, who had been sitting in the back of the car, joined in and shot Police Constable Geoffrey Fox, aged forty-one, as he sat behind the driving wheel of the unmarked police vehicle. The three men who had set out that night to steal a Ford Corsair—but had failed to find one—were on their way to rob a rent collector when they were stopped by the police. But now they were on the run and made their escape as quickly as their battered old vehicle would carry them. They hid the car in a garage Witney rented in Tinworth Street, Vauxhall, where police found it two days later.

Police always pull out all the stops on a murder inquiry, but when three of their own colleagues are the innocent victims of such a savage attack from dangerous armed men who could easily stage a repeat performance, there are no holds barred. Within hours they had 'turned over' petty criminals of all types in a concerted bid to find the killers. Their determined efforts were immediately rewarded with the capture, within six hours, of a frightened John Witney, a small-time crook with ten previous convictions, including an eighteen-month sentence for conspiracy to rob.

Duddy fled to his home town of Glasgow, hoping to hide with friends with whom he had shared his earlier criminal life. But, within three days, he too, was in police custody.

Only Roberts remained free and police knew that he was, by far, the most dangerous of the three and would not hesitate to kill again to remain at liberty. They had checked his thick file at the Criminal Records Office and recalled that his life of crime, often accompanied by violence, had started when he was only fifteen years old. He was then, in 1951, placed on probation for two years for receiving. Three years later, at the Old Bailey, he was sent for Borstal training for assault with intent to rob. Two years later he joined the Rifle Brigade at Winchester and, after a short tour in Kenya, was posted to the steamy jungles of Malaya at the height of the terrorist campaign. Roberts was a proficient marksman, became a corporal and eventually joined a special jungle tracking unit which meant completing a jungle survival course. It was this knowledge which helped him evade police after the triple murder.

After leaving the army, Roberts was soon back to a life of crime and, while serving eighteen months for store-breaking and theft, he was questioned about an attack on an elderly man at Stoke Newington, London, in November 1958. He was eventually charged with robbing the old man, aged seventy-nine, with violence and sentenced to seven years in prison. The man had subsequently died from his injuries and, ironically, had he died just two days earlier, Roberts might well have hanged for the attack. For the old man's death came just one year and three days after it happened—only two days outside the time limit under which a murder charge could be brought. The judge then described the young Roberts as 'a brutal man' and told him: 'You yourself have come pretty close to the rope.'

Surprisingly, Roberts proved a model prisoner in Maidstone and Winchester gaols and was allowed to benefit from the hostel scheme for rehabilitation. He was sent to Bristol, lived in a hostel and was allowed to go out to work every day. He was employed as a lorry driver and later as a bricklayer where he earned above-average wages. It was in Bristol that he met Mrs Lilian Perry, the wife of a former Bristol policeman, in a pub in the city's Gloucester Road. When he was free, Roberts moved into Mrs Perry's home in Filton Grove, Horfield, where she lived with her daughter and son-in-law. He started his own sub-contracting business, sometimes earning £58 a week, but it eventually failed and the ex-convict moved to Maida Vale, back in London, with his new girl friend. He had long since left his striptease dancer wife, Mitzy. Unable to make enough money honestly and satisfy his gourmet palate, Roberts decided to organise a small gang and carry out raids. He picked Duddy and Witney and together the trio enjoyed early success in their escapades. They always went about their life of crime 'tooled up'—armed—'in case anyone gets in the way'. Roberts was always the armourer, providing his partners with guns before each raid and taking them back afterwards to hide away.

But now he was on the run, not for a petty raid or robbery, but the murder of three policemen. Although police knew within hours whom they were looking for, it took them ninety days and one of the strangest searches in criminal history to find him. Because Harry Roberts had gone to ground—literally. He had moved into a copse at Thorley, right in the centre of the dense and extensive Epping Forest, on the outskirts of London, and established a 'permanent' hideaway. It was superbly camouflaged and almost impossible to detect, even from a few yards. His knowledge of jungle survival had stood him in good stead. What is more, he survived in this manner for nearly three months, even though police were fully aware he was in the area and combed the woods every day with armed patrols and tracker dogs. Harry Roberts had, maybe, not learned that crime does not pay, but he had certainly learned his army lessons very well.

But even Roberts had to eat. His main point of contact with the public was at the Farm Shop, a tiny store in Thorley village where, once a week for six weeks, he spent about £2 buying food. He was even recognised from newspaper photographs by the shop owner as he walked into the store, dressed in a fawn jacket and dark trousers and usually covered in mud. But she did not report the man who usually bought beans, eggs, luncheon meat, fruit and butter and always paid in half-crowns, because, she said, 'people laughed when I mentioned it'. Furthermore, farm workers, working on the edges of the Forest, noticed smoke—obviously coming from Roberts's fire—but again nothing was done because they believed it came from a children's camp fire. Roberts gained confidence and began visiting the nearby small towns of Sawbridgeworth and Bishop's Stortford.

He once went into a leather shop and shoe repairer's to buy leather to make holsters for the two guns he still had in his possession. By this time he had grown a ginger beard which helped disguise what should have been the most easily recognised face in Britain.

In Shepherd's Bush police station, from where he was leading the hunt, Detective Superintendent Richard Chitty kept special squads of armed officers standing by to follow up every 'Roberts seen' alarm. Apart from local officers, these included men from the Scotland Yard Flying Squad and members of the regional crime squads. But it was the simplest of mistakes which led, eventually, to the capture of Harry Roberts. He allowed the batteries in his tiny transistor radio to run out and missed the news that police had found his jungle-style hiding place while he was out. The next day in Thorley he came face to face with two traffic department sergeants from Hertfordshire. And the man police had thought might try to stage a 'shoot-out' because he had vowed never to return to prison again, gave himself up without so much as a fight. He just pleaded with the two policemen: 'Please don't shoot me.' The cheap gunman who had thought himself a master criminal was captured at last.

Raymond Morris
The monster of Cannock Chase

Hardened Scotland Yard detectives, especially those assigned to the Murder Squad, are not normally noted for outbursts of emotion. Some of the sights they encounter during their daily work would turn the stomachs of men unfamiliar with the contortions of violent death. The sight of little Christine Darby, aged seven, lying nearly naked, her arms outstretched and her knees raised and splayed was almost too much even for Detective Chief Superintendent Ian Forbes, as he then was, when he arrived at Cannock Chase in Staffordshire, just before dusk on 22 August 1967.

Mr Forbes, one of the most brilliant detectives ever to work at the Yard, revealed his initial feelings years later in his memoirs, *Squad Man* (published by W. H. Allen). He said:

> I stood looking at a body only just visible beneath brushwood and undergrowth. I was seeing for the first time in my long career as a detective the pathetic, sprawling victim of a child killer. Involuntarily, I clenched my hands. I had seen the hideously inflated body of a strangled woman dragged from the river Tyne. I had seen a man peppered by shotgun bullets who looked like a collander, murder victims stabbed to death and drenched in their own blood and men with vicious razor slashes which gave them gruesome, bloody grins from their mouths to their ears. I had become immune to such scenes of violence, but now . . . . A hardened detective of fifty three, with nearly twenty nine years service behind me, I suddenly had butterflies in my stomach. They were quickly replaced by a mood of intense anger. The first reaction was activated by a fear that I might not catch the killer. The second mood took over as rage dictated that, come hell or high water, I would hunt down the murderer.

Alongside Mr Forbes stood Detective Sergeant Tom Parry, father of a 7 year-old daughter, also named Christine. He looked in horror and said: 'Good God, guv'nor. That could have been my little girl. We've just got to find this bastard.' They did fourteen months later when he tried to snatch another little girl. But the hunt which ended in a life sentence for Raymond Leslie Morris—described by Mr Forbes as 'the most evil and sadistic man I ever had the ill-luck to encounter'—was a masterly example of police thoroughness which culminated in a stroke of luck the tireless officers never thought would come their way.

During the months that led up to his arrest, police eliminated from their inquiries more than 25,000 car owners, interviewed 80,000 people and examined about 1,375,000 vehicle taxation files. Their strongest clue throughout came from a witness who claimed she saw a frightened little girl crying in the front passenger seat of a grey coloured Austin A55 or A60 car. With the help of the manufacturers, car dealers, garages, and Interpol, owners of similar vehicles were traced to thirteen different countries as far away as Australia and the Far East.

Although any murder inquiry is treated as urgent and important, the death of Christine had an added significance. Only nineteen months earlier, the bodies of Diana Joy Tift, aged five, and Margaret Reynolds, aged six, were found in a ditch only a mile from the spot where Christine had been discovered.

All three children lived within a seventeen mile radius of each other and near the A34 trunk road which runs through Cannock Chase. Furthermore, there were remarkable similarities in the manner of their deaths: all three had been coaxed into cars while playing near their homes and were murdered after savage sexual assaults. Police realised they might be looking for one killer who could strike again at any time. So did thousands of local mothers who were terrified one of their children might become the next victim.

Then, on 4 November 1968, 10-year-old Margaret Aulton, preparing for the following night's Guy Fawkes celebrations on some waste ground in Walsall, was approached by a man who offered her some fireworks. She walked to his car, a green and white Ford Corsair and, as she peered inside, the man grabbed her by the arm and tried to push the frightened girl into the vehicle. She struggled and managed to escape. The man panicked and quickly drove away, but not before the scene had been witnessed by Mrs Wendy Lane, an 18-year-old housewife. She knew Margaret but did not recognise the man. Luckily she made a mental note of the car's registration number which was later traced to Morris, a 39-year-old works' foreman. Morris had already been interviewed by the police during the early stages of the inquiry into Christine's murder, mainly because he was then the owner of a grey Austin A55, similar to the one detectives were fairly certain was used to abduct the young girl. At that time they could not prove anything against him, due to his persistent denials and the unshakeable alibi corroborated by his young second wife, Carol.

But the fact that he now owned the car that Mrs Lane was sure she had spotted, made police almost certain that Morris was their man. There was one further important piece of evidence against him. Margaret, in her struggle to escape from his clutches, had noticed her attacker was wearing a distinctive silver watch with a bracelet. Morris was wearing a similar watch when he was arrested.

He obviously realised the significance of the watch because when he was later searched by a reception officer at Winson Green prison, Birmingham, he had tried to conceal it by strapping it to his ankle. While this was taking place, detectives were making a thorough search of his flat, opposite Walsall police station. They found photographic equipment and a number of pornographic pictures with him shown indecently assaulting little girls. Detectives were now convinced they had the murderer but, despite the welter of evidence against him, Morris remained conceited and arrogant during questioning and his wife insisted on backing his story.

Suddenly the situation changed. Mrs Morris was shown the pornographic photographs of her husband assaulting her own 5-year-old cousin in their flat.

They had been taken with a delayed action device on his camera. Raymond Morris's alibi disappeared as his shocked wife made a second statement to the police admitting she had earlier told lies to shield him. He had not been with her at the time Christine Darby was abducted and neither had he been at home at the time Margaret Aulton was attacked.

In fact, when Morris stood trial at Staffordshire Assizes in February 1969, his wife gave evidence against him, a rare occurrence in English courts but one that convinced the jury of his guilt. Sending him to prison for life, Mr Justice Ashworth commented:

> There must be many mothers in Walsall and the area, whose hearts will beat more lightly as a result of this verdict. It must have been a nightmare for the mothers and fathers of Walsall over the last months when they heard a child may be missing.

One question remains: did Morris also murder Diane Joy Tift and Margaret Reynolds? Only he knows. There was never any evidence produced against him. But there have been no more child murders in the Cannock Chase area since he began his long sentence.

The Kray Twins
Directors of 'The Firm'

They were identical twins: one a homosexual, the other a ladies' man. One was certified insane, the other impersonated him at the mental hospital to prove his sanity. Together they murdered, ran extortion and protection rackets and were the managing directors of 'The Firm', considered by both police and criminals to be the most evil and vicious organised gang in the history of crime in Britain.

But their empire of brutality toppled at the Central Criminal Court in 1969 when the Kray twins, Ronald and Reginald, then aged thirty-five were gaoled for life. Mr Justice Melford Stevenson, widely regarded as one of the country's toughest judges, recommended to the Home Secretary that their crimes warranted the minimum of thirty years behind bars. After a dramatic and criminally historic trial which lasted forty days the stern-faced judge contemptuously dismissed the self-styled kings of London's gangland in three short sentences: 'I am not going to waste words on you. I sentence you to life imprisonment. In my view society has earned a rest from your activities and I recommend that you be detained for thirty years.'

Ronnie Kray, convicted of two sadistic murders, grimaced at the judge's pronouncement. As he was led from the dock, flanked by four burly warders, his only reaction was to point his fingers, pistol fashion, at someone in the public gallery. His twin, Reggie, showed no emotion as he followed his brother to the cells. Their elder brother, Charles, then aged forty-two, was sentenced to serve ten years for being an accessory to one of the killings. In addition, four of the Kray henchmen, who had stood in the dock alongside them, were also given life sentences and three other members of the gang were sentenced to a total of nineteen years in prison. Ronnie Kray, known to his men as 'The Colonel' had been convicted for the murders of George Cornell, a bookmaker's clerk, and Jack 'The Hat' McVitie, an out-of-work small-time gambler. Reggie was convicted for the savage death of McVitie and being an accessory to the killing of Cornell. Their trial had been one of the most sensational in modern British legal history and day after day the court was told horrifying tales of how the twins had administered their criminal empire. The jurors were shocked to learn of the cold-blooded manner in which Ronnie had calmly shot Cornell at point blank range in the busy saloon bar of the Blind Beggar public house, Whitechapel, in March 1966. Cornell had virtually signed his own death warrant the night before, after a violent row with the mercurial twins, during which he called Ronnie Kray 'a queer'. It was an insult the homosexual could not take from anyone outside his own closely-knit circle of family and friends, and his retribution was quick, sharp and permanent.

The following night, shortly before 8.30pm, Ronnie Kray, accompanied by one of his toughest henchmen, John 'Scotch Ian' Barrie, walked into the public house where Cornell was sitting on a high stool at the bar with two friends. The juke box was playing 'The Sun Ain't Going to Shine Anymore'. The unsuspecting Cornell glanced casually round and had time only to say cockily: 'Look who's here' before he was blasted from his stool and lay dying on the bar floor, a lethal bullet from the Kray gun having passed through his head.

The sickening story of the Krays became even more ghastly when the jurors learned how McVitie came to die. Of all the cold-blooded killings recorded in the archives of Scotland Yard, this must rate as one of the worst. Its premeditation almost defies belief and its savagery can be described only as animalistic. 'Jack the Hat' was his own worst enemy and had been foolish enough to let it become generally known among the gossiping circles of London's underworld that he disapproved of the Krays' methods. It was after he had angrily argued with the twins' friends that the pair lost their patience with the balding would-be gambler. McVitie immediately became a prime and convenient target who would satisfy the brothers' craving to be always on equal terms. Following the death of Cornell, Ronnie had goaded his brother daily saying 'I've done mine, now you do yours'. Reggie could stand it no longer and plans were made to execute 'Jack the Hat', the victim whose nickname derived from the fact that he constantly wore a trilby to cover his balding head.

He was lured to a drinking party at a flat in the tough East End, an area where nobody, even the respectable, argued with the demands of the ruthless twins who were uncrowned kings of the territory. Possibly with some reluctance, but clearly with no foreboding of how the night would end, McVitie accepted the invitation from the brothers Christopher and Anthony Lambrianou, two of the Krays' most vicious and trusted lieutenants. Everything was prepared for his arrival and it was agreed that Reggie should be the executioner. As McVitie walked into the 'party' in the small flat in Evering Road Reggie took careful aim as he levelled an automatic pistol at his victim's head and squeezed the trigger. Inexplicably, the firing mechanism failed. Had everything gone as planned McVitie would not have known a thing, only sudden blackness. In the event he terrifyingly realised what was in store and frenziedly threw himself at a near-by window in a desperate but futile attempt to escape the brutality he knew would follow. Ronnie and his cohorts dragged him unceremoniously back into the centre of the room and Reggie, his eyes wide with anticipation, produced a sharp twelve-inch-long carving knife. Terrified and bathed in sweat, like an animal frantically seeking escape from its restrictive cage, McVitie struggled for freedom. But Ronnie, who had done his job, held McVitie tightly from behind, pinioning his arms, while Reggie picked up the knife and plunged it into his face. Then he punched his bleeding victim over the heart and repeatedly sank the blood-stained blade into the sagging body of McVitie with the background accompaniment of his brother screaming over and over again, 'Kill him Reg . . . ., Kill him'. McVitie crumpled to the floor, mortally wounded and gasping for breath. But the savage butchery was not yet over. Reggie Kray straddled his dying victim and plunged the knife twice into his neck twisting it at the same time to make sure its deadly work was done. The elation of the blood-covered twins subsided and both calmly began organising their alibis and the disposal of Reggie's 'equaliser'.

The Krays felt completely safe and beyond the law and their total arrogance was manifested much later when they were charged with 'Jack the Hat's' murder. Ronnie told the police: 'Your sarcastic insinuations are far too obnoxious to be appreciated.' Reggie, when he was charged, snapped coldly: 'Not guilty.' Despite the heavy sentences they received for these two killings, the Kray twins' total contempt for law and order was demonstrated yet again when they made their second appearance at the Old Bailey some months later, this time for the murder of Frank 'The Mad Axeman' Mitchell, whose escape from Dartmoor they had planned and financed. During the trial, at which the Krays were found not guilty of murder, it was stated that Mitchell disappeared and had never been seen again after spending a week as the guest of the twins—along with a woman also provided by them—at a flat in East London.

Murder was a sideline, 'The Firm's' real business centred around racketeering involving clubs, betting shops, dubious businesses, gambling and blackmail. Their empire proliferated and was organised and adminstered like a huge collection agency. Teams of 'heavies' toured the East End of London and later moved into the smart West End, demanding 'commissions'—protection money. Victims were always given a choice: 'Either pay up, or we will put you out of business.' Those who refused often fled, leaving their sometimes lucrative businesses in the hands of the Kray twins. Those who agreed found themselves increasingly bled for larger sums.

It was this real fear of 'The Firm' which hindered police inquiries when it was decided, after top level discussions at Scotland Yard, to compulsorily liquidate the Krays' business enterprises. Only much cajoling by the police investigating the gang, and a faithful promise that nothing anyone said would be used until after the Krays were arrested and safely in custody, persuaded a few brave businessmen to come forward with enough damning facts to make a case. Their courage became contagious and many others, who for years had lived in the shadow of fear created by the twins, decided once and for all to shake off the yoke of gangsterism which had weighed them down for more than a decade. Many were given armed guards to protect themselves and their families during the agonising months between the Krays' arrest and their final appearance at the Old Bailey. The police genuinely feared that attempts would be made to 'nobble' their hard-won witnesses. As a result, some of the most vital were moved to homes in different areas to avoid interference.

There was another facet of the Kray twins' character which misled scores of famous people, usually those connected with the entertainment business. For there was nothing the two sharply dressed brothers enjoyed more than the night life of London's fashionable West End and being seen and photographed in the company of show business personalities. Their grinning faces were constantly being snapped with their arms flung familiarly around people like singer Billy Daniels, actors George Raft and Edmund Purdom, politicians Tom Driberg and Lord Boothby, boxers Joe Louis and Freddie Mills.

There is no doubt they had a 'personality complex'. It was almost certainly an attempt to shake off the psychological chains of their poor East End upbringing and their many earlier brushes with authority which had seen them both in prison, on courts martial charges whilst in the army, and sometimes the butt of audience criticism while both fairly successful but undistinguished professional boxers. The only chance they had of joining what they considered to be the élite set was to buy themselves into the company. Even when they knew Scotland Yard had established a special squad to smash their empire, Ronnie and Reggie still boasted at expensive night club dinner parties how they would outsmart the two senior detectives assigned to the case, Detective Chief Superintendent Fred Gerrard and Detective Superintendent Leonard 'Nipper' Read. They went so far as to buy a boa-constrictor as a pet and named it Gerrard, much to the amusement of their society friends. They dined out regularly on the story of how Gerrard had disappeared and, on the best possible advice, they had bought yet another boa-constrictor, which they were assured would find the missing snake. They called the second one Nipper. Indeed it was not long before Nipper found Gerrard.

One story they never recounted—and it is probably a significant insight into their characters—was how they bought a string of ponies and used them to play Cowboys and Indians in Epping Forest. Not many of their impressionable friends would have laughed if told how Ronnie stalked his brother during one of their western fantasies and so startled Reggie's mount that it bucked and threw him to the ground. Furious, Reggie chased the animal and punched it so violently on the nose that its legs buckled beneath it.

Notice his anger was not directed at his brother, from whom he was inseparable. Despite quarrels, they would do anything for each other and this had been demonstrated clearly on at least two occasions. The first was when Ronnie was serving part of a prison sentence at Long Grove mental hospital Epsom, Surrey where he was being treated after being certified insane. On the day Reggie visited, they exchanged places. Ronnie walked to freedom and Reggie hopped into the hospital bed to impersonate his brother. Five months later when he was recaptured, Ronnie claimed the switch was done to prove his sanity, a view upheld by a panel of experts who returned him to prison to serve the remainder of his sentence. The second was after beginning their life sentences and they had been sent to separate prisons. Both pined so much for each other that the Home Office finally agreed, on medical grounds, to accommodate them under the same roof, but in different cells at the top security wing of Parkhurst prison in the Isle of Wight.

Charles Kray has since been released on parole, still emphatically protesting his complete innocence.

Frederick Joseph Sewell
Gunman who killed a hero

Eight policemen and a widow went to Buckingham Palace to be honoured as heroes by the Queen after Frederick Joseph Sewell was sent to prison for thirty years. The widow was Mrs Maureen Richardson, whose husband Gerald had been shot dead in cold blood as he tried to arrest Sewell who was armed with a 7.65 mm automatic revolver. Superintendent Richardson, head of Blackpool Borough Police, was awarded the George Cross posthumously. Eight of his men shared another George Cross, four George Medals, two British Empire Medals and a Queen's Commendation for Brave Conduct.

The 23 August 1971 was a bright, warm, summer's day. Thousands of holidaymakers were strolling towards the beaches along Blackpool's Golden Mile. It was, as one described later, a good-to-be-alive day. Then in less than twenty minutes nine shots were fired; £106,000 worth of jewellery was stolen; Superintendent Richardson lay dying in the back of an ambulance and two of his men were injured by gunshots.

Forty-five days later, 7 October, 228 miles away in London, Sewell, then described as the most wanted man in Britain, was arrested. So ended one of the most intensive manhunts ever mounted in Britain.

Sewell, a heavy, thick-set bully, and four others made their first visit to Blackpool the week before the shooting to reconnoitre the jeweller's shop in The Strand, and the immediate vicinity. Then after a week of planning in a café in South London where Sewell was a car dealer, they returned to carry out what one of them described as a 'simple job'. But their plans went awry when the gang panicked, leaving a trail of rings and bracelets from the shop to their waiting getaway car. As Sir Peter Rawlinson QC, the Attorney General, said at their trial later: 'Their incompetence as robbers, was matched only by their ruthlessness in the use of firearms to evade arrest.'

Their first mistake was made while they were still in the shop scooping up trays of jewellery; such was their haste that they overlooked Mr Joseph Lammond, the shop's sales manager, slip into his office and set off the alarm. Within seconds the police were alerted. First on the scene was Police Constable Carl Walker, driving a patrol car, who saw the gang running to their stolen getaway car. After chasing them for just over a mile he trapped them in a *cul-de-sac*. Sewell who was driving, slammed his car into reverse gear, and knocked the police car across the street. Constable Walker continued the chase in his damaged vehicle, however, until he saw the five men abandon their car. 'I ran after them. I had already heard shots. I passed two policemen and I could see two other men ahead. One of them turned and pointed the gun at me'. The man with the gun was Sewell. In quick succession he loosed off two bullets at the officer from a distance of about twelve yards. Both missed. Describing the incident later PC Walker said:

I ran on. I kept at him. As I ran towards him he fired from about six feet. I rolled up like a ball. Something hit me in the leg and I went down. As I went down the gunman went to the rear of a parked van nearby where there were two other men. I think I got up. The man who shot me had his back to me. Then he turned and came towards me. I went down again. He leant over me. He pointed a gun at my head. I turned my head away. The gun was about two feet away. Then a police car arrived and the man ran and got into the van and drove away.

PC Walker was helped into a house and other officers took up the chase. Police Constable Ian Hampson, then aged twenty-eight, concentrated his attention on John Patrick Spry, one of the gang who was also armed. As the officer pulled up his car behind the Triumph, Spry shot him at close range in the chest, only a fraction of an inch from his heart. But still the police pursued the gang. Sewell was finally cornered by Superintendent Richardson who felled him with a Rugby tackle. Both men wrestled in the road; Sewell, gun in left hand, desperately trying to shake off the officer who had a fierce grip on his throat. Then within three seconds two shots were fired. The first tore a hole in the sleeve of the officer's uniform. The second hit the Superintendent in the stomach. Sewell escaped through a maze of back streets. The other four were later arrested. With the help of an accomplice, a woman, Sewell hid in the boot of a car and was driven to the Lake District and then to London by a circuitous route.

By this time a massive search was on for Sewell, then aged thirty-eight, whose name had been given to the police by one of the members of his gang. Detective Chief Superintendent Joe Mounsey, head of Lancashire CID, was put in charge of the case. It was obvious by now that Sewell would be back in London.

After a telephone conversation between his Chief Constable, Mr William Palfrey, and the then Commissioner of the Metropolitan Police, Sir John Waldron, it was agreed that Mr Mounsey should centre his investigations at Tintagel House.

This was a unique situation; never before had a provincial detective been allowed to lead a murder hunt in London. Under his command were men of the Flying Squad, the Regional Crime Squad and many of his own officers from Lancashire.

Several rewards were offered, including one by the *Daily Mirror* of £10,000 for information leading to the arrest of Sewell. It was this which finally persuaded an informant to betray the address of Sewell's hiding place. At 6.45am on 7 October, a grey foggy morning, Mr Mounsey divided up his team of more than 200 officers into seven squads. All were given a secret briefing at which they were given the addresses of seven houses in London. After dispatching his men he decided to lead personally a raid on a terraced house in Birnam Road, Holloway. The front door was forced open and the officers, Mr Mounsey leading, ran upstairs and shouldered open a bedroom door. Sewell, naked, a gun beside his bed, was awake, but was given no chance to move as he reached for his gun. He was taken to Holloway Police Station and locked in a cell while Mr Mounsey, who had worked tirelessly those six weeks, reported to his chief from his temporary office at Tintagel House. He also made a point of thanking personally all those who had worked with him. As he left to take his prisoner back to Blackpool a crowd of about 200 Londoners cheered him as he drove north. At Blackpool four and half hours later he was given a heroe's welcome by a cheering crowd of more than 500. Sewell was booed as he was driven into the police station where until the morning of 23 August, Superintendent Richardson had been in charge.

At his trial Sewell was sent to prison for a total of eighty years concurrently, for murder, attempted murder, robbery and conspiracy, with a recommendation that he should serve a minimum of thirty years. The epitaph to Superintendent Richardson was probably best spoken by his killer: 'He was too brave'.

Edward John Paisnel
The Beast of Jersey

This sadistic disciple of Black Magic who preyed on children and young women in Jersey for more than ten years, often subjecting them to horrifying acts of sexual assault and perversion, began his life sentence in September of 1971. A well-respected local building contractor, and the first man to denounce the sadist who had terrorised the island's 72,000 inhabitants, when drinking in his local public house, Paisnel was a Jekyll and Hyde character nobody suspected. For his daylight activities, repairing and patching up local homes, chatting happily to children who called him 'Uncle Ted', even at one time caring for orphans, he showed none of the traits of the monster he became when darkness fell.

For at night Paisnel worshipped at a grotesque shrine he had built to the Gods of Evil and Black Magic. It was here that he worked himself into a frenzy before purposely setting out under cover of darkness to savage his next victim. When he was finally brought to justice, the court at St Helier was told of fifteen separate acts of sexual assault, including rape and sodomy. One woman explained how, on a night in March 1960, she was at home with her 14-year-old daughter, her husband sick in hospital. Both were asleep when the telephone rang and the woman, dressing hurriedly, went downstairs to answer the call. Suddenly from the shadows a man appeared and pushed her into a chair where he gagged and bound her. The sight was so terrifying that the woman fainted, for the man was wearing a hideous rubber mask, a wig of fuzzy black hair and a coat edged with inch-long nails. Around his wrists were thick bands of elastic also studded with wickedly sharp nails. The struggle roused the daughter who was immediately carried off by the unknown assailant. Later the girl returned, saw her mother and said: 'I have been raped. Thank goodness you are alive. I thought you were dead.'

The jury heard from two other young girls, one aged seventeen, and the other twenty, how they had been raped in separate attacks by a man wearing a similar costume. The elder girl had been attacked in the countryside and knocked over a hedge. The younger one was carried from her bedroom to an adjacent field where the man assaulted her while holding a pair of scissors to her throat. The next witness was a distressed father who told the court how in 1964 he heard cries coming from his 16-year-old son's bedroom. The boy had told him that a masked man had just escaped after committing a violent sexual assault. The father had grabbed his loaded shot gun, and ran from the house and fired several cartridges into bushes, still rustling in the moonlight. A 17-year-old boy explained how he was awakened from a deep sleep by a man shining a bright torch into his eyes. He told how his brother, who was sleeping in the same room, was assaulted and described how the man opened the French windows and 'took me to a hut and assaulted me and said he would cut my throat if I cried.' Witness after witness told similar horrifying stores about the man who was known as 'The Beast' by all the islanders.

It was only later that police discovered how the victims, especially the children, had been selected. Often, when following his trade as a builder, Paisnel would be alone in homes where he was working. If the family had children he would memorise the layout of the property and note where the children slept. Then at night he would cunningly steal back to the bedrooms and carry off his victim. The attacks created such terrible lasting impressions on several young people that they refused to testify in court, mentally unable to re-live the gruesome details of their assaults.

Paisnel's career of Black Magic worship and perversion came to an abrupt end almost by accident on the night of 10 June as he was driving through the darkness to find his next victim. Unluckily for him it was that day that the body of a young girl had been found murdered and police sealed off all roads around St Helier and extra officers had been drafted into the area to maintain check-points. Then, as he approached one set of traffic lights in the car he had stolen earlier the same day, Paisnel was forced to slow down. Immediately he believed police activity was aimed at finding him and it was then he made his first mistake in nearly eleven years. He revved the engine and raced through the red light, soon being chased along the narrow country lanes by a police car at speeds approaching eighty miles an hour. What he did not realise was that the police thought their speeding quarry was merely an erring motorist. But finally Paisnel's car was overtaken and forced to a halt. The alarmed builder leapt from the vehicle and ran across adjacent fields. It was not total darkness and Police Constable John Riseborough, a stocky Rugby player, realising this was no ordinary motorist, quietly stalked him.

Suddenly the two met and the young policeman hurled himself in a flying tackle, grabbed Paisnel about the knees and threw him to the ground. For five minutes the two wrestled and fought until another police officer arrived to help in the arrest. A few minutes later Constable Riseborough learned why his uniform was ripped and his hands scratched and bleeding. In the headlights of his car he noticed Paisnel's long blue jacket with its lapels and shoulders closely studded with inch-long nails. Around his wrists were the nail-studded bands. The two policemen searched his clothing and found the terrifying rubber mask hidden in the lining of his coat. In the car was a woman's black wig and a yard-long piece of knotted sash cord. The frightened builder hurriedly explained that his weird garb was to protect him against judo and karate attacks. At St Helier police headquarters he was interviewed by Detective Inspector George Shutler, who had worked tirelessly for eleven years, even forgoing holidays in his efforts to catch 'The Beast' he was convinced was responsible for at least twenty brutal sexual assaults. Of the moment they came face to face Mr Shutler said:

As soon as we met I knew we had the right man. We had never met before but I was not surprised when he was brought into my office. He looked exactly as I had always pictured him in my mind's eye. He had been described to me more than a dozen times by various witnesses. I had lived with this man's description since 1960. Face-to-face he fitted perfectly the picture I had built up.

Paisnel's behaviour in the detective's tiny first floor office revealed for the first time the true character of 'Uncle Ted'. A cross, fashioned from reeds and not unlike those distributed to church congregations on Palm Sunday, had been found in the stolen car. Mr Shutler held it up in front of Paisnel whose face turned puce, his eyes bulging. He quickly recovered some composure, but stammered, 'My master would laugh very long and loud over this.' He was asked: 'Are you afraid of the cross?' A smirk twitched the corners of his mouth as he snapped back: 'Not particularly. There is a much more powerful emblem than yours. Our cocoon is getting larger, yours is shrinking.'

This interview was interrupted as Detective Sergeant James Marsh returned from searching the rambling Paisnel home. In an upstairs bedroom, behind a red curtain, the sergeant had found an alcove covered with brown felt and black material. This was Paisnel's Black Magic altar. On another wall was a large, black wooden dagger, suspended over a chalice, and a china dish containing toads. Sergeant Marsh told the Inspector:

> I was bending down, examining something on the floor when I noticed a cupboard. It began to move. I looked again and found that the whole cupboard was fixed on hinges. I struck a match but there was a sudden draught which blew out the light. It was very eerie. For several minutes I pulled and tugged at the cupboard and suddenly it swung open, revealing a secret room, leading to a loft.

In this room Paisnel stored the paraphernalia for his weird Devil-worshipping rites. 'The Beast' was captured and his reign of terror over.

But his Black Magic continued in prison, where he fashioned tiny soap effigies of Mr Shutler, piercing them with sharp pins as he summoned the power of his Master to curse the detectives who had hunted him for so long.

chapter four

Juveniles

Children and their parents   Pay mothers to care   Police truancy patrols
Teenage dial-for-advice scheme   The policeman and his drug addict
son   Recidivists at twelve years of age   Murder for pleasure   The influence
of violence in films   Pupils burn their schools down   Children in prison

Society gets the children it deserves, according to one of Britain's leading
experts on juvenile delinquency—an observation many fear will have frightening
significance when the present generation of teenagers attain adulthood. Even a
casual glance at the crime statistics is sufficient to detect a trend which, if
unchecked, could lead to a decade of violence, the like of which has never been
experienced in this country. Parents will ignore it at their peril and will have
much to answer for when their children, quite justifiably, indict them for
culpable negligence and wilful ignorance. Those who criticise the young out of
hand with a shrug and a sigh, should pay them the common courtesy, if nothing
more, of at least trying to understand them, feeling more at ease pouring out
their problems with an anonymous stranger over the telephone, than having a
heart-to-heart chat with their parents. In some cases the children are as young as
eight years old. It must surely make one wonder whether children of such tender
years really deserve the parents they get.

   Children, from the beginning of time, have been getting into trouble, and the
present generation is certainly no exception. Only the causes and the effects
have changed. Governments, here and abroad, have allocated millions of
pounds, and learned men and women have dedicated their lives to attempting to
rationalise and solve the problems of the young. But still, those who have most
contact with them, except their parents, it seems, fear the 1970s will break all
statistical records for juvenile crime, with violence causing the gravest concern.
An analysis of this aspect of the problem has rarely been more simply or
sympathetically explained than in a lecture given late in 1973 by Dr Mia Kellmer
Pringle, director of the National Children's Bureau, to an audience of police
chiefs and local government officals.

Research had shown, she said, that violence, and vandalism which often accompanied it, was probably linked to the 'most basic emotional needs and to the extent to which these are met or remain unfulfilled'. These needs fell into four main categories: the need for love and security; the need for new experiences; the need for praise and recognition; and the need for responsibility.

These needs have to be met from the very beginning of life and continue to require fulfilment, to a greater or lesser extent, until the end of life. If one of these basic needs remains unmet, or inadequately met, then one of two reactions follows: fight or flight, attack or withdrawal. Society reacts much more strongly to those children and young adults who respond by fighting, attacking—probably because this is seen as a challenge to authority; because it arouses feelings of aggression and revenge; and because by force we can control its outward expression, at least temporarily. But there is little evidence that meeting aggression with coercion brings about any lasting change; rather, a vicious circle is set up—with escalating violence and inevitably more forceful control. The need for love was probably the most important of the four classifications. When it is not met adequately, then the consequences are pretty disastrous later on, both for the individual and for society. Our prisons, mental hospitals, borstals and hospitals for the maladjusted, contain a high proportion of individuals who in childhood were unloved and rejected; their number is high too, among the chronically unemployable and among what I have termed the able misfits. Anger, hate and lack of concern for others are common reactions to being unloved and rejected. Vandalism and violence are an expression of these feelings. This same reaction can be seen in embryo, when a young child who has been scolded or smacked, goes and kicks his doll, or the dog, or a table. Through a loving relationship, children learn to control their anger or to use it constructively; without affection, it remains primitive and grows more vicious and vengeful with increasing physical strength.

The second of Dr Pringle's priorities—the need for new experiences—is essential to the development of a child's intelligence. The more dull and uneventful life is the more boredom, frustration and restlessness is created.

This is shown clearly by the contrast betwen the eagerness, alertness and vitality of normal babies whose life is filled with new experiences and challenges; and the aimlessness and boredom of the adolescent with nothing to do and nowhere to go. In seeking, legitimately, for the excitement of new experiences, where few are to be found or unattainable, the forbidden, risky or dangerous are liable to acquire an aura of daring and excitement. What may start as a lark, an expression of high spirits and the desire for adventure, can turn into vandalism and violence. This happens all the more readily, the longer and more pervasive the boredom and frustration of their lives. One outstanding fact is that violence and vandalism are predominantly male activities. Why should this be so? One explanation may be that boys and men have a greater desire, perhaps even need, for experiences which are challenging or dangerous. Another is that physical punishment and violence are more often meted out to boys than girls, which is likely in turn to provoke aggressiveness and violence.

Many parents who throw their hands in the air in a despairing gesture and mutter, 'I don't know what will become of you' would do well to ponder what Dr Pringle calls the third basic need—praise and recognition. To grow from a helpless baby into a self-reliant adult, she explains, requires an immense amount of emotional, social and intellectual learning.

It is accomplished by the child's modelling himself on the adults who are caring for him. The most effective incentives to bring this about—which requires continuous effort, sustained throughout the years of growing up—are praise and recognition. Eventually a job well done becomes its own reward but that is a very mature stage; and even the most mature adult responds and, indeed, blossoms, when given, at least occasionally, some praise or other form of recognition. Unfortunately we give praise and recognition to achievement and not to effort. In consequence, this need is readily and often satisfied in the case of intelligent, healthy, adjusted and attractive children. In contrast, the intellectually slow, the culturally disadvantaged, the emotionally deprived or disturbed, get far less, if any, praise and recognition. Yet their need is very much greater. Whatever small successes they have, inevitably demand much effort and perseverance; yet they receive less reward because they achieve less. Worse still, those who are rejected by their parents, and regarded as failures by their teachers, are wholly deprived of the satisfaction of this need by adults. The only avenue open to them is to win the admiration and recognition of their mates. Being accepted as a member of a gang, or better still becoming its leader, is one means of achieving this. Then, it is not behaving in a way an individual would not do by himself but is enabled to by being carried along by the contagious excitement and safety of a group—all these are characteristic of gangs and able misfits—rejected, affectionateless youngsters, whose ability is unrecognised—may be the 'brains'.

The need for responsibility, the last of the four formative desires required by the growing child, is met, says Dr Pringle, at a very early age through possessions, toys for example, over which a child is allowed to exercise absolute ownership. Children who are denied the opportunities to exercise responsibility will fail to develop a sense of responsibility for themselves, for others, or for material objects.

The upbringing of such children, also, often lacks training and self-control, in waiting and working for what they want, and in treasuring their own and other people's property. In consequence, such young people tend to be impulsive, unwilling (and unable in some cases) to postpone the immediate gratification of their impulses, and contemptuous of the rights of others. Among them one would expect a high degree of vandalism and violence.

On leaving school many youngsters drift into boring, repetitive, and mentally undemanding jobs. The advances of technology and automation have taken much of the physical demands out of work, too, leaving stores of pent up energy unused. Unemployment, which often faces the less able and intellectually slow is another factor which hits the young. The effect is plain and disturbing. As Dr Pringle comments:

> Enforced idleness, boredom and little money in his pocket tend to under-mine further what little self-respect is left to the adolescent who has for years been caught up in a web of multiple disadvantages. Feeling that society disowns him, may well engender a feeling that he in turn owes nothing to society.

These then are some of the problems confronting the young; their causes make an almost never-ending list. Prominent among them must be their environment, cramped living conditions with little or no facilities for play; overcrowded classrooms; lack of parental interest and control; commercial exploitation; undue, and often unpleasant, influences from television, films, magazines and newspapers; the sensationalising of exploits by the notorious and infamous; and an adult society too busy worrying about their own problems to pause and ponder the plight of others. No wonder many youngsters feel that to command attention they need to resort to outrageous acts of violence, theft or drug taking.

Happily, Britain has no monopoly where juvenile delinquency is concerned. In the autumn of 1973 France played host to thirteen other European countries who sent ministers to a three-day conference at Nice to discuss 'Children in Danger'. The French minister for public health and social security, Mr Michael Poniatowski, advanced an interesting plan, which is now being considered by the British Government. He suggested that mothers of 'difficult' youngsters should be paid to stay at home and care for their children in cases where they needed to leave them to go out to work. The thought that some mothers would actually get a 'wage' for performing their moral duty as a parent is unattractive, to say the least, but it must be considered against a background of ever increasing juvenile crime. For example the number of juveniles brought before the courts in Britain during the ten years from 1963 increased by 80 per cent. The same disturbing figure was recorded for West Germany. France had a staggering rise of 150 per cent. Even Switzerland showed a jump of 46 per cent during the same period.

Realistically, Mr Poniatowski explained that the most difficult preventive measures for children and young people at risk were those designed to help the family. The place of the family in society was fundamental and should be assured without penalising the mother, who through economic necessity, was forced to go out to work. The state, he argued, should recognise the role of a mother as an 'economic activity' and where necessary pay her to stay at home to bring up her family. Undesirable as the scheme is in many ways it could, in time, have a great stabilising effect on the young and even save money. This would be achieved, if the mothers played their part industriously, by reducing the number of policemen needed to concentrate on catching their wayward off-spring, saving the time and expense of courts and social workers and ultimately doing away with the need to provide costly accommodation in remand homes and borstals. A more settled home life would almost certainly cut down the incidence of vandalism which with each year presents the nation with a multi-million pound bill.

An interesting experiment conducted by Glasgow police in 1973 demonstrated how children respond to supervision. Senior officers in the Shettleston area of the city were becoming concerned at the increasing number of thefts from houses, shops and parked cars. The robberies bore all the hallmarks of children being the culprits, but were taking place when they should have been at school. So, for an experimental period of eleven days special 'Truancy Patrols' were set up in the area with extra officers patrolling the streets during school hours. At the end of the period there was a noticeable decrease in crime in Shettleston. The period of operation, however, had obviously been too short for any sound conclusion to be reached so a second experiment spanning two months, between April and June, was approved by the Chief Constable.

Four constables, all young men, and a sergeant were drafted into the area and told that all children seen on the streets between 9am and 4pm, except during the lunch hour, should be stopped, asked why they were not at school, and then taken either to their homes or their schools, whichever was nearer, so that the reasons given by the children could be checked either with their parents or teachers. At the end of the experiment truancy dropped to almost nil in most local schools. During the two months 665 truants were caught by the police, and of that total nearly a hundred were between the ages of seven and ten. When the figures were compared with those kept by the school attendance officers it was found that of the total 264 who were listed as persistent truants, 181 of these came from problem families. During the months, April, May and June, crime dropped by nearly 20 per cent compared with the same period the previous year.

Going to school is a problem for some children, as this experiment in Glasgow proved. Being at school also creates problems for children, especially those in the 14-16 age group. This is the period which brings teenagers face to face with emotional problems never before experienced. Aware of this, the Home Office and the Department of Health and Social Security launched a seven year experiment at selected high density schools with between 600 and 1,000 pupils. One unknown factor which educationists were keen to study was the effect such huge groupings would have on the individual child. Four big secondary modern or comprehensive schools were chosen in and around the Blackburn area to pilot the scheme. Each school was assigned a social worker who was provided with an office where children with problems could be referred to them for interviews. At the outset only children sent along by the headmaster, or headmistress, or a teacher were seen. But as the social worker became more and more part of the school scene children began to seek advice voluntarily, not waiting for the staff to make an appointment for them.

The social workers entered into the spirit of the scheme to such an extent that juvenile delinquency was soon reduced by about one third. At the end of the seven years the Blackburn education authorities were so impressed with the results that they persuaded the social workers to stay on and even recruited more for other schools. By visiting children at home after school hours and during the holidays the social workers were able to discover problems which without their help would never have been detected or resolved.

Another experiment in West Germany designed to penetrate the barrier of silence and lack of confidence between child and parent is also proving successful. The country's Child Protection Society selected three major cities to establish an SOS telephone service day and night for teenagers with problems. The service is a cross between the Samaritans and the Citizens' Advice Bureaux in Britain, but aimed specifically at the young.

One of the organisers said:

We do not ask for callers' names and addresses. We are more concerned with their worries and how to fix them as soon and as best as we can. We do not keep any files, except the names of experts and specialists we can call upon at any time to help us. We believe our anonymity principle is the best way to get young people to trust us. We are all mothers so we try to talk to our callers like mothers and give them first of all, some calming sympathy. If they need medical, legal or other official help we tell them whom to contact or arrange an appointment for them, if need be. We do not see ourselves as experts—just universal aunties applying common-sense with heart.

Many of the problems dealt with by the service involve worries about sex, school, work, home life and drug addiction. Drug taking, without doubt, is becoming an increasing problem among the young. It is a problem few of their parents encountered or experienced during their adolescence and therefore they find themselves ill-equipped to deal with it within the confines of the family home. One parent who suffered the anguish of discovering his son was a drug taker was Police Inspector Reg Gale, who from 1970 until his retirement in 1974 because of ill-health, was chairman of the Police Federation, the policeman's trade union. It is difficult to imagine his horror when he discovered that his youngest son had been taking drugs at the early age of twelve and was injecting himself with heroin at sixteen. Six years later, though convinced the boy had been cured of the habit, he was again found in possession of illegal drugs and was fined £50. To any 'ordinary' parent the shock, the shame and the grief would have been impossible to hide. But to a senior policeman, whose colleagues were firmly of the view that anyone caught taking, pushing or possessing drugs should be 'stamped on' and dealt with severely, it was a shock which ironically made him change this deeply held view. To the consternation and anger of many of his colleagues Mr Gale began to air his new attitude towards drug-taking. In fact, after a series of newspaper, magazine and television interviews on the the subject he launched an appeal for drug rehabilitation projects entitled 'Action in Distress'. He said:

> I had now learnt that fighting the drug taker doesn't work. The deeper problems involved usually can be met only with understanding and the parent is often best suited to be a kind of sheet anchor. We have to find an alternative to the courts as a means of dealing with people arrested for possessing drugs—some form of social rehabilitation.

His advice to other worried parents was simply:

> If you don't know what it is about, consult someone who does. It is sometimes better to go to a non-qualified worker in the drug scene than to a medical practitioner.

A survey conducted by the Home Office Research Unit into drug-taking by under-16-year-olds published in 1973 concluded that fines were the most effective form of punishment in preventing re-conviction of first offenders. For those with previous convictions probation proved to be the best deterrent. Among the sample of nearly 300 children were boys and girls aged twelve and thirteen. One shocking case involving a 12-year-old girl, not included in this survey, came to the notice of the authorities during a trial at Winchester. Two youths of eighteen and nineteen were charged with having unlawful sexual intercourse with the girl, who looked, it was admitted, much older than her years. So 'hooked' on drugs was the girl that she allowed the two boys to have intercourse with her in return for some pills. Astonished at what he had heard, Judge Louis McCreery told them:

> It is abundantly clear that you would not have become involved with this girl had she not forced her attentions on you. It is an appalling thing to think that a girl of twelve should be loose on the streets telling men she will do anything, including having sexual intercourse, in return for drugs. I have rarely met a more frightening picture of a girl of that age.

Even prosecuting counsel was moved to comment: 'The degree of depravity is surprising.' The youths were given a conditional discharge for twelve months.

The drinking of alcohol and the ease with which young children can obtain it is also giving the authorities, especially the police, cause for grave concern. One headmaster in the West Country was forced to write to parents threatening to expel or hand their children over to the police, after he found several boys returning to afternoon lessons under the influence of alcohol. Inquiries showed that the boys were missing their school lunches to visit a local supermarket where they could buy beer, cider and spirits, with few questions asked by the busy check-out staff. Research on the juvenile drink problem carried out in 1972 and 1973 showed that the north-west of England had more teenage 'drunks' than any other part of the country, including London. In fact when the figures for Liverpool, Bootle, Salford, Manchester and other parts of Lancashire were added together it was found that a quarter of all boys aged between fourteen and eighteen convicted of drunkenness came from this one area. It is perhaps significant that Liverpool and Bootle had the worst record for drunkenness among all age groups outside London.

Although these findings are not conclusive in any way they do tend to indicate that in some cases bad parental influences can corrupt children at a very early age. Although the age of criminal responsibility is ten there is ample proof that many children launch themselves, or sometimes are launched by their parents and contemporaries, on a career of crime at a much earlier age. One of many examples concerned a 10-year-old boy whom detectives in London seriously regarded as a professional thief. He was caught by chance breaking into a house and his fingerprints were taken. As a result the police were able to clear up twenty-three hitherto unsolved thefts and robberies.

On closer investigation the police also found that the boy was the leader of a gang which comprised his two younger brothers aged nine and eight. Their technique at breaking and entering was a classic case of copying well-tried and proven methods—the older boy would shin up a drain-pipe, climb through an open window and then calmly stroll downstairs to open the front door to let his brothers in. In one week alone they netted more than £1,000 worth of valuables, including jewellery, none of which was ever traced. Comprehending such audacity and daring by three virtual 'toddlers' makes the mind boggle but actually disposing of the stolen property through a 'fence' must surely have involved someone older. Detectives had another shock, again in London, when they set out to break up a sophisticated gang of violent thieves. When arrested the three 'men' they had been hunting had ages ranging from ten to fourteen. One of their 'jobs' was to break into an elderly widow's home, while she was there. Within minutes they pocketed every valuable item they could lay their hands on and fled through the front door, leaving the woman in a severe state of shock. On the pavement outside, the eldest boy asked: 'Wasn't there a meter in there?' Without a word they returned to the house, terrorised the old lady further and robbed both gas and electricity meters. One senior detective, in a North London area prone to teenage crime, said:

You can label some of these children quite accurately as recidivists by the time they are twelve. There are some kids you know are away on holiday if they are not arrested for a week. You just sit back and wait for a call from some county police force. During the summer we are flooded with inquiries from all over the country about them.

Social workers who have interviewed some of these children are alarmed, not so much at the crimes they commit, but by their couldn't-care-less attitude when questioned. One summed it up as: 'They don't give a damn for anyone or anything so long as they get what they want.'

These youngsters aroused the suspicions of an alert policeman . . .

. . and one was just a bit reluctant to go quietly

The problem of juvenile crime was taking on such proportions in the Camden area of London that the local council called a 'summit' meeting of heads of department of all organisations concerned in any way with children, in the hope that someone would be able to come up with an idea that would help either to cut down or even contain the growing teenage crime wave. Violence by children under fourteen was causing the greatest concern, with one case of assault on a police officer by a 12-year-old boy, demonstrating the lawlessness in that area. Magistrates who were called to the meeting explained how demoralised they were, feeling that they had insufficient powers. Recent experience had shown them that there was evidence that children under the age of ten—and so outside the law—were deliberately being used by older children and adults in carefully planned crimes. They had also detected an attitude of utter contempt for both the courts and the police by many of the youngsters who had no fear of the consequences and openly ridiculed their light punishments. Inevitably, it is the elderly and infirm who fall victim to these young 'monsters', as one social worker described them. The plight of one of them, Miss Rose Allison, aged eighty-one and blind, typifies the fear of the aged. Miss Allison, who lives in a flat on the Peabody Estate in Camden needed two white walking sticks to help her get about to do her shopping. Suddenly she was chosen as a victim, a plaything and a figure of fun by the local children. Whenever she went out they would chase after her, swear, jeer, laugh and spit at her.

Being blind, Miss Allison would sit for hours listening to her radio set until the children outside her windows discovered this gave her pleasure. Gangs of them would take turns to create a din to drown the sounds coming from her set. 'I don't know why they do it or pick on me. I don't think they really know how cruel they are being', said Miss Allison, who during the Second World War helped to evacuate hundreds of children from London. 'Everyone was so friendly then', said the old lady sadly.

This callous lack of thought for the feelings of others is widespread throughout Britain, escalating from tormenting the old to murder. The weak, the old and the defenceless are natural victims, as was a 19-year-old youth in Edinburgh early in 1973. Chronically ill with asthma the youth was waiting alone at a bus stop when he was attacked by a 15-year-old boy who stabbed him to death in a frenzy. At his trial he said he had 'decided to stab somebody', because he 'approved of boys being stabbed'. Lord Brand, the Scottish High Court judge, could barely disguise his disgust when he sentenced the youth to be detained during Her Majesty's pleasure. He told him:

> This is one of the most disgraceful cases of murder that has ever come to my notice. It seems to me that if the public at large had heard the shocking evidence which we have heard in this court the clamour for the restoration of former methods of punishment would be even louder than it is. It appears to me that this murder was not committed for greed or lust or even on account of hatred, because the unfortunate and chronically ill youth whom you murdered was unknown to you. It appears that the murder was committed for no other reason than the pleasure of inflicting extreme violence.

Although the motives behind this crime are typical of many of the worst sorts of teenage violence now plaguing the country it differed in one important respect. This youth acted alone whereas the majority operate as gangs or in small groups. There is considerable evidence that many of these packs of marauding thugs are established within the school framework with bullies demanding protection money from smaller boys. One 14-year-old Northumberland boy, coincidentally also an asthma sufferer, ran away from home, because he could not keep up the demands of 15 pence a day. He simply left a note for his parents saying: 'I am sorry to do this but I just cannot cope.' A bully boy the same age was given a custodial sentence after admitting thirty-two cases of demanding money and assault on his school-mates. He admitted being the leader of a protection gang. Outside normal school hours these gangs manifest themselves in the guise of football fans, terrorising other supporters and innocent by-standers. After a 'friendly' match in Glasgow a 16-year-old boy, who was merely walking past the ground and had not been a spectator, was set upon and stabbed to death. More than forty youths were in the gang that struck him down.

It has become an accepted fact that wherever teenagers gather, ostensibly to watch a football match, an orgy of violence is likely to follow. Why? Perhaps the following comments, freely expressed by hooligans after matches in different parts of Britain, will help to enlighten if not explain.

'I lead a gang of about 150 of my mates at Chelsea. When it comes to a fight we use anything we can lay our hands on, bricks, bottle, pipes . . . you name it.' 'Of course we like watching the match but we like a good brawl, too.'
'We used to be able to take chains and coshes with us but the coppers stopped all that when they started searching us.'
'We got steel caps put into our boots so that we can get some real power into them. If you are kicked by them you won't get up in a hurry.'
'Part of the fun of going to a match is having a good punch-up and putting the boot in the rival supporters afterwards. I look forward to it—I've got nothing else to do.'
'We get niggled when our team loses.'
'It's exciting when we see the boys kicking and punching each other and we want to be a part of it', said a girl fan.

One father, who was present in court when his 17-year-old son was fined £100 for his part in a soccer riot, had very definite views on how to channel the boy's violent tendencies—he marched him straight to the nearest army recruiting office and made him 'sign on'. Aghast at the violence that accompanied the opening of the 1973 season, Mr Len Shipman, president of the Football League said: 'More ruthless action is imperative and I hope that it will be taken on the Government's direction. Fines will not stop the violence. The time has come for the return of the birch.'

The courts, too, decided to take stronger action, using their maximum powers to punish. Mr Peter Goldstone, the North London magistrate, who imposed heavy fines on one group of supporters told them: 'Hooliganism is terrorising city after city. It must be ruthlessly stamped out. Ordinary, decent people dare not walk the streets near major football grounds, and the courts have a duty to stop it.' Another magistrate in West London took the same stern line telling one thug: 'You are a miserable creature. You are a coward and an absolute rotter.'

A survey conducted by the Institute of Research Techniques at the London School of Economics on the causes of violence spanning a six-month period during which 1,565 boys aged between twelve and seventeen in London were interviewed concluded: 'Tolerance for minor violence is fairly widespread and there is a hard core of at least 10 per cent who seem attracted to or even enthusiastic about the use of violence generally.' Some of the findings were startling, to say the least. Nearly 200 boys admitted that in the six months prior to being interviewed they had committed serious acts of violence. Some quite freely admitted they had thrust broken bottles into other boys' faces; had tried to rape girls; smashed up cars with hammers; stabbed other boys; set fire to buildings; fired revolvers at people. Five per cent volunteered that 'shooting looks like fun'. Among other admissions were: 'I threatened to kill my father'; 'I broke into a house and smashed everything I could find'; 'I deliberately dropped a lighted cigarette into a shopper's bag'; 'I threw the cat on the fire'. Asked if they would be willing to shoot or stab someone, more than ninety boys said they would if their girl friend had been insulted. Over thirty said they would shoot or stab 'if they were in a bad mood'.

The study was aimed at discovering what influence violence shown on television had on the young. Dr William Belson, who led the research team, concluded that one of the main causes of increasing violence among the young was the easy-going attitude towards aggression shown on television.

Mrs Mary Whitehouse, who for many years has led a crusade aimed at cleaning up television programmes agreed with Dr Belson's findings, and added that violent films, such as 'The Clockwork Orange', were also a bad influence. Several eminent judges also criticised the film during a spate of ghoulishly violent assaults and murder committed by youths who had either seen the film or had read the book. Judge Desmond Bailey, sitting at Manchester Crown Court, had no illusions about the effect and influence of the film after he had heard how a 16-year-old youth had savagely attacked a boy three years his junior. He said:

We must stamp out this horrible trend which has been inspired by this wretched film. Cases like yours present, in my view, an unassailable argument in favour of the return as quickly as possible, of some form of censorship to prevent this sort of exhibition being released on the screen or stage which is evil in itself. If that happens it will be very salutary in that those salacious creatures who appear to dominate what is called show business today are compelled to earn a more respectable and more honourable livelihood instead of inciting young people to violence at the expense of their victims.

This was the second case in less than three weeks in which, said the judge, a 'despicable bully had attributed his behaviour to having seen this dastardly film'. Sending the youth to Borstal he added: 'We appreciate what you did was inspired by this wicked film but that does not mean you are not blame-worthy.'

At Oxford Crown Court where a boy of sixteen was accused of battering to death a 60-year-old tramp a psychiatrist said: 'It seems to me this boy was acting a part modelled on the characters in this book.' Mr Justice Ashworth agreed, adding: 'Play acting in a most ghastly fashion.'

Both prosecuting and defending counsel agreed that 'The Clockwork Orange' had influenced the boy. The Crown said: 'It was something done, something carried out, as a result of the film the boy had talked about and the book the boy had read and the prosecution are bound to say the makers of the film would have much to answer. The defence added: 'Many people have much to answer for, whether they be authors, film producers, television directors, or those who allowed such films and plays to be shown. They are producing a canker to be stopped at once.' It seemed, said the boy's counsel, that 'the devil had been momentarily planted in his sub-conscious.' Warner Brothers, who made the film which was seen by more than two million people in London alone, defended the showing of 'The Clockwork Orange'. It had been given a certificate restricting audiences to over eighteen and a spokesman for the producers said:

> As far as we are concerned, although the film could disturb average people, it would not make them turn to violence. If someone is mentally disturbed it might affect them but then they can be troubled by everybody and everything. It would be impossible to try and legislate against every film or book that could possibly influence just a few people. When people go to see Westerns they don't start shooting each other, when they see love films they aren't immediately unfaithful.

Curiously, Mr Anthony Burgess, who wrote the book was also critical of the film version, accusing the makers of projecting violence for its own sake. That was 'damnable' he said, pointing out that he was not involved in the making of the film. He also condemned the judges who had attacked his book. He pleaded:

> For God's sake let us know what we can write. These bloody judges and other people are just playing around on the fringes of a very difficult subject. Let us put the ball in their court and let them tell us what we may or may not write about. I just want to see what the ideas of the average legal or religious mind are about art.

Of the film he said: 'It was a good film, though boring in places, But it should have been more violent, because only by piling on the violence could the absurdity of violence be shown. We should have been able to reach a stage in violence where we were just laughing at it. This was what I tried to do in the book.'

'The Clockwork Orange' cult came and went within the space of twelve months, proving beyond all doubt that even the portrayal of violence can have an evil influence on the impressionable young in their formative years. While assaults, and in a few cases murder, are mainly confined to older children, violence in the form of senseless vandalism is largely the preserve of a younger age group, say six to twelve. It is estimated that vandalism at schools alone, costs the ratepayer more than £10 million a year and the annual bill is rising at an alarming rate. Arson, especially, is giving grave cause for concern. In 1962, for example, arson accounted for fifty-three of the 602 school fires reported. In 1973 there were 400 cases of arson out of 1,230 fires. In 1974 arson cost £9 million in damage. Statistics show that the number of cases of arson double every four years, which if unchecked would mean 1,000 deliberate school fires by the year 1980. Although setting fire to his school is probably, psychologically, a healthy but unfulfilled dream of most school boys, other forms of vandalism reveal a quirk which in many ways is far more frightening.

At one school in East London, for instance, a gang of young vandals broke in and enjoyed an orgy of battering to death some guinea pigs, mutilating tropical fish in a tank and then ended their escapade with a game of football with a bird cage, the terrified creature still trapped inside. A similar case was discovered in Guernsey in the Channel Islands when two youths broke into a nursery garden and decapitated seven ducks with a carving knife. Such horrific acts, by those so young, almost defy belief, certainly comprehension. Perhaps the magistrates in Guernsey, however, came close to finding a punishment, which although did not fit the crime, was a salutary lesson to the two boys responsible. They ordered them to be birched, the older of the two boys to receive twelve strokes. In the case of the younger boy, aged only fourteen, his father appealed against the sentence on the grounds that his punishment, four strokes, was excessive and wrong in principle. The appeal was dismissed and the boy received his punishment at the hands of a local prison officer witnessed by a doctor and a prison governor.

Punishing children has been a problem for society since the eighteenth century when courts began to deal with the misdeeds of the young. Before this the parent was responsible for the actions of his offspring, a state of affairs recommended by many of the youth of today. For, as the State has now undertaken to educate and punish our children many parents are beginning to wonder what their role is in the family. A wise move to restore this imbalance of responsibility began in London in 1969 when the Metropolitan Police set up a series of Juvenile Bureaux aimed at keeping children out of trouble and out of the courts, too. The scheme is now being tried in many parts of the country and is proving a success.

When a young offender is caught, the arresting officer hands to the bureau chief, usually a chief inspector, all the relevant documents in the case so that a deeper investigation can take place, not only into the alleged offence but also into the child's home background, his parents' attitudes and outlook, his school performance. In fact, no piece of information is too minute before a decision is made on how the best interests of the child should be served. If, of course, inquiries show that the case against the youngster is too thin and cannot be conclusively proved, no further action is taken. If, however, there is little doubt of his guilt the bureau officer, always dressed in plain clothes, begins a home inquiry in an attempt to discover from both the parent and the child why the crime was committed. Reports are also prepared by the probation service, the education authorities and the social services department. With all this information before him the chief inspector then has to decide what action to take; to prosecute, to caution or to drop the case. Although by deciding to drop the case it means that the police play no further part in the inquiry, it does not mean that the child is left to feel he has 'got away with it'. Often the papers are handed to one of the other social organisations better equipped to help both the child and his family. Where it is decided that a caution will have the right effect, both parents and the child are called to their local police for an interview either with a uniformed Superintendent or Chief Inspector, not connected with the Juvenile Bureau. The caution can take many forms but usually is delivered in a kindly but stern manner, leaving the child in no doubt that if there should be a 'next time' they may face each other in a court.

A caution can only be given to a child if he or she admits the offence. A denial leaves the police no option but to bring a charge so that the facts may be determined by the juvenile court magistrates. The victim of the alleged offence must also be prepared for the police to deal with the matter by caution. If this permission is not forthcoming then the police must prosecute. Although it is not officially in the rule book it is a well known fact that the obdurate 'victim' is sometimes gently persuaded to be lenient for the sake of the child. Once inside the superintendent's office the child usually stands while his parents are seated beside him. Often the experience is awe-inspiring, leaving the child feeling contrite and determined not to go off the rails again. Sometimes, the child is sent from the room after his 'ticking off' leaving his parents, especially if they have been awkward, to listen to a few home truths, with the accent being on the home.

The success of the scheme in London alone can be measured by the figures published at the end of 1972, when 10,000 children were dealt with by caution (a third of all known juvenile offenders), and few of them got into trouble a second time. Another scheme designed to make the young stop and think before committing further crime is administered through the juvenile court and is aimed largely at hooligans and vandals. This is the Attendance Centre where magistrates can order a child to spend between twelve and twenty-four hours of spare time on Saturday afternoons under supervision. The Centres are usually run by either retired police officers or active serving officers who have a special understanding of the young. A variety of activities are available, including physical training, handicrafts and lectures.

Failure to attend regularly could mean that the child would be reported to the court where the magistrates would have to decide to inflict a stricter type of punishment, usually of a custodial nature. Although the Attendance Centres cannot claim to have been an overwhelming success they are a popular form of punishment with some magistrates confronted with football hooligans. Sending them to the centres on Saturday afternoons means that they are unable to attend matches, so keeping them out of trouble for several weeks.

Inevitably, some children, especially the persistent offenders, must be taken from their homes to receive discipline and training. One problem, however, is that there are insufficient places available to provide the corrective training so urgently required. For example, less than two weeks before Christmas 1974, there were between twenty and thirty children in adult prisons simply because the courts had nowhere else to send them. Borstal training, probably the strictest regime a young offender could face, does not seem to have achieved the desired results. Figures published by the Home Office showed that four out of five 16-year-old boys discharged from borstal in 1970 were back inside on re-conviction within two years, many only managing to stay out of trouble for nine months. In fact, 65.2 per cent of all former Borstal boys were found guilty of a futher offence after their discharge.

The Children and Young Persons Act provided for the phasing out of detention centres and yet five years later they were still being used. In fact, due to the lack of finance to provide the new and wide range of residential facilities envisaged under the Act, juveniles were being sent to remand centres in even greater numbers. In 1969, the year the new Act came in, for instance, the number of youngsters sent to detention centres was 1,383. That figure had increased by nearly 1,000 by the end of 1973 and was still rising.

When asked about future plans for housing juvenile offenders, Mr Alexander Lyon, Minister of State at the Home Office, told the House of Commons that a scheme was being drawn up to provide Community Homes for about 8,750 young offenders. Some of these homes would have what he called 'secure units' in which there would be a tough regime with very strict discipline. It would certainly be tougher than the old approved school system, he warned. It is a sad comment on our present way of life that there is now a growing need to lock away young boys and girls to protect society when not many years ago a hearty cuff round the ear from the local policeman and a sound thrashing from father at home would in most cases have been the end of the matter.

chapter five

The gentle art of fraud

How banks are duped into lending millions   When does legitimate business become fraud?   How fraud is becoming international   How a Fraud Squad detective caught the men who squeezed £12 million from banks   The great insurance fraud   The Poulson empire and how he dragged his victims into a web of graft and corruption.

Of all the world's criminals, the one who, more than any other, must be a master of his craft to succeed, is the fraudsman. It is he, above all, who is the supreme confidence trickster, a man of guile, subtlety and often extraordinary accountancy skill. Not for him the dingy atmosphere of a four-ale-bar, plotting his next 'job' with his swarthy, ape-like friends. Not for him the trappings of a slum-terraced home, living off the State's social security handouts. You do not find a good fraudsman in those surroundings. Rather, you would look into the best Mayfair clubs, check a few Park Lane addresses, peer closely under the bowler hats in the City's stockbroker bars or join the cocktail set in the best five-star hotels. For that is the habitat of the true professional fraudsman, confidence trickster, the men with the panache and sheer nerve to deceive, not only the gullible, but the best financial brains in the City. For fraud, after all, is the three card trick of the sophisticated criminal world—now you see it, now you don't.

But a fraudsman's greatest asset—apart from his often genuine business acumen—is his sheer nerve to go ahead and deceive banks, insurance companies and sometimes individuals into giving him millions of pounds for 'surefire' enterprises based entirely on promises he has no intention of keeping. Often they present merchant bankers with fictitious sets of accounts and profit forecasts, and amazingly prise millions from them as a result. The public are not immune either. There are many cases of unsuspecting small investors pouring life savings into grand-sounding enterprises only to find, usually months or even years later, that their money is totally and irrevocably lost. This, of course, often has tragic consequences and is the main reason the public conscience is stirred into anger against the fraudsman. They do not mind, it seems, if he takes a banking house for an expensive ride. The public attitude in these cases is simply that the banks can afford it and small savers cannot. There is some truth in this, of course. Losses of this sort can come out of bank profits, whereas the individual is not allowed to recoup his life savings through a large income tax rebate. Further, there is the argument that the banks, with all their specialised knowledge and expertise, should know better and institute more thorough checks on people to whom they are prepared to lend fortunes. But, surprisingly, even the most conservative bankers get caught out and, it seems, are just as susceptible to the clever trickster as the pavement punters who squander their money in 'Find the Lady' schools. But to deceive the banks and the stockbroking community by their starched front of respectability, efficiency and enterprise, is the hallmark of the good fraudsman.

He plays for very high stakes and realises that if he manipulates his, or rather the banks' and investors', money sufficiently cleverly, his chances of spending time in prison are minimal. His fraud may be exposed and he may be successfully put out of business, but, if he is agile enough to find his way through the legal maze, he is likely to come out the other side with his fortune intact. For one of the biggest problems facing any Fraud Squad officer is proof of intent to defraud. It sometimes happens that, by the time the police have been called in to investigate apparent irregularities in a firm, the books have been 'cooked' and the money dispersed through complicated and occasionally untraceable 'business transactions'. More often, the money has been salted away in foreign banks, out of reach of the British authorities, earning interest and awaiting collection in some sunny clime by the successful swindler.

Occasionally, of course, the fraudsman is successful to the extent that he is able to remain in the City, amiably mixing in the wheeling and dealing of financial life. Former Detective Chief Superintendent Francis Lee, now retired, but once the famous head of the City of London Fraud Squad, used to laugh inwardly as he walked through his multi-million pound 'patch'. Bowler-hatted 'gentlemen' would suddenly blush as they spotted him, raise their hats and mutter 'Good morning, sir' as he passed. Others would hurry to the other side of the street for fear of recognition. 'It's amazing how many businessmen in this City have something to hide. They think I know all their secrets. And sometimes they are right—I do', he once confided.

Another Fraud Squad officer, also with wide experience in the City, once explained:

> The dividing line between fraud and what passes for accepted business practice is often very thin. It is said no man could make a million without bending the rules, even a little. We are not interested in the rule benders. It's the rule breakers we are after. And there are more than enough of them to keep us going.

Fraud has been described as crime's growth industry. And certainly both the

City and the Metropolitan police Fraud Squads (they come under one overall umbrella but, as far as possible, retain their own identities) are busier now than ever before. City officers for example, have an estimated £50 million worth of fraud under investigation at any time. The figure for the Metropolitan police is considerably higher. Furthermore, fraud is spreading its wings, not only to increasingly affluent provincial centres of Britain but, more importantly, internationally.

The internationalisation and computerisation of business, together with virtually instant world-wide communications, has given the better fraudsmen a global hand to practise their art. It is no longer unusual, for instance, for, say, an American bank to loan a British firm capital to expand its business activities in, for example, Australia. If that company turned out to be a 'front' organisation for some illegal dealing, the American bank would find great difficulty in recouping its funds which, by the time its suspicions were aroused, could be deposited snugly in Cayman Islands banks, other 'front' companies apparently unconnected with the first, or officially 'lost' in bad business deals. This situation only makes life more difficult for the investigating Fraud Squad officer who has no authority to examine books of account, or even interview suspects or witnesses in other countries without the explicit permission of those concerned.

The classic example of this was the massive cut-price motor insurance fraud which swept Britain in the late 1960s, dragged on into the early 1970s and has never been fully explained. The result of the fraud was that 750,000 British motorists were left without insurance cover, millions of pounds disappeared into thin air and have never been found, and company law was revised so it could never happen again. In all, fourteen cut-price insurance companies were wound up along with strings of brokerages, some of which had direct links with the fraudulent companies. Between them they grabbed around £40 million in premium income from the unsuspecting motorists who invested in more than two million useless motor insurance policies. Many of the motorists, unable to obtain cover from the higher-priced but eminently respectable British Insurance Association firms, managed to fulfil their legal obligations and stay on wheels by insuring with the cut-price fringe firms. As they collapsed, one by one, the 'bad risk' motorist had little alternative but to seek cover from one of the others. In this way, some people paid money into six or seven different firms, only to find, at the end of the day, there was none left. They were then either forced to pay the very high 'bad risk' rates demanded by the BIA firms, or go off the road altogether. One of the men behind a large chunk of the fraud was Robert Jacobs, an undischarged bankrupt, who called himself Michael Knowles.

A dark, debonair young man in his late twenties, Knowles, as he was generally known, loved the high life, the fast cars, pretty girls, penthouse living. Basically, his swindle revolved around three of the firms—the Irish-American, the London and Cheshire, and the London and Midland insurance companies. Irish-American, based in Nottingham, was started by Knowles with money (he told his friends) from an American millionaire named Eugene Sutton who did not wish to feature on the board of directors 'for tax reasons'. He found a willing 'front man' in Ian Porter, an equally young but unsuccessful insurance broker from Tunbridge Wells, who became chairman of Irish-American after purchasing a nominal £100 in shares. With the insurance company offering rates as much as one-third lower than those of the BIA companies—and Porter channelling all his brokerage business through the firm, Irish-American finished its first year of trading with an impressive premium income of more than £1 million. Things were looking good. Then the pair purchased the Chester-based London and Cheshire insurance company from a man named Robert Leckenby. This firm was already sinking fast and losing about £45,000 a year when Knowles instructed front-man Porter to take it over for £74,000—£10,000 down and £1,500 a month. Porter immediately cut the London and Cheshire rates to those of Irish-American and, once again, the formula worked. Money began pouring in, from £123,000 when they took it over to about £2 million. Later, the obliging Mr Porter registered a third company for the Knowles empire—the London and Midland. This took only about £250,000 before the balloon finally burst and the swindle was exposed.

In the meantime, however, the flourishing group was taking money, not only via its own brokerage group of Dickinson and Co, but from thousands of brokers throughout Britain who were receiving a staggering 20 per cent commission, far higher than that offered by the reputable firms. The next of Knowles's problems was to get the money out. And he did this via a string of 'shell' companies, including a non-functioning bank, The Merchant Bank of Guernsey, which he had purchased for a nominal £2,000. The bank was later described as 'a hole in the world through which money vanished'.

So the scene was set for a fraud on a grand scale: as fast as the premium income was coming in, Michael Knowles was instructing the luckless Mr Porter and another 'front' man, Henry Mason, who was running the London and Midland on his behalf, to sign cheques to these non-functioning companies—including the bank. The money disappeared as fast as the 'shell' firms collapsed. Eventually Knowles disappeared, too, with about £500,000, much of which had been in cash and stored in two suitcases. There were rumours that he had fled the country and was enjoying the high life on a West Indies beach or in the South of France. But eventually he was found in London and finally sentenced to eight years in gaol for his part in the fraud. His mystery millionaire, Eugene Sutton, was never found. Theories were rife that he never existed at all and that he was merely a figment of Knowles's imagination. In fact, a London printer, later imprisoned for printing forged bank notes, is now believed by police to have been the real Mr Sutton. Mr Porter was charged at the same time as Knowles but was acquitted by the jury. Mr Mason was never charged with any offence. But the Knowles empire collapsed leaving motorists without insurance cover and very much poorer.

And what happened to Knowles's money? Nobody knows to this day—and Knowles is not saying. At the Knowles trial, prosecuting counsel told the jury:

The (Irish-American) insurance company was particularly suitable for misuse in that . . . when the company had sufficient money, it was siphoned out for fraud, ultimately in the biggest sum of cash which could be removed . . . leaving the main company altogether insolvent . . . premiums came in every year and this could attract people wishing to siphon off large sums and . . . in such cases it was essential to create a large confusion in the transactions between various accounts and books of the company.

It was not until Knowles had fled with the cash that investigators were able to uncover what had actually taken place. Even then, the trail was not easy to follow. For he had been involved in various dealings, mainly concerned with re-insurance, with firms in Holland and Belgium. Further, some of his links stretched as far as South Africa where he had been involved in insurance business before starting Irish-American in Britain. There were also suggestions that much of the money initially used to start some of these companies—not only those in the Knowles empire—had come from Mafia funds in Nebraska, where their laws, particularly relating to the establishment of companies in insurance, were as lax as those in Britain.

The truth or otherwise of these theories, has never been proved and is never likely to be established. One reason is that British Fraud Squad officers, although the nearest thing this country has to international policemen in that they now often travel abroad during the course of their inquiries, have neither the time, nor receive the international co-operation necessary to uncover such information. So, once again, the international fraudsman stands a good chance of escaping if he is able to keep, literally, just one jet plane ahead of the pursuing law.

The Knowles case highlighted one alarming loophole in the Companies Act, 1948, which enabled the fraud to get off the ground in the first place. This was that any new insurance company had to satisfy the then Board of Trade that it had assets of £50,000. This sort of money, by itself, was chicken feed for any firm hoping to encourage a premium income of millions and nowhere near enough—for this was the object of having the money anyway—to pay out any large and urgent claims which might come its way. And, even more astonishing, the money had to be available for one day only—and that was when the Board's examiner demanded to see it!

The situation was exactly the same when another well-known insurance swindler, Dr Emile Savundra, was running his Fire, Auto and Marine insurance company which eventually folded with about £1 million missing from the company. Dr Savundra has now been released after serving his six-year term for his part in the FAM collapse, still protesting his innocence and threatening to take his case to the European Commission of Human Rights in Strasbourg.

Fortunately, the Companies Act loophole has now been effectively sealed. But other aspects of this and many other similar cases involving fraud, show just how fine is the line between breaking the law and merely 'bending' it. The law ruled that Knowles had committed an offence, several in fact, in the way he misused money from the three insurance companies. But what of the brokers who were taking their 20 per cent commission? Many of them certainly knew what was going on but jumped on the band-wagon in a get-rich-quick effort.

They gladly took the money from their unsuspecting motorist customers knowing that, within a few months at the most, the cut-price market would fail and the motorist, without any possible refund coming his way, would have to spend more money trying to obtain cover elsewhere. Further, although some of the younger brokers, without much experience—vast numbers of them were surprisingly naive about the business—could be forgiven for their ignorance, what about the 'elder statesmen' of the industry? Surely they knew that such fly-by-night concerns could not last long? Yet they, like the others, were happy to let their customers think everything in the garden was rosy. They were guilty of moral fraud at least.

When the dust of failure had settled around the bones of the cut-price insurance fiddles, Fraud Squad officers in many forces, especially London and the Midlands, began doing a little arithmetic. They finally worked out—and it took years—that the insurance firms had grossed around £40 million, of which only £20 million had been accounted for. So what happened to the rest? And who has it? Well, much of it is neatly locked away in private bank accounts in Switzerland, Liechtenstein, North Africa, the Middle East and even Britain, earning vast amounts of interest. Some has already been collected and, no doubt, spent. Other amounts have been transferred to accounts in the USA and Canada.

Insurance, however, is only one aspect of a wide-ranging fraud activity that is growing daily, not only in size but in complexity. It is this very involved nature of the offence that is worrying the legal profession and the police: the lawyers because they are concerned the defendant may not get a fair trial because the jury may be unable to understand the evidence; the police because they feel too many guilty people are acquitted for exactly the same reason.

In the end, the problem comes down to: can a lay jury, composed of plumbers, joiners, clerks, bus conductors and whatever, fully comprehend the masses of complicated documentary evidence that is virtually a prerequisite of any company fraud case? And is the jury system fair, either to the law or the defendant, in such situations? If not, what are the alternatives? It might be useful to examine an actual example of where both the police and the lawyers were faced with this very dilemma.

A large and well-known national company went broke. Its books were in a mess and its affairs were complicated and had international ramifications. After several years, accountants and examiners appointed by the Board of Trade completed their investigation and discovered that there were grounds for believing the head of the firm had been involved in fraudulent activities. The police, pursuing their own inquiries had reached the same conclusion and the man was charged with a number of offences involving fraud.

After lengthly committal proceedings, he was sent for trial and a date was set. Only then was the full extent of the problem realised: the case could last for up to a whole year and involved hundreds of detailed financial accounts, files that had taken experts months to understand and inter-company balance sheets comprehensible only to a qualified few. Already the initial problems were enormous. For a start, judges, by the very nature of their profession, are generally elderly men. But the case was to last a year. Suppose, it was argued in legal circles, that the judge died after the case had been in progress for, say ten months? Would the entire procedure have to start again? And what of the cost in such circumstances? Leading counsel are not exactly the cheapest people to employ, their fees sometimes running into scores of guineas per working day.

Then came another problem: how to select a jury that was able to sit for perhaps a year. So many categories of people would be automatically excluded—pensioners, young mothers, the self employed, the sick, and scores of other would-be jurors. Even after all that, what would be the chances of a jury being able to understand what was going on? After all, it took the best accountancy brains years to sort out the mess. What chance would a lay jury, probably familiar with nothing more complicated than household accounts, have of piecing together such a complicated financial jigsaw puzzle? Probably none and everyone realised it.

So, presumably with the agreement of the Director of Public Prosecutions and, possibly, the Attorney-General, a deal was struck. The problems were outlined to the defendant, a household name in Britain and the offer was: if he agreed to plead guilty to lesser charges on the sheet, not directly involving fraud, he would receive a fine—paltry by his millionaire standards—and the whole thing would be settled. No gaol, no heavy cost of legal fees, hardly any interruption to his well-ordered Mayfair lifestyle. He agreed, appeared in court for just a few minutes, was fined and that was the end of it. Out of court he walked, a perfectly free man, much to the disgust of the Fraud Squad officers who had sweated long and hard to bring him to justice. One who had been involved in the case just shrugged his shoulders and delivered the classic policeman's reply when asked what he thought: 'It's my job to get him here—not convict him'.

That was one solution, but few would agree it was satisfactory. Inevitably the case sparked off appeals for law reform when dealing with such fraud cases. Many eminent lawyers began arguing for the jury to be replaced by a panel of learned and experienced assessors who understood finance and business and had more than a passing familiarity with a balance sheet. In this way, it was argued, trials would certainly be fairer and evidence could be completed much more quickly, thereby saving not only time but money. However, nothing has been done to end the present ludicrous situation or to institute badly needed reform. If it costs the State many thousands of pounds to institute proceedings against someone it believes to have broken the law, surely it can legislate for a simple change that would ensure the money has not been wasted.

But, if the wheels of the law are grinding slowly on the jury issue, police are concerned that judges should hand out stiffer sentences when defendants have been brought to court and eventually convicted. As has been seen, fraud investigation is often a long and laborious job with many disappointments at the end of an inquiry. There may be grounds for thinking in fact, that some judges are not playing their full part in the fight against crime especially when a master fraudsman, finally brought before the court, is given such a light prison sentence that he considers his crime profitable. After an Old Bailey judge had passed a particularly paltry sentence at the end of a long case, senior fraud squad officers were so furious that some suggested that in future, it would not be worth investigating frauds of less than a million pounds because the necessary work would take too long and the results (so far as the punishments were concerned) were not commensurate with the effort.

Ellis Eser Seillon and his partner Elias Fahimian, both of Middle Eastern origin but who had been in Britain for some years, operated a £12.2 million fraud which was so audacious in its concept that it fooled the banks for years. In the end, the Standard Bank found it had loaned the pair £4.4 million and the Co-operative Bank a staggering £7.8 million. A little time after the fraud was discovered, a senior executive of the Co-operative Bank died, some said because of the strain and pressure resulting from the massive deception.

Seillon ran a small chemical works in London, a tiny affair mainly concerned with re-packaging drugs on a small scale. One of his closest friends was Fahimian, who dealt mainly in the property markets. The Vietnam war was at its height and Seillon convinced the banks there was a great deal of money to be made from the drugs that the USA 'urgently needed' for its troops. Although his existing arrangement with the Co-operative Bank—he had been a customer of theirs for years—limited his overdraft facilities to only a few hundred pounds, he told them he had secured a deal whereby he could import vital quinine supplies, virtually by the shipload. Moreover, a giant American chemical and drug company, based in Chicago, had agreed to buy the supplies from him. The bank agreed to go along with the deal for a trial period to 'see how things go'. Within weeks, Seillon was producing shipping documents to show the quinine had been sent to him, agreements from the American firm to indicate they were prepared to buy it. The Co-operative Bank checked with the Chicago company's bankers for a credit rating and found the firm was most reputable, well backed and could easily afford deals of the kind Seillon had apparently secured.

As the shipments increased, so Seillon needed more and more funds to finance the enterprise. Backed by Fahimian, he went to the Standard Bank in London, gave them the same story and received large credit availability. With all this at their disposal, the pair began buying up property in London and re-selling it within days to one of their wholly-owned subsidiaries at hugely inflated prices. Then, armed with perfectly legal documents that showed the apparent worth of the property—thereby concealing its true market value—they went to the banks for even more money. And they got it. They even produced a 'Persian princess', a pretty young girl in her early twenties, who they said was interested in buying the properties from them. They also 'opened' a fictitious chemical plant in Kings Lynn to process some of the drugs they were 'importing'. In the end, as the police later discovered, there was no quinine, no chemical plant in Norfolk, no agreement with an American firm—and no Persian princess. All were phonies.

After a trial which lasted seventeen weeks, Seillon was given five years imprisonment and Fahimian four years. But it took the police a long time to discover the truth and unravel the massive complexities of the fraud. The amount of sifting and probing by detectives led by Detective Superintendent Bob Fowley of the City Fraud Squad, can be judged by the number of exhibits presented at the trial—3,735 of them! And even then, as police will readily admit, 'we never really got to the bottom of it. Several other banks were involved for lesser sums which just had to be written off.'

The first alarm that something might be wrong did not reach the police from official bank sources. It was a quiet 'tip on the grapevine' that first started them making preliminary inquiries. And even after several months they were not certain they would ever have enough evidence to bring the pair to justice. But when the unscrupulous duo finally went to prison, Mr Fowley was highly praised for 'one of the best pieces of detective work seen for many years'. He and his colleagues discovered that the 'Persian princess' was none other than Simone Dowlatshahi, the Persian-born au pair girl employed by Elias Fahimian, who probably never really knew what was being hatched. In the end she disappeared to New York with a one-way ticket purchased in cash at Heathrow airport. The agreements from the American company, detailed on their official-looking notepaper, were pure forgeries. Seillon had obtained their real letterheads by earlier writing and offering a deal in which the company showed no interest but replied out of courtesy. Shipping company letterheads were obtained in the same way. Armed with these, he and Fahimian went to a small Polish-born printer in East London and had the letterheads copied. From then on it was easy to forge any documents and dream up an 'deals' they liked. The banks fell for it and provided the funds. However, when the Co-operative Bank asked for a credit rating on the American company and received a five-star reply, they let the matter rest there. Nobody bothered to inquire with the company itself about transactions with Seillon and his partner in crime. Had this simple step been taken, the whole racket would have been immediately exposed and killed at birth.

The case highlights two important points: the sheer audacity and cheek of the fraudsmen to carry on such a charade and their meticulous planning in making it work for them for so long, and the gullibility of the banks, even the biggest and most experienced, in falling once again for the criminal 'three-card trick'. The final irony is that, as police were later told, the American troops in Vietnam did not use much quinine; it had largely been overtaken by other drugs. Furthermore, if it had been shipped to Seillon in the amounts scheduled on the forged papers, it would have needed a storage space as big as Hyde Park!

But frauds come in all shapes and sizes and skilled crooks have tried all manner of deceptions to relieve the public of its money. In most cases they find it remarkably easy. It never ceases to surprise the police just how willingly investors, anxious for a quick and lucrative return, are prepared to part with their hard-earned capital. And if this means the chance of purchasing otherwise expensive goods on the cheap, so much the better. Norman Jackson Dunstance realised this and gently robbed the public—and, in this case, the Press in unpaid advertisements—of over £547,996. The method, as Fraud Squad officers said later, was so easy 'that even a baby could do it'. All the persuasive Mr Dunstance did was operate the classic long firm fraud, a well-known get-rich-quick device which hardly ever seems to fail. In this case, the former Royal Air Force pilot became a regular customer of the perfectly reputable Coronet Wine Co, of Billet Road, Walthamstow, London.

At that time it was run by Ronald and Arthur Cairns who, with an annual turnover of about £190,000 a year, were showing a regular, if small, profit. But they needed room to expand, for wine was a growing business in Britain, with an increasingly affluent society spending larger and larger amounts on wines from all over the world. Primarily they needed a warehouse and Dunstance, who at the time called himself Norman Cameron, offered them a £2,500 loan to buy a warehouse to keep their increasing stocks. The Cairns took up the offer immediately but, by this time, Dunstance the customer had become Dunstance the potential buyer of the company.

After long and detailed negotiations, Dunstance actually purchased the thriving little firm for the niggardly sum of £5,000. Within days of taking over he changed the company policy and credit was no longer allowed. The new order was cash in advance and a cash-and-carry scheme. Mail ordering of wines—at least a dozen bottles at a time—began bringing in more money although Dunstance employed only two part-time labourers to complete the storage and packing.

Before the end of 1968, the stockily-built Scot had weighed up the situation and decided everything was ready to make a quick fortune. He began advertising in the national press on a considerable scale, offering a bottle of whisky at only 43s 6d. Again the stipulation was no orders of less than a dozen bottles. But the drinks were so cheap that groups of individuals throughout the country banded together and formed purchasing syndicates. Within days, the money was flowing into the Coronet offices at an ever-increasing rate. In November alone, its bankers cleared no less than 16,000 separate cheques. But towards the end of that month, Dunstance vanished, leaving only a note for his landlady saying he was going to Paris for a few days. Even then the money still flowed in—but no orders were going out. After receiving a number of complaints, the police finally broke into the locked Coronet premises and discovered 1,600 unopened letters, mostly containing cheques for new orders. Board of Trade investigators were called in and eventually Mr Christopher Naylor was appointed Official Receiver to sort out the terrible tangle of disappointed would-be customers, including one syndicate of 400 teachers, who all stood to lose their money. Wine suppliers were also screaming for payment—but Mr Dunstance was nowhere to be found. After leaving for Paris he never returned to his flat in Ravensdale Mansions, in East London. Mr Taylor, after spending weeks in the Coronet offices, told a meeting that the firm had no less than 15,487 known creditors. It had still £105,000 in the bank and other assets of £114,500. Even so, the debts of

£547,996 meant that each creditor was likely to get a dividend of just 2s 9d in the £. Eventually they each received 21p when all the company's affairs were cleared up.

Meanwhile, Mr Dunstance was enjoying the high life in the Bahamas after a long and expensive holiday in New York. Apart from taking much of the firm's cash with him, he also bought £112,000 worth of diamonds. After five years, assuming the police and everyone else had forgotten all about him, he stupidly returned to England and London. But Scotland Yard has a long memory and Mr Dunstance was picked up at Heathrow airport only seconds before boarding a plane for Las Palmas. He had been stopped by a Customs official because he was carrying £500 with him—when the limit then was only £300. It was a silly mistake and one that was to cost him six years in gaol, a sentence he started in September 1973. Not surprisingly, he at first denied he was Dunstance, or Cameron, but the police confronted him with people he had duped five years earlier. The game was up and the 'plausible rogue', as Judge Gwyn Morris described him, began a sentence that would give him plenty of time to ponder his mistakes. But Dunstance's 'long firm fraud' was only one of many such instances of where the innocent have been robbed by the wily and the shrewd. It is a favourite method for the trickster to make a quick fortune and disappear. Many of them are never caught and some even succeed in repeating the performance elsewhere, obviously with a new name and background.

The work of the busy Fraud Squad detective, however, embraces a much wider field than fraud in its purest sense. Any company thought to be concerned with malpractice of one form or another would come within its orbit. And this is why it was Fraud Squad officers who concerned themselves in the notorious Poulson affair. Though there were no allegations of 'fraud' there were plenty of corruption and the 'adjusting' of certain accounts. It is often difficult to see much difference between corruption and fraud in the Poulson case. He regularly obtained contracts by methods which, at the best, were dubious practices and, at worst, clear deception. In a sense, John Garlick Llewellyn Poulson will go down in history as a tragic figure. He was a man of humble origins who dragged himself to the top of his particular business ladder by his own bootlaces, became a millionaire—then lost the lot due to bad management, his refusal to delegate authority and massive 'hand-outs' to people he thought could obtain building contracts for his firm. It was these hand-outs, nothing less than bribes, that landed him and some of his main business friends in gaol after an inquiry by Assistant Deputy Commissioner James Crane, head of the Metropolitan and City of London Police Fraud Department, and Detective Chief Superintendent Ken Etheridge.

But, to understand how this remarkable man went from an ambitious but penniless would-be architect, to international business millionaire with world-wide political friends, to bankrupt and gaol-bird, it is necessary to know something of his background. He started his business life in 1932 with £50 he had borrowed from a relative and was not even a qualified architect. However, he was soon winning small contracts from the local council at Pontefract in West

Yorkshire and, later, the West Riding County Council. Poulson was also accepted as a member of the Royal Institute of British Architects by the now defunct 'common consent' system, a device whereby non-qualified people were given membership on the basis of their experience and quality of work. He ran his one-man firm from a small office in Ropergate and, by sheer hard work and not a little skill and talent, he was soon employing others. Within only a few years, John Poulson became the very personification of what most northerners respect most—a self-made man. His tough, unyielding, hardheaded, arrogant, sometimes dictatorial approach amassed him considerable wealth.

After the Second World War, with so much re-building to be done, Poulson went from strength to strength and, in 1954, designed and built the house of his dreams, a £60,000 mansion he called Mannasseh, on the countryside fringes of grimy Pontefract. Four years later it was chosen as 'House of the Year' by a leading magazine because of its architectural excellence, absence of ostentation and scores of unusual features including electrically-operated curtains. A few years later, the now white-haired John Poulson had reached the pinnacle of his success. He owned a Rolls and a Bentley, employed 750 people in the biggest architectural and design practice in Europe, kept a permanent suite at the Dorchester Hotel in Park Lane, became a Freeman of his native borough, chairman of the National Liberal Party of Great Britain (a Conservative organisation) and a millionaire.

Moreover, he had opened offices in London, Edinburgh, Middlesbrough, Lagos and Beirut and courted a host of influential political friends. But the Poulson business empire was a giant beast of its species and needed some feeding. Finding enough contracts to keep everyone busy was no easy task. So Poulson used the simple but quite illegal device of 'buying' contracts by bribing people with the power to grant them.

It is arguable that, in the early days at least, Poulson did not realise the full implications of what he was doing. For, despite his business success, he was not the most intelligent or articulate of men. And, anyway, so far as he was concerned, he was doing only what everyone else in the building industry was doing. If it was all right with them, it was all right with him. Furthermore, he was, at heart, a generous man who often gave money to people in need and asked nothing in return. The contracts he 'won' were big and lucrative. They included a £1½ million hospital in Gozo, Malta, the £3 million Aviemore sports complex in Scotland. He was also appointed consultant architect for the Cannon Street Station project in London and the development of several other stations. His firm also won prizes, for an M1 motorway bridge design and a fly-over on the A13 road at Barking.

By the middle 1960s, the Poulson empire was concerned not only with architecture, but embraced design and construction work as well. It also included a firm called Open Systems Building which was to market a 'revolutionary' building principle based on pre-cast construction. Its directors included Sir Bernard Kenyon, former clerk to the West Riding County Council, Mr Reginald Maudling, and Mr W.H. Sales, former chairman of the Yorkshire

Division of the National Coal Board. The firm had been initially formed by Mr T. Dan Smith, who was a close friend of Poulsons and nicknamed 'Mr Newcastle' when he became the first chairman of the Northern Economic Planning Council.

Then, in 1970, the once-mighty empire began to crumble, and accountants Cooper Brothers were called in by Mr Poulson's bankers to examine its affairs. Mightily though they tried, there was no saving the hopelessly confused and financially unsound firms in their existing condition. Mr Poulson resigned and, two years later, he filed his own petition in bankruptcy. And it was at this point that Britain's most sensational bankruptcy hearing began when Mr Poulson's relationship with scores of councillors, local government officials, top civil servants and members of Parliament came under the microscope. For the first time the public learned exactly how Mr Poulson amassed large fees, more than £120,000 from his home town of Pontefract alone, a figure which rose to more than £300,000 over a ten year period. But, as architect, Mr Poulson exercised his right to recommend builders—and chose Open Systems Building, a firm which by then he owned through his wife, Cynthia. In fact, Mrs Poulson was his 'front' in many of his firms because RIBA rules forbade him to control them. Over a period of years he obtained a virtual monopoly of contracts in Pontefract and how he did so is in itself a microcosm of how he operated elsewhere.

Alderman Robert Egan, a former Mayor of the town, received £455 from Mr Poulson and a free holiday on the south coast. Poulson's explanation for the gift was: 'He was a friend of mine. He was ill one period and I helped him out. I didn't see anything wrong in helping him and he certainly didn't help me and couldn't.' Alderman Joseph Blackburn, OBE, JP, twice mayor of Pontefract during the 1960s when Poulson won most of his contracts, received no less than £4,700—which he repaid to the Trustees once Mr Poulson went bankrupt. He also had regular use of a Poulson company car. Mr Poulson's explanation: 'We loaned him a car for a period while he was without his own.' He never did explain the money. Mr Fred Rook, town clerk to the Pontefract council, a close friend of Poulson's, received a free Mediterranean holiday and became secretary of Open Systems Building when he retired. Poulson's explanation: none at all. Interestingly, it was disclosed that, in 1966, Poulson won a contract from the local water board for £831,000. Clerk to the Board at that time was none other than Mr Rook and one of the Pontefract council representatives was Alderman Blackburn from the West Riding County Council. Poulson won his share of the available contracts, particularly junior and comprehensive schools. In all, over a number of years, he succeeded in obtaining work worth £6½ million on fifty-four different contracts. Two of the people on the county council at that time were Alderman Blackburn and Councillor Egan. Clerk to the county council then was Sir Bernard Kenyon who, in 1966, became chairman of Open Systems Building and two other Poulson companies, while still the top official in the county. When Sir Bernard's name appeared in the bankruptcy proceedings, Mr Richard Crossman, Labour Minister for Housing and Local Government from 1964 to 1966, commented:

I was surprised to read that Sir Bernard Kenyon . . . for the last
three years before his retirement managed a number of Poulson companies
although Mr Poulson had contracts with the council. Even more remarkable,
this top level integration of local government and local business was
formally approved by the council . . .,I suppose it is possible to
believe in the Immaculate Conception of County Clerks, but I cannot see
how effective discipline can be exerted over minor officials in the
planning department who wish to render a few favours to outside
interests when their Chief Officer is permitted this degree of licence.

The man who had brought out all this—and much more—at the Wakefield
bankruptcy hearings, was Mr Muir Hunter, QC, representing the creditors. He
and his junior, Mr David Graham, are two of Britain's foremost authorities on
bankruptcy law and together they spent months sifting through complicated
balance sheets, account books, letters, all manner of documents, in a bid to
discover what had happened to the Poulson fortune and why he went broke
owing more than £250,000. Week after fascinating week the hearings went on
and more and more public figures were mentioned. Mr T. Dan Smith, who had
been acquitted at a corruption trial at the Old Bailey in 1971, had received
£155,000 from Poulson. And Poulson's explanation: 'Well, he advised on
housing layouts and housing developments and eventually he went into public
relations.'

For Poulson had now moved outside Yorkshire and worked his way to the
North-East, a depressed area with a vast development potential. Again the
contracts poured in and the largess went out. The Smith family received many
free holidays from Poulson, including one in Italy, another in Palma and two in
Greece. Much of the money provided by Poulson to Smith went in promoting
the Poulson empire interests among local councillors and officials. Smith even
employed influential local councillors in his public relations' firm, among them
Roy Hadwin, Lord Mayor of Newcastle in 1967-8 and Robert Urwin,
vice-chairman of Chester-le-Street Urban District Council who received £500 a
year as a consultant. He once wrote a letter to Smith which included the phrase:
'We are trying to break this in various ways. It is not one of our controlled
councils.' Mr Urwin was also a member of the Durham County Council.

Another prominent, and certainly the most influential North East figure then
to join Smith in his Poulson promotion exercises, was Alderman Andrew
Cunningham. His public service record was impressive. Three times chairman of
the Felling District Council, chairman of the Durham County Council and
chairman of the Durham Police Authority. He was also a full-time area leader of
the General and Municipal Workers Union. When he joined the Poulson payroll
on a part-time 'consultancy' basis, Felling council decided to build a £2 million
housing project. And the consultant architect who got the job: John Poulson.
The contract did not even go out to tender.

Alderman Cunningham, whose wife also went on the Poulson payroll as a
consultant on interior design (a subject she knew nothing about), was chairman
of the Durham County Council from 1963 to 1965. During that time Poulson

obtained £725,000 worth of business for work on three schools and a technical college. Alderman Cunningham failed to 'declare his interest'. He also exercised his powers as chief of the Police Authority when it came to the building of a new police headquarters at Sunderland. The local borough architect was originally given the design but, three years later and without any reason being offered, Cunningham arranged for Poulson to take over the work. But that was not all. Cunningham, the standard bearer of public service, was also chairman of the Northumbrian River Authority which needed a new headquarters building. And who got the work? John Poulson. But, in this case, his scheme was considered too elaborate and costly and was abandoned. Even so, he obtained £40,000 in fees. In return, Cunningham received an annual salary—from Smith—of £1,000 a year and his wife, Freda, who worked in Poulson's Newcastle office, £1,500 a year. Further, the couple enjoyed £672 worth of holidays including a trip to Lisbon, money they later repaid to the creditors.

In all, Poulson obtained about £10 million worth of work in the North-East, including the police headquarters, the Felling flats (which later proved unsound and had to be strengthened), a swimming pool in Eston and a £4½ million redevelopment of Stockton High Street. But, if local councils had money to spend, the nationalised industries had more, especially the National Coal Board which was, in the 1960s, spending huge sums on modernising its pithead facilities. Poulson, for instance, built about ten pithead baths during this time. Again the pattern became familiar. Chairman of the Yorkshire Division of the Coal Board from 1957 until 1967 was Mr Bill Sales. When he retired he got another job—as chairman of Open Systems Building.

In the meantime, Poulson had designed the new £1 million tower block which became the Board's Doncaster regional headquarters. In fact, for various reasons, he designed it three times and took three separate sets of fees. Poulson had done Mr Sales another favour, besides providing him with a lucrative post-retirement job. He purchased for him (through the Wakefield Building Society of which Poulson was a director) a superb home set in folding acres of grounds. This later went on the market at over £100,000, though Sales—or rather, Poulson—had paid only just over £12,000 for it from the National Coal Board. The Poulson pattern of business was now well established—'grease the right palms' and the work would come flooding in.

In the 1960s, a boom period for Poulson and his companies, the national hospital building programme received a substantial financial boost. Mr Poulson managed to grab a share of what was going. His practice had long specialised in hospital design so it was only to be expected that some of the work would come his way. In fact, nearly half the fees paid out by the Leeds regional hospital board went to Poulson firms: £134,000 for St Luke's Hospital, Huddersfield; £470,000 for a reconstruction job at St James's, Leeds; £480,000 for the Airedale Hospital, near Keighley. And, at the bankruptcy hearings, Mr Muir Hunter wanted to know why Mr William Shee, secretary of the Leeds Hospital Board, received substantial payments from Poulson. The reply: 'The Ministry recommended that when he got to the age of sixty, I take him on as a consultant.'

But Mr Shee, while still serving with the Board, became a major shareholder in Ovalgate Investments, another Poulson company which intended to develop the town of Harrogate. Then the ever-generous Mr Poulson decided to hand out some benefits to Mr Jack Merritt, the Department of Health's man on the Leeds Regional Board for eleven years until 1968. Apart from monies which Mr Merritt received from Mr Poulson, he also took advantage of holiday offers. And one of them was arranged through Mr Reginald Maudling. A letter to the Conservative MP, written on Poulson's behalf, said: 'Dear Mr Maudling, A personal friend of Mr Poulson's, a Mr A.J. Merritt, Principal Regional Officer at the Ministry of Health, Leeds, who has been extremely helpful to the firm in that capacity, is retiring at the end of this year and wishes to take a sea voyage in January/February 1968. Mr Poulson wonders whether your travel agent would be able to do anything to assist in this connection.'

When Poulson was winning his hospital contracts, his plans had to be submitted to the Ministry headquarters at Whitehall and one of the men responsible for handling such matters was Mr William George Wilson, who was Assistant Secretary, on the Hospital Building Division. He later joined the Poulson organisation at £15,000 a year but returned to the Ministry when the Poulson empire collapsed. That, however, was much later. Meanwhile Mr Poulson was going up the ladder; local councils, county councils, nationalised industries. The next step was Parliament. He soon established an impressive list of valuable contacts at Westminster. Apart from Mr Maudling, then Deputy leader of the Conservative Party, former Home Secretary and Chancellor of the Exchequer, there was the late Sir Herbert Butcher, a taxation expert and Conservative MP for Boston-in-Holland, Mr John Cordle, the Tory member for Bournemouth and Christchurch and Mr Albert Roberts, the ex-miner Labour MP for Normanton.

Sir Herbert, who became a director of several Poulson companies, received fees totalling £21,666. Mr Cordle, who got £5,928 from Mr Poulson over a number of years, was a West African affairs specialist and spoke in the Commons about the port development scheme at Bathurst, capital of Gambia, and the enlargement of the local airfield. Much of the money for the scheme was being provided by the British government. 'I believe it would please the British taxpayer if they knew that such money as was being provided by Her Majesty's Government was finding its way into the pocket of British contractors', he said.

On the other side of the Commons sat Mr Roberts, a man with considerable influential contacts in the Spanish and Portuguese governments. He was employed by Mr Poulson as a salaried consultant and received a total of £11,500. Furthermore, he helped the architect with his biggest-ever contract—a £15½ million scheme in Portuguese Angola. In addition he visited people in Saudi Arabia and Malta on Mr Poulson's behalf and saw contacts in London, sometimes taking them for lunch. Then there was Mr Maudling who joined Poulson as a non-executive director in 1966 at £2,000 a year. Later, when in Opposition, he became chairman of another Poulson firm, but insisted that the

£9,500 he was due should go to the Adeline Genee Theatre Trust in East Grinstead, Sussex–Mrs Maudling's favourite charity. Nonetheless, he was able, with his background in banking and his overseas contacts, to assist Mr Poulson considerably. Mr Maudling's son, Martin, was also a Poulson company director, then earning £4,000 a year. But later, like his father, he resigned.

During the 1960s, John Poulson gave away nearly £350,000 and when he went bankrupt, he announced debts of about £250,000. The result of the bankruptcy hearings was that the extra-mural activities of all these MPs, local government councillors, aldermen and officials, became public knowledge. When Mr Heath, the then Prime Minister, announced a full Fraud Squad investigation into the allegations made at Wakefield, Mr Maudling resigned as Home Secretary. He felt that this was the only course since he was officially head of the Metropolitan Police and it was officers from this force who were carrying out the investigation. At one point, the bankruptcy hearings and the police inquiry were going on simultaneously which made life difficult for the police, Mr Hunter, and especially Mr Poulson.

As Mr Poulson sat answering embarrassing questions about his complicated business life, detectives were interviewing Mr George Pottinger, one of Scotland's top civil servants, about his dealings with the Pontefract architect at his luxury Poulson-built villa at Gullane, East Lothian, alongside the famous St Andrew's golf course. Pottinger–known among his underlings in the civil service as 'Gorgeous George' because of his sartorial elegance–had earlier been suspended from duty following allegations made about him at Wakefield, but on full pay of nearly £10,000 a year. It had been claimed that he had been influential in obtaining the £3 million Aviemore winter sports complex contract for Mr Poulson when he had been seconded to assist Lord Fraser in organising and promoting the scheme. Further, that in return for securing the contract he had received clothing, several holidays abroad, a Rover 2000 car, £3,650 in cash–and his luxury villa that became the envy of the exclusive Gullane area.

Both Mr Poulson and Mr Pottinger denied the allegations and claimed that what Mr Pottinger had received had been entirely 'out of personal friendship'. But long before his subsequent arrest and conviction at Leeds, Mr Pottinger knew the game was up and even 'doctored' official files in St Andrew's House, Edinburgh–home of the Scottish civil service–to hide his guilt. But there was enough evidence in Poulson's own files to convict the pair of them. And much of this had been found, deliberately hidden away in a remote attic in Mr Poulson's office block–two lorry loads in fact.

If there was any genuine friendship between them, they were an odd couple. Mr Pottinger, haughty, sophisticated, brilliant, academic, ballet and opera lover, accomplished author and raconteur, graduate of Oxford and Heidelberg universities; Mr Poulson, harsh, arrogant, blunt, brash, as roughly hewn as the craggy rocks of his native West Riding. They had nothing in common, except, perhaps one thing–money and their love of it.

An indication of just how far apart they were academically and intellectually was seen when Mr Poulson became chairman of the National Liberal Party and

Mr Edward Heath was the guest of honour. Mr Poulson had to make a speech of welcome but it was Mr Pottinger who wrote it. And, in view of what had been taking place between the Scot and the Yorkshireman, one sentence was quite remarkable: 'Our respect for you is our recognition of your personal integrity—a quality sadly lacking in many who are engaged in public life today'. Mr Pottinger wrote many speeches for Mr Poulson—and many letters, too. These included one, signed by Sir Basil Butcher to a Government minister, requesting that Mr Poulson be considered for a knighthood!

But, as the police inquiry progressed, so the net tightened around Mr Pottinger, Mr Poulson and others who had benefited from his unique brand of business enterprise. However, particularly during the early part of their investigation in the North-East, detectives were not receiving all the co-operation they might reasonably have expected. Their inquiries into town hall graft and corruption were often met with a wall of silence. It became so bad at one point that officers returned to Scotland Yard for a top level conference and urged that councils which refused to assist the police should be threatened with prosecution for obstruction. The detectives faced a typical cold shoulder, at Newburn Urban District Council in Northumberland. They were refused permission to copy minutes and other documents without payment. Eventually the council agreed to police demands—but sent a £40 bill to the Director of Public Prosecutions. Mr Colin Walker, the council clerk, was later quoted as saying:

> They wanted copies of minutes and records extending over a period of years. We were busy dealing with arrangements for local elections and my staff was working overtime already. They (the police) have gone now and I hope they will not be pestering us again. Mr Poulson was our consultant architect for six or seven years. He designed our swimming baths, library, shopping centre and some housing.

Later the police moved to nearby Middlesbrough, where Mr Poulson once employed no less than twenty-two local councillors. They told officials they were particularly interested in documents relating to developments at Eston, Middlesbrough and Stockton, all now part of Teesside. The pattern was followed in more than thirty councils in Yorkshire and the North East. Next they went to Scotland and established a temporary inquiry headquarters in Edinburgh. Again their inquiries met some opposition. But, according to Mr Barry Payton, the former town clerk of Wandsworth and now a practising barrister, this reluctance was not surprising. He explained:

> Some local government officers are frightened and fear they might lose their jobs. I have spoken to many of them and, given a syllable or two, all have told me the same thing: Why should we do the same thing you did? You were young enough to resume your legal career, but we are not. The way the people in Wandsworth got rid of you shows just how easy it is to fire a town clerk who does not toe the line. Helping the police fully is more than our jobs

are worth.

Mr Payton called in the police only five days after starting his £7,000 a year job in Wandsworth because he found there had been corruption in the previous administration. Scores of people were questioned including councillors, businessmen and outside contractors. There was a trial at the Old Bailey and a local alderman served a four-year sentence. At the same trial T. Dan Smith was acquitted.

But the result of the inquiry was that Mr Payton lost his job. He explained: 'I know that, officially, I resigned but I was left with no choice. I could not continue under those circumstances. I was rather in the position of the club secretary reporting a senior member for doing something wrong. The secretary may have been perfectly right but the other members would round on him for making a wash.'

Even after his resignation, Mr Payton kept in close contact with the world of the town clerk and eight of them, he said, had admitted refusing to co-operate with the Poulson inquiry detectives. Mr Payton added:

All town clerks know who is fiddling in their authority and just how big or small it is. Some fear that if they say too much now they may by accused by the police of being an accessory to dishonesty by keeping quiet for so long. I have been told that some town clerks and other officials who have been co-operating with the detectives have been 'black-listed' by their councils. It is bound to happen. There is a lot at stake. Some councillors whose reputations are perhaps not all they might be would be extremely upset if some poor local government officer, attempting to do his duty, spilt the beans about what the councillors had been up to.

Still, co-operation or not, the police investigation went on relentlessly. Then, in June 1973, they made their first arrests. John Poulson was picked up at his home near Pontefract (he had long since sold his beautiful show house at a £30,000 loss) and, simultaneously, other officers went to Mr Pottinger's villa. But he was having dinner at the adjacent golf club with several of his friends, including a judge.

Dinner over, he returned home, was arrested and taken to Leeds where he and Mr Poulson were charged with conspiracy. Just two weeks later, Mr Poulson was arrested again, this time with Alderman Andrew Cunningham (Mrs Cunningham was also arrested and charged some time afterwards). A fortnight after that came a further arrest for Mr Poulson, this time with Mr Graham Tonbridge, a 74-year-old retired estates and rating surveyor for the Southern Region of British Railways. Again, the charges in all cases related to corruption—in Mr Tonbridge's case to the huge Cannon Street Station redevelopment in London. Next to be arrested, again with Mr Poulson, was George Braithwaite, secretary of the South West Metropolitan Regional Hospital Board. He was accused of showing favour to Mr Poulson over hospital building contracts. All of these, apart from Mr Tonbridge (who was given a suspended sentence because of his age) and Mrs Cunningham, were eventually sent to prison. Mr Poulson, who has suffered from ill health for years, seriously doubts whether he will come out alive. As for the others, Mr Pottinger's once illustrious civil service career lies in ruins; Mr Cunningham will never again step along the corridors of North-East power. Neither will Mr T. Dan Smith, who was later arrested and sentenced to imprisonment. Mr Braithwaite has lost his job with the Hospital Board and Mr Maudling who, of course, was never accused of any dishonesty in his dealings with Mr Poulson, has only recently been invited back to the Conservative Front Benches. Councillors all over the North and North East have lost seats they held for years because they had become tainted with the Poulson image.

In all, it is a sorry end to what once was a thriving empire. However, although the ramifications of the Poulson scandal are immense and its consequences still being felt in councils virtually all over Britain, police know full well that local government graft and corruption still thrive. Every man, it is said, has his price and councillors in positions of power and authority, and well placed to 'do someone a favour' are no exception. Mr Poulson, it is obvious now, was only doing what he thought—in the early stages, anyway—everyone else did. Certainly it is true that most firms in the building industry employ 'trouble-shooters' to get council contracts for them. One firm placed their 'trouble-shooter' in the Central Hotel, Glasgow, and gave him an annual six-figure sum as 'running costs and expenses'. For this he had to make sure the firm secured lucrative contracts throughout Scotland. How did he do it? Simply by bribing councillors and council officials. 'It is easy in Scotland. There is so much local graft and corruption and nobody thinks twice about it. It is virtually an accepted fact of life', he said in the late 1960s.

It is known, for example, it has cost up to £1,000 to obtain a drinks' licence for a public house north of the border. Officially they are free, but some local councillors have to be taken care of. But that is not to say all councillors, or even a majority, are 'on the fiddle'. Most of them are honest, hard-working people, anxious to promote their district and assist in its prosperity. But there are enough bad apples in the local government barrel to cause concern. And the equation is simple: if a firm wants a big contract badly enough, it will take every available step to get it.

The bigger the contract, the more money there is at stake. And the bigger the stakes, the more certain the likelihood of an illegal approach to a few hand-picked councillors in the hope of making sure there are no hitches in the contract being signed and sealed. It happens and is unlikely to be stamped out completely, mainly because it is difficult to detect and would require almost a full-time army of Fraud Squad officers to keep a constant check on every possible instance. In that sense, Poulson was an exception, but even then, detectives privately intimated they had found enough minor cases of graft among local councils to keep them going for years.

But the luckless Mr Poulson was dealing in strictly small change when measured against some of the daring frauds which were attempted during 1974 alone. Some of these, of course, were successful and a few went unreported to the police.

However, in that one year alone Deputy Assistant Commissioner James Crane, the quietly spoken but painstakingly thorough head of the Metropolitan Police Fraud Squad and his dedicated team of 111 detectives—including women—saved no less than £170 million from going into criminal coffers.

This is a staggering amount of money by any standards but is indicative of the way more and more criminals are turning to fraud. As Mr Crane explained: 'It is becoming much easier to open a bank account than a safe these days. But our problem is that a lot of fraud is never reported because, generally, people don't like to be shown up as having been foolish. This applies as much to company chairmen and directors as to the public.'

It was a good year for the Fraud Squad which maintained its impressive 80 per cent conviction rate. But Mr Crane insists that the £170 million total of 'money at risk' would have been considerably greater had all major fraud attempts been reported to the police. 'Money at risk' is official police jargon for amounts which would have bolstered the criminal exchequer but for prompt police action.

The extent to which fraud is Britain's biggest growth industry can be assessed from one simple fact: Fraud Squad officers are now handling nearly 400 cases at any one time, three times the figure of 1972. Similarly, the amount of 'money at risk' has almost trebled over the same period. And all but £40 million of it is centred in possible fraudulent operations inside the London area. This means that Mr Crane's officers, and another thirty-three detectives under Chief Superintendent Keith Taylor, who heads the City of London Fraud Squad, are usually handling three cases each at any one time. Both senior officers agree that this sort of workload is much too heavy.

However, enticing experienced CID officers into the Fraud Squad is usually difficult because the work lacks the glamour of a sensational murder inquiry or Flying Squad operations. In fact, much of the Fraud Squad routine is boringly dull, entailing hours and hours of mulling over lifeless documents, account books and combing through official records at Companies House where registration certificates and records of share issues are kept.

Furthermore, investigations often grind on for months, even years, and usually at a slow pace that many detectives would find unbearably frustrating. Good Fraud Squad men are therefore, by definition, detectives with unending supplies of patience who know their way round a balance sheet and are astute enough not to be bamboozled by the smooth double-talk of some clever fraudsman. Fraud officers have another problem. Their legal powers are often insufficient to bring known criminals to justice. For, until a suspect is charged and has appeared in court, detectives have no legal right to examine documents and financial records used to commit a fraud. Yet charging a criminal is often impossible without access to their documents. A detective knocking at the door of a suspect company chairman can be—and often is—told to clear off. Unless the officer has sufficient evidence from other sources to charge the fellow, clear off he must.

This sort of ludicrous situation is causing growing concern at Scotland Yard and at Old Jewry, where the City Fraud Squad has its offices. Many senior officers are pressing for new legislation which would give them access to bank statements of individuals or companies they suspected of being engaged in fraudulent activities. Similarly, they would like powers to examine relevant books and documents. At the moment they have to rely almost solely on evidence gathered freely from disgruntled shareholders or people who have been defrauded. But, again, victims of fraud, as Mr Crane has explained, are sometimes reluctant to come forward and complain because they are afraid of looking silly.

It is as though society is aiding the criminal and not the law enforcement officers; solving a complicated fraud with one hand tied behind your back can often be a soul-destroying business, especially when you have to watch the confident fraudsman laughing all the way to the bank. One experienced fraud squad officer explained:

> It's a bit crazy, really, particularly when you think of the sort of money these people can get away with. It can run into millions and often does run into hundreds of thousands. If we were able to apply for permission to examine suspect bank accounts in the early stages of an inquiry, it would save us a lot of time and trouble. Similarly, if we could get a warrant to enter a company premises and insist on seeing the books, this again would cut the corners. At the moment it can take ages before you ever reach that stage of an investigation. The real savers in this situation would be the public. More fraudsmen would be caught—and a lot quicker. This would mean we would have more time to investigate other frauds, and so the thing would snowball. Equally, fraudsmen, knowing we could examine such documents and accounts, would be very reluctant to operate some of the swindles they involve themselves in at the moment. It would be just too risky. Until we get some new law which entitles us to conduct these examinations, many frauds are going to remain undetected.

Mr Crane expressed similar views:

> It is clear that many highly sophisticated businessmen are turning to fraud. The cases we handle are becoming more and more complicated and more difficult to investigate. But we don't have enough men and we lack sufficient powers. This limitation on our powers often enables a good fraudsman to escape prosecution. In some ways, City journalists have more power than a Fraud Squad officer, because a company often feels obliged to make a statement to a newspaper when an inquiry is made. But if a Fraud Squad detective makes a similar inquiry he is often told it is none of his business. But don't run away with the idea that the fraudsman has the upper hand. Time is always on our side. The gaols are full of people who thought the police would never catch up with them.

Meanwhile, in the absence of such legislation, Mr Crane usually offers this piece of sound advice to all new officers joining his fraud department: 'Always follow the money. Inevitably it will lead to an oak-panelled door and behind it will be Mr Big.' It is a tip that has paid off in scores of cases.

Even so, Fraud Squad officers beginning a new inquiry, especially if it concerns a large company, are often treading on egg-shells. The slightest sniff of a Fraud Squad investigation and that company's trading position can be ruined overnight. Credit can dry up, manufacturers, fearful for their money, will refuse to deliver their goods and share prices tumble to an irrecoverable level. If, in the end, the investigation revealed there had been no fraud, the company would be in a position to scream blue murder and demand immediate and large sums in compensation. As Mr Crane put it: 'Any Fraud Squad inquiry is like a stab in the back to a company. We cannot afford to put a foot wrong.' So, in addition to his unending patience, any officer joining the squad must also be something of a diplomat. The 'bull at a gate' approach—often successful in some aspects of police work—would be totally useless in a fraud inquiry. Furthermore, in a field of criminal investigation where, more than any other, financial temptations to 'forget' a certain line of inquiry could produce fat bank balances for detectives, graft and corruption is virtually non-existent. The Fraud Squad is proud of its reputation for fair dealing and integrity, a reputation painstakingly accumulated since it was started nearly twenty years ago after the Government became alarmed by an outbreak of 'bucket shop' frauds. Furthermore, fraud officers, not surprisingly, have cultivated their own jargon. While detectives in other areas of criminal investigation use the language of the underworld, the fraud investigator talks of 'kite-flying' and 'cross-firing cheques' and 'cube-cutting'.

Cube-cutting is a fraudulent operation used in the shipping business by scheming forwarding agents and underwriters. They either understate the cubic capacity of their cargo or the ship which is to carry it. In plain language they steal shipping space and so increase their profit. It is a device well known among the City's shipping fraternity and a few of the less reputable agents and underwriters have been known to indulge in it from time to time.

Although more than a few criminals lurk under the 'bowler hat uniform' of the 'City gent', most Fraud Squad officers reject insinuations that the square mile of London is full of crooks. Rather, it is the very reputation of the City for honesty and 'my word is my bond' that attracts the fraudsmen, because a good London address gives any fraudulent company a mark of respectability and is virtually a prerequisite to any good fraud operation. Nearly all large-scale fraud inquiries over the last ten years have involved firms with a central London office as its centre of operations.

For example a man selling advertising space in a bogus commercial directory might not influence many company directors if he announces that his head office is in Scunthorpe. But if his office is in the City, he stands a better-than-even chance of reaching the right man in the organisation he is about to swindle. For this has been one of the best money-spinning frauds in recent years. And, as in many other frauds, thousands of people who have been duped out of large amounts of money have been reluctant to complain. Simply, it works like this: a salesman walks into an office and announces he represents a particular firm of trade directory publishers and produces a fat volume crammed with all kinds of well-printed advertising. The directory, he is careful to explain, goes into more than 100,000 offices and is widely used by the most reputable firms in the country.

Furthermore, for only £400 (or whatever the figure might be) the firm could be included in the next issue. The patter is smooth and sounds impressive, the well-bound directory has the look of authority. And, the final convincing piece of evidence, the firm the salesman represents is listed in the official telephone directory and has an office in Central London. The unsuspecting company director, seeing the apparent business potential in getting his firm prominently displayed in such a widely-read manual, happily signs an order form, agrees the advertising layout and hands over a cheque for the £400. What he does not know is this: the directory shown him by the salesman is the only one of its kind and has been specially made up by the fraudulent firm in the City. It does not circulate to 100,000 companies and never will. The whole operation is a total fraud. But, such is the gullibility of large numbers of people, the fraud does not stop there.

Many of these salesmen, representing different fraudulent companies, used to meet in a little afternoon drinking club off Park Lane and compare notes, or rather order forms. In their brief-cases they carried forms for 'repeat' orders. The original signature would then be cut from the first order form and carefully stuck on the 'repeat' form. A few months later, another salesman would go along to the unsuspecting firm to 'collect the cheque for our next issue'. Any company official disputing that such an order had been placed would then be shown the photocopied 'repeat' form, complete with what appeared to be a genuine signature. 'Sorry, old boy, you must have forgotten about it', the salesman would say. 'But we did not receive last year's directory', the official might complain. 'Really? We certainly sent you one. I'll ring the office today and make sure one is put in the post to you tonight.' Usually, with this reassurance, the official would hand over yet another cheque for £400.

If, by comparing notes, the salesman decided that one particular firm was 'an easy touch', that company might easily find itself writing cheques to several different bogus directory publishers. It is a fraud brilliantly simple in conception and easy to operate. Unfortunate firms who have been 'conned' in this way have paid out small fortunes for the privilege. Several salesmen and their bosses have been jailed for this type of offence but others are still pulling the same trick and getting away with it.

The country's present economic plight has also produced a new type of fraud—the 'advanced fee swindle'. A surprisingly high number of firms, faced with having to borrow large amounts of money but having exhausted their traditional sources, have turned to crooked money brokers. The brokers 'guarantee' the hard-up company whatever it wants to borrow, often in excess of £100,000. They charge a sizeable fee for their service which results in the victim being handed a document. This piece of paper, he firmly believes, can be used as collateral at a bank. In fact, the thing is worthless and actually says, in the tiny print at the bottom, that it cannot be used for raising money. The unsuspecting firm, having paid out a fat fee, is left holding just another bit of useless paper.

In a large number of fraud cases, firms and individuals who are duped have only themselves to blame. But such is the plausibility of the expert fraudsman, it is not difficult to see how he succeeds. For instance, there was the case of the Canadian who wrote to scores of major British companies claiming to be the head of a 1,000-shop retail outlet in Canada. British manufacturers saw this as a golden opportunity to increase their markets and quickly invited the Canadian to come and inspect their goods.

He would come, he replied, but only if the manufacturers would pay his fares and all expenses. Within a short time he was in Britain, touring large numbers of manufacturers and talking in terms of large-scale purchases. Each firm he visited—not realising others were involved—paid his air fare, hotel and other substantial expenses. In this way he was swindling firms all over the world out of more than £100,000 a year. Only one British company actually made any checks on the Canadian's claims—and discovered he had previous convictions for fraud. When confronted with this he remained totally unmoved. 'Splendid. If only all my customers took as much care we would soon catch this fellow who is going round impersonating me. Well done. And now to business, gentlemen . . .'

But one of the biggest headaches for Fraud Squad detectives in recent years has been the enormous growth of what have become known as computer frauds. These are enormously difficult to detect, often even more difficult to prove and, occasionally so well managed that they can never be detected at all! Computers are brilliant pieces of machinery but they can only operate on information they have received. So, if some clever programmer decides to make himself and a few accomplices a large amount of money, all he needs to do is 'feed' the computer incorrect information. For example, an unscrupulous computer expert could even invent an entire company, provide it with bank accounts, employees and so on. All he needs to do is supply the computer with details of the non-existent firm, provide it with a healthy bank balance and hey presto! The 'firm' is in business and monies can be drawn on the 'account'. It could take months, even years, to discover the truth of the situation.

In the same way, goods can be falsely assigned from one company to another, bogus debit and credit notes manipulated into and out of businesses, with the crooks at the end of the line making money by selling the goods they had no right to receive in the first place. One Fraud Squad officer summed up the situation like this:

The more computerised the firm, the easier it is to swindle. And finding the source of the fraud is often like trying to literally find a needle in a barn full of hay. It's one devil of a job.

Even simpler for the fraudsman, but just as difficult for the police, is the illegal use of credit cards and cheque books. Barclaycard and Access have lost millions of pounds to thieves who have stolen these little plastic credit cards and fraudulently used them to obtain goods and cash. American Express and the Diners Club have had similar experiences and, no doubt, will continue to do so. The less people deal in hard cash and the more they rely on credit cards, the easier it will be for the fraudsman to operate. Frauds of this kind became so prevalent that Scotland Yard was forced to establish a special squad of detectives to deal with it. The Cheque Squad has been very successful but will never be able to wipe out this type of crime. After all, a bank clerk would never be able positively to identify a person who walked in, produced a £30 cash card and a corresponding cheque book, forged the signature on the card and made off with the money. A new cheque book normally contains thirty cheques. Therefore, a thief who steals a new book along with a cash card can easily make himself over £900. A professional could multiply the operation many times and successfully escape with thousands.

Similarly, with, say, an American Express card, a determined fraudsman could not only obtain plenty of cash, but kit himself out with a substantial wardrobe and even buy an air ticket to some other part of the world before he was even suspected. 'A good operator can do a lot of damage with one of those things and you would be amazed just how careless people are with them. They leave their wallets and coats lying around all over the place, making life very easy indeed for the crook', a Cheque Squad officer said resignedly.

Not all frauds, of course, are big. In fact, most of them are small and involve only a few thousand pounds. But even these illustrate the ingenuity of the fraudsman and the lengths to which he is prepared to go to secure himself a quick cash return. It was only because a printer queried spellings on Imperial Cancer Research Fund identity cards and rang the Fund to check, that a neat little fraud was found to be operating in London and the Home Counties. The gang had issued ninety unsuspecting collectors with forged identity cards and they received 45-per-cent commission on the £6,500 they had collected from pubs in only six weeks. The gang took the rest and the Fund received only £200.

And towards the end of 1974, Judge Bush said at Birmingham Crown Court that fraudulent claims for non-existent child dependants were now so numerous that genuine claimants were finding it increasingly difficult to obtain their legal entitlement. Even the Royal Courts of Justice themselves have not been immune from the small-time fraudsmen. A loss of £10,000 was discovered after a special audit by a team of fifteen accountants. They examined 129,000 writs and found some had been falsified by staff. One of the employees who pleaded guilty had told the police: 'I started doing this because I saw others doing it'.

Labourers operating 'The Lump' system in the building industry have certainly defrauded the Inland Revenue of millions. Moves were made in the Finance Act, 1971 to remove this danger by insisting that all 'lump' labour paid tax at source unless the person was in possession of a tax exemption certificate issued by the Inland Revenue. Not surprisingly, forged certificates soon appeared on the market and quickly developed into a multi-million pound fraud. Inland Revenue investigators, already in possession of exemption vouchers for more than £1,500,000 are 'extremely concerned' about the situation and are convinced that many more such vouchers are being passed around the building sites of Britain. In one case which came before the courts towards the end of 1974, it was discovered that one Irish labourer had not paid any tax since arriving in Britain in 1958. He owed over £5,000 but had over £1,000 in his pocket when questioned by police.

But that sort of money was not for the man who was undoubtedly King of the Con Men. He was suave Charles Percival De Silva, a handsome Singalese who, during his twenty-six years as a high-living fraudsman, was believed to have parted the rich and gullible from around £3 million. Even tough Scotland Yard detectives had a sneaking regard for him. One said: 'He was one of our best clients, a perfect gentlemen.' For, every time he was caught at 'one of my little games' he would submit gracefully, without fuss or temper.

Charles De Silva arrived in Britain from Colombo, Ceylon, in 1947, the well-educated grandson of the second richest man in the island. Within weeks he was spreading his undoubted charm around the fashionable West End of London, dining in the best restaurants, often passing himself off as a close relative of Ceylon's Minister of Finance. His object: to become known and respected by London's Establishment and the wealthy.

Four years later he received his first term of imprisonment, for attempting to swindle Selfridge's of more than £2,000 of then scarce nylons. On his release from prison, De Silva moved into Claridge's and boasted about his involvement in a £200,000 gun-running plot to overthrow General Franco. A few months later he was declared bankrupt with debts of £109,000. But that did not stop him. He looked around all the time for 'mugs'—people he could part from their money. He once found an impressionable but wealthy man who was trying to lever himself into a position of influence. So De Silva used 10 Downing Street as the 'front' for his masterly operation. He managed to obtain an invitation, through a friend, to a social function organised by Lady Dorothy Macmillan. At the party, to which he took his astounded friend, he handed Lady Dorothy a cheque for one of her favourite charities. De Silva's companion was duly impressed, so the superb confidence trickster had no difficulty in persuading him to part with a considerable amount of cash 'for an unbeatable' scheme.

Once he met an American multi-millionaire with a particular liking for young girls. De Silva saw his opportunity and took it. He arranged a party for the American and organised a team of prostitutes who, he insisted, dressed as schoolgirls. The unsuspecting American was completely fooled by De Silva's casual story that the girls had been provided by the Mother Superior of a convent school, and handed over £25,000 for the name of the fictitious nun. On another occasion he was jailed for six years after trying to sell £700,000 worth of non-existent trawlers from Sweden to Ceylon. His name was never out of the newspapers and was once linked with the £600,000 theft of three Old Masters from Amsterdam. He was also convicted of trying to sell forged plates for £1 and 10s notes.

Charles De Silva lived well, often stayed at Claridge's, dressed in 160 guinea Savile Row suits and drove around in a chauffeured Rolls Royce which he had bought on hire purchase—having made only one payment, of course. But he was no gourmet. During his heyday he would order his £40-a-week chauffeur to drive to a transport café in King's Road, Chelsea for his favourite breakfast of bubble and squeak (fried potatoes and greens) and fried eggs.

But as a gambler he was first class. He spent well over £100,000 in casinos in the Riviera and Las Vegas and, on many occasions, won large sums of money. He never kept it for very long, operating always on the principle that there was 'always another mug round the corner'. He was generally right. On one occasion, when he was broke, he persuaded several firms and wealthy individuals to part with a small fortune for a chinchilla business he was going to start in Ceylon. Needless to say, the business never materialised.

Even his suicide, in 1973, occurred in such circumstances that his friends had their suspicions about whether it was genuine. He booked into the Divan Hotel, in Euston, under the name of Sir Charles Paris. The next morning a maid found him dead from an overdose of drugs. A young woman he lived with in Roland Gardens, South Kensington, suggested that he knew he would go to prison again when he faced a jury—the case was due the following month—at the Old Bailey. 'He just could not stand that', she said. But friends who had known Charles De Silva for years were not convinced. And some were certain that, despite the body, he somehow faked his death to avoid another term behind bars. But this time there was no 'con' trick, Charles De Silva had, in fact, died. And even the King of the Con Men could not cheat death.

chapter six

Security against thieves

The role of security companies   Can the police go into the security business commercially?   The problem of 'walk-in' thieves   Is some theft economically justifiable?   Bank robberies and the men responsible   The pathetic men—The problem of forged paintings and antiques

It is only in the context of the vast cash losses, incurred every day by businesses large and small, that the growth of Britain's private army of security companies can be justified. In a perfect or near perfect society, the need for such firms as Securicor, Security Express, Group 4 and the like, would be totally unnecessary. In these circumstances, affairs could be quite adequately handled by the local police force.

As it is, these firms are becoming more and more necessary as company accountants examine their balance sheets and realise that enormous amounts of cash and goods are disappearing every day, thereby slashing vital profit margins that could mean the very real difference between staying in business and going bankrupt.

For losses suffered by companies in all kinds of businesses are now so colossal that, as one security expert put it, they sound just like long telephone numbers. So, before examining the role of the security organisations, it is important to see why they have become so essential to everyday commercial and business life in Britain, the USA and most countries in the Western world.

Possibly the biggest single loss suffered by firms in the retail, manufacturing and construction industries every year is what they euphemistically describe as 'shrinkage' and, more often, 'wastage'. In other words, pilfering and shoplifting. Taken individually, the loss of, say, a pair of stockings from a shop counter may seem barely worth a mention, or the loss of a single plank of wood from a builder's yard hardly worth reporting to the police. But added together nationwide, they add up to a staggering estimate of around £700 million a year in Britain alone. And yet, because these thefts—for that is exactly what they are—are usually of apparently trifling proportions, few people ever get hauled before the courts. The result is that industry, in its broadest sense, has to 'write off' this amount every year.

The retail industry suffers greatly. It is still too easy to walk into a shop and slip something into a bag without detection. But Britain's annual shoplifting bill comes to more than £100 million a year and is growing. Even so, that is not the worst part. For retailers estimate that 'shrinkage' due to staff pilferage tots up to £200 million annually and this is even harder to detect and stop than shoplifting.

Together they add up to a critical 2 per cent of gross profit margins. This, in an industry which relies on a quick turnover on a small profit basis to make its livelihood, can be little less than crippling.

Despite the figures, retailers often do nothing about them. Some even deliberately refuse to acknowledge the problem exists and merely increase prices by 2 per cent to level out their profit margins. In the end, the honest customer usually pays the thief's bill. Officials of the British Security Industry Association have described the twin evils of shoplifting and pilfering as having now reached the proportions of a moral epidemic.

In the manufacturing and construction industries, the situation, in terms of hard cash, is even worse. Here, it is estimated, on the same 2 per cent 'shrinkage' rate, losses amount to £372 million a year, of which £248 million is due to employee pilferage. Taken overall, the total figures indicate that thefts of this type alone amount to more than £2 million every day. This is, by far, greater than other losses due to forms of crime such as wage snatches and armed robbery. Some criminologists have described it as the greatest single crime in the western world.

Interestingly, the reluctance of employers to do much about it is based on their fear of upsetting either their workers or customers. Many retailers, for example are loath to install closed-circuit television equipment, although this has proved to be an effective deterrent, because they feel customers would object to be 'spied' upon from a central control room by unseen store detectives.

Moreover—and this applies to all industries where shoplifting and pilfering are rife—employers feel staff objections would cause industrial unrest and upset the often delicate relations with trades unions which would count the installation of such 'Orwellian' devices as an unacceptable intrusion on their members' privacy. So employers, even in time of spiralling inflation, are faced with the sole alternative of turning a blind eye.

It is a far from happy situation but, in many ways, the employers have only themselves to blame. Large numbers of them, especially supermarket chains and large department stores, often put temptation on a plate. New recruits, often after only a few days training, are put behind a counter or cash check-out till without any question of references or background information. In these circumstances, it is simple for them to fill their shopping baskets, siphon goods out through the loading bay—or merely show a personal cash profit through deliberately overcharging unsuspecting customers.

A director of an Oxford Street store explained: 'It's virtually impossible to stop this sort of thing happening. We are just having to live with it. I agree it is a sad reflection on the integral honesty of, not only the customers, but our employees as well. But many of them just regard pilfering as one of the perks of the job. It is almost an expected part of their wage packet, a sort of tax-free bonus.'

Commercial companies obviously do not have the shoplifting problem, but they do have staff pilferers, who genuinely see nothing wrong in writing personal letters on company notepaper, taking pens and pencils home or simply 'borrowing' from the petty cash box. However, by far their biggest problem comes from what the police describe as 'walk-in' thieves who are after much bigger pickings than a few pieces of notepaper.

For the 'walk-in' thief is often a professional who knows his business and exactly where he can dispose of the stolen goods—usually on the not-too-particular second-hand market where cheap 'bargains' are always quickly snapped up.

The 'walk-in' thief relies almost entirely on the gullibility of office and factory workers. His favourite trick is to stroll into an office and announce that he has arrived to repair and service the typewriters. Within minutes he will have found a 'serious fault' with at least one which, he assures unsuspecting staff, can be dealt with only on the workbench. Then, with the typewriter tucked under his arm, he wanders out and is never seen again.

Another example, which happened in the London offices of a major international company, shows just how daring these thieves can be. Two of them wearing white overalls and driving a van, pulled up outside the firm's glass-fronted multi-storey office block as workers were arriving to start the day's work. After a cheery 'Good Morning' to the jovial commissionaire, they explained they had come to inspect the valuable crystal chandelier, the impressive centrepiece of the prestige foyer.

Watched by the commissionaire and workers waiting to board the lifts, they climbed their ladders for the 'inspection'. Within minutes they had detected rust and erosion which made the chandelier unsafe. It would have to come down and be taken away 'for a few days' to be repaired, they explained. Shortly afterwards the 'workmen' had loaded the finely-cut crystal into their van and have not been seen since. Moreover, it was several days before anyone even realised there had been a theft at all. Nobody had taken the trouble to question the two men, ask for a business card or even a receipt for the glassware. The cost: several thousands of pounds.

Even twenty years ago, around half the crime committed in the City of London involved thefts other than by forcible entry. But 'walk-in' thieves now enter offices and factories in Metropolitan London at least 100,000 times each year and latest figures indicate they made off with £1,020,000 worth of goods and equipment—an amazing average of more than £100 per theft.

In the City of London, where this type of offence is one of the biggest headaches for Commissioner James Page and his overworked policemen, a sustained crime prevention campaign resulted in a significant 22.5 per cent drop. But the problem is still growing and there is no sign that the 'walk-in' thief is being greatly deterred elsewhere.

It is already apparent that, given this serious situation, more and more firms are turning to the professional security organisations in an effort to cut down, wherever possible, on the activities of the 'walk-in' criminal, the shoplifter and the pilferer. Most moderately-sized firms have for years relied on the security firms to handle delivery of their staff wages and, in many cases, take responsibility for night security patrols.

But, as experts have now reached the sad conclusion that bad security is costing Britain about £1,000 million a year in various types of theft, vandalism and fire, these specialised companies, with their technical knowledge and resources, are becoming increasingly a familiar part of our everyday business life.

The reasoning behind their growth is simple. Companies are finding it cheaper in the long run to pay, say, £20,000 a year to a security firm for their professional services, than to fork out £50,000 in higher insurance premiums for possible fire, theft, damage by vandals or having their wages or takings snatched from a member of their staff in the street.

With the growing use of computers in business houses, protection against vandals is vital, especially when it is realised that anyone with a decent magnet or a handy half brick could damage a computer to the extent where the unfortunate company could be literally put out of business because of irreplaceable information banks being lost.

It is often said that total security is totally impossible. But, with the growth in crime and the increasing sophistication of the criminal fraternity, companies are taking the view that security of personnel, offices and factories, equipment and information, should be a major item in their cost analysis calculations. Security services are not cheap and costs, given pay rises, petrol prices, higher pensions, are likely to double within the next five years. Even so, the services of top security organisations are in increasing demand and the trend is certain to continue.

So who are they, these private armies, fringe police forces or, as they have been sometimes called, uniformed gangs of professional strongmen? And what is their role in relation to the official police authorities? Are they effective and worth the vast sums spent on hiring their professional services?

Britain has many security companies, ranging from the small firm which specialises in guard dogs for building sites to the large complex groups which supply a complete security service. The bigger firms, such as Group 4, Security Express and Securicor, will undertake everything from bullion carrying, escort duty, wage collection and packaging, night guards and closed circuit television, to providing store detectives and strongboxes for personal valuables.

They will advise firms and individuals alike on the most efficient methods of caring for their property. Many are staffed at senior levels by former detectives and retired security experts from the armed services. Their organisations are usually reliable, efficient and any losses they incur at the hands of criminals are fully insured.

The leading firms in this country operate under the umbrella of the British Security Industry Association which has devised its own meticulous code of ethics and operational practice as one sure-fire method of ridding the industry of the twilight firms whose background and *modus operandi* were open to question. Several of these firms with a dubious pedigree flourished briefly until the mid-1960s and succeeded in giving the corporate security watchdog a bad name. But, by and large, these have now been put down and the remaining firms can, generally speaking, be regarded as perfectly honest and respectable.

While staff recruitment, at the top levels, comes from the upper echelons of the police force, men of wide experience in dealing with the criminal mind and thereby best equipped to counter it, recruitment at ground level is from all walks of life.

The security companies themselves claim to have an efficient vetting system for winkling out the 'bad eggs' among their recruits (and it is unofficially accepted they have access on a private arrangement basis to Scotland Yard's Criminal Records Office). But the police, while agreeing the security firms often do a good job, especially in the crime prevention field, are often critical that the security guard recruits are drawn from men rejected by the police for character defects. Too many recruits, they claim, are people who see a uniform as providing them with some sort of instant power; men who are basically unreliable or occasionally prone to violence at the slightest provocation.

In some cases this is undoubtedly true. Police are certain, though often they lack the vital proof, that more than one wages snatch, bank robbery, or safe blowing operation has been the direct result of important information passed to the criminals by a security guard who either could not keep his mouth shut or deliberately looked for money from the villains. However, these instances are few enough to leave the security industry with a good name.

As recently as the 1960s security company vehicles were relatively easy meat for determined criminals who would stop at nothing—even murder—to grab a large cash haul. But times have changed. The days of overpowering security guards inside their vehicles by using gas or ammonia and breaking the rear doors with pick-axes are gone.

Vehicles now used for carrying cash, bullion or any other valuables will now defy virtually anything would-be robbers can throw at them—including small bombs. They are, by and large, armour plated machines with specially reinforced flooring to resist bomb or land mine attack. They are fitted with specially-designed air conditioning to ward off any gas threats and windows are bullet proof. Finally they are in constant radio contact with their base so that any threat can be immediately reported and the police quickly alerted. The result of these improvements has been a dramatic drop in the instances of attacks on security vans.

But for Brinks Incorporated, the Chicago-based security firm with offices and subsidiaries in London, even these measures were not enough when it came to providing safety for valuable bullion which had to be carried across Europe. They have introduced a massive articulated and fully armoured vehicle with gun ports so crews can defend themselves with weapons in countries where security guards are allowed to carry them. Even the radiator is fully protected. Also it will travel up to 650 miles without having to stop to refuel.

Even with vehicles such as these, Britain's top flight security firms, which between them employ about 60,000 men and women, realise the system is not foolproof. After all, the criminals have only to entice the driver or his mate into becoming the 'inside' man for their team (and several security guards have slipped through their company security net and have later been found to have criminal records) and the best security systems are totally useless.

So they attempt to solve the problem by strictly adhering to the 'need to know' principle. In other words, when a man leaves work after one shift he has no idea what he will be doing the next day until he reports for duty. In this way the companies minimise the risk to their clients—and the temptation to their staff. Daily work schedules are completed only by the most carefully vetted and trustworthy members of the firm. In other words, a guard could find himself on patrol duty at an office block one day and driving large amounts of bullion or cash the next. Though far from perfect, it is a pretty secure system which, by and large, seems to work effectively, especially when it is realised that something in the order of £1,000 million is transported around London alone every day without mishap.

All the major banks and companies with sizeable amounts of cash being handled regularly, now find the services of the security companies invaluable. So do governments who trust them to transfer gold reserves from place to place. When the late President De Gaulle, for example, decided to call in all of France's gold reserves during an economic crisis, the gold deposited in Britain was stored for several days in the vaults of a security firm until sufficient Air France planes arrived at Heathrow to fly the valuable metal home to Paris. The operation was top secret and, even now, details of how it was done are sketchy. But the firm's senior management are said to have spent some sleepless nights until the last of the gold was safely airborne.

But security firms have no special standing in relation to the police. So far as the police are concerned, they are merely individual private companies undertaking contracts on behalf of clients and for which they draw a fee.

And, despite the often close liaison between the two, police officers generally speaking, tend to look down on security guards as second-raters, would-be officers who have failed to match up to the required physical or educational standards. Further, despite the fact that all large security companies have schools and courses for a comprehensive grounding in security work, policemen consider their training inferior and certainly not of the quality required at the Police College at Bramshill, Hampshire.

Mr R.L. Carter, senior lecturer in industrial economics at Nottingham University, in a comprehensive paper for the Institute of Economic Affairs, published towards the end of 1974, argues that perhaps the police should themselves go into the private security business on a commercial basis, employing civilians, rather on the same basis as traffic wardens, to do the job. This would eliminate the need for the government to employ private firms for 'politically sensitive' tasks, such as dealing with aliens at airports. He said:

> The security companies are constantly widening the range of their activities, some of a type the police are ill-equipped to undertake. On the other hand, the police have the capital resources to undertake some of the more politically-sensitive activities of the security companies.

Mr Carter contended that police communications networks and garaging facilities would enable them to operate the cash carrying services without much problem. Given Home Office encouragement and the right organisation he felt the police should be able to supply such services at a price equal to or lower than the manned security firms. The question of public accountability would then be firmly resolved, and the cash-carrying services would be able to co-operate closely with other branches of the police.

While it is doubtful that Mr Carter's ideas would win much support amongst serving police officers, or indeed amongst the security companies themselves, some of his ideas undoubtedly have commercial merit:

> Organisationally, such a service could operate as a separate branch of the police, using existing facilities as far as possible, and responsible direct to each chief constable, but with national co-ordination. It could be staffed by civilians, including retired police officers, the security guards being given a status similar to traffic wardens.

He made it clear he was not suggesting existing business generated by security companies should be taken over by a government-operated service but he considered that if the police proved they could operate a more efficient and cheaper service, that result naturally followed. If at the same time the private security companies proved their efficiency, that would justify their continued existence.

It was accepted that many chief constables would not have the business flair and imagination required to compete with the private companies, some of which have displayed considerable enterprise and flexibility in recent years.

Therefore, Mr Carter suggested, such schemes should be started experimentally in areas where they would be welcomed by the local police chief. Commercial merit or not, some chief constables, already unhappy about the 'Pinkerton Rides Again' security companies, will consider they have enough work on their hands already without going into business on their own, or at least the community's behalf. Even Sir Robert Mark, the liberal-thinking and far-sighted Commissioner of the Metropolitan Police, who, generally speaking, is in favour of security firms on the grounds that they can be influential in reducing crime, is unlikely to give the matter too much consideration.

One or two of the Nottingham lecturer's ideas for trimming theft figures generally could, however, win him more friends among the police. For example, Mr Carter believes that all homes should be required by law to have minimum standards of protection—quality locks, window catches and so on—as a deterrent to thieves and burglars. And he takes his argument a step further by advocating similar reasonable standards for industry, commerce and public authorities.

Mr Carter considered that only if loss prevention and the arrest and punishment of offenders could be provided at no cost to the community, would it be worthwhile trying to reduce theft losses to nil. In practice, it was for the community to decide how much theft activity it was economical to prevent.

> If a community's objective is to obtain the maximum satisfaction from its productive resources, it should not employ resources on theft prevention which could yield larger benefits in other uses . . . . The benefit obtained from resources employed in theft prevention may be measured by the reduction in losses caused by thieves (that is, by the reduction in the value of the property stolen and destroyed and personal injuries suffered by the victims), and it is reasonable to assume that the amount of this benefit is directly related to the community's expenditure on theft prevention.

These are certainly major points of discussion and debate but, in the meantime, the police have the job of catching thieves and security firms of all descriptions the task of outwitting them. Banks, for instance, now have sophisticated alarm systems, particularly in the USA but increasingly so in Britain, to defeat the hold-up specialists and safe-breakers.

More and more banks are installing closed circuit television equipment which scans the counter constantly. At the first sign of a hold-up, bullet-proof shutters quickly slide down to protect staff and money. So the thief, or bank robber, is then in the position of having to nobble the television equipment and the security staff who man it.

This creates more difficulties for the criminal and is, in itself, sufficient to deter many but, by no means, all. However, it is likely that, as such security methods spread in Britain, determined robbers will resort increasingly to violence to multiply their funds. This has already happened in the USA where gangs silence the security staff first and worry about the money afterwards. Having achieved their first object, the second becomes comparative child's play.

Undoubtedly the biggest zone for bank robberies in the United Kingdom is Northern Ireland where they have become such a feature of life that they hardly justify a mention in the newspapers any more. The overworked officers of the Royal Ulster Constabulary, furthermore, have hardly any chance of catching the bank thieves who disappear into the ghetto areas and are never seen again.

Many of these raids take place on Fridays when banks normally handle a great deal of money to pay company wages and so on. In fact, Fridays have now become known in Ulster as 'pay day' for robbers. And, although a large number of these raids are carried out by terrorists to finance the purchase of arms and ammunition, the IRA is by no means always responsible, though they nearly always get the blame. Frustrated RUC detectives point out that, in the present climate, 'any thug can stage a bank robbery to line his pockets and be virtually certain of getting away with it'. And it must be remembered, these robberies take place in an area where security is a way of life and far more stringent than in the rest of the UK.

However, clever robbers who do not wish to run the risk of being seen and possibly identified—despite their masks—at bank robberies, can resort to blowing the bank's safe and vaults. But these operations require great skill, clever and meticulous planning and an intimate knowledge of the bank's existing security arrangements. It is no use, for example, trying to break into a bank via the windows or doors. These are all wired to an alarm system which would bring the police to the scene within minutes. Even ceilings—and sometimes floors—are wired to warn off intruders.

So the would-be robbers have to discover a method of either effectively silencing the alarms or by-passing them. Having done that they need someone in the gang with the skill to open the safe or the vaults—also without raising suspicion. Clearly, therefore, while a hold-up gang needs only a team of thugs, with no specialised knowledge, the safe-breaking fraternity need a group of highly skilled experts. They need an electrician with the know-how to silence the alarms; they need an explosives expert who can 'blow' the safe without killing his colleagues or someone who can handle laser equipment to burn a hole through the metal. Depending on their plan, they may also require people with tunnelling experience and so on. They also need some 'inside' knowledge of when vaults are likely to be full, the simplest way to get to it and the easiest way to beat the alarms.

Mr David Holdsworth, Chief Constable of the busy Thames Valley police, had obviously been thinking along similar lines when he said at a public dinner in 1973:

Something like 1.7 million crimes are reported to the police every year in England and Wales, most of them thefts. We believe that something like 50 per cent of them would not have been committed if members of the public had taken some elementary precautions to protect their own property. You leave your valuables unlocked in your cars, you scatter cash carelessly in your homes and offices; you leave food, credit cards, cheque books, clothing and radios all over the place. You are careless, irresponsible and apparently determined to make life easy for the thief. And then you have the effrontery to criticise the police for failing to prevent crime!

It has often been argued by leading economists that theft, when taken totally as a loss to the community, the costs of insuring against it, the cost of police investigation, the employment of security services in attempts to stop it, probably costs Britain as much as 2 per cent of its national income at around £850 million a year. Given that rather dramatic figure, the economic argument then centres on exactly how much money should be spent in stopping thieves going about their business. In other words, whilst it would be theoretically possible to stamp out all theft, given enough finance and resources, the capital cost of mounting such an exercise—and maintaining it year after year—would probably exceed £850 million.

Naturally banks insist that their staffs are totally trustworthy, but criminals nearly always obtain vital information from a clerk in financial difficulties, a nightwatchman who is prepared to take a knock on the head for a share of the takings, or someone else prepared to betray trust. Without it, few bank raids could be carried out in this way. The days of the genuine 'peterman' who, armed with only a stethoscope could open any safe by cleverly manipulating the combination lock tumblers, are over. Skilled locksmiths have made sure of that. Nearly all modern safes and vaults cannot now be opened in this way. Some are even strong enough to resist gelignite and laser beam treatment and it is this, more than anything else, which has restricted the activities of this type of bank robber.

However, supermarkets, department stores and other premises which deal in large amounts of cash have, surprisingly, been rather slower than the banks to install this sort of security equipment. The robbers have, therefore, turned their attentions to these sources of ready cash and made some spectacular 'killings'. In fact, their annual haul has been bigger in total, than the Great Train Robbery where £2½ million was stolen. But it was this one crime, by its sheer size, skill, planning—and not least the 30-year sentences which were handed out after the conviction of the robbers—which captured the public imagination and lingers still in the public memory.

It happened in August 1963 but is still regarded as a classic crime, is still revamped and re-told by newspapers and magazines, is still a topic of conversation at bars and the sentences even now are the subject of debate and controversy in legal circles.

It will be remembered that the gang ambushed the Glasgow-London night mail train near Cheddington, Buckinghamshire—after altering the signalling equipment so that driver Jack Mills was forced to bring the train to an unexpected halt. His co-driver, David Whitby, climbed down from the engine and walked along the track to investigate. Some of the hooded gang jumped on him, hurled him down the bank and told him: 'If you shout, we'll kill you.' Other members of the gang, similarly dressed in balaclava hoods, uncoupled the two leading coaches of the train which contained the 120 mailbags they wanted. Inside the bags was the fortune in used banknotes they were after.

In the cab, experienced driver Mills was waiting for the return of his colleague. Suddenly he was jumped upon by another member of the gang and battered over the head with an iron bar. After a brief struggle Mr Mills was forced to drive the 'valuable' section of the train down the line to a road bridge. Inside the coaches were five unarmed Post Office guards, blissfully unaware of what was happening outside. They were quickly overpowered and the mailbags thrown over the bridge to a lorry waiting on the road below. Within seconds the gang had disappeared. The entire operation, which had obviously been planned, rehearsed and detailed down to the last second, was completed, from start to finish, in just thirty-five minutes.

The gang drove to Leatherslade Farm only twenty miles from the scene and there divided their loot. Each man got about £140,000 for his efforts and it was probably only because of the stupidity of two unknown men, who had each been paid £10,000 to remove every trace of the robbers at the farm, that police were able to follow their trail so soon. The men never turned up and the farm was left littered with informative clues that proved vital to the police inquiries.

The man who led the police investigation was Detective Chief Superintendent Tommy Butler for whom tracking down the gang became something of a personal crusade. His success was remarkable and he eventually captured every one of them. Only one, Ronald Biggs, succeeded in escaping the net—after being sentenced to thirty years in prison and escaping from Wandsworth fifteen months later. He is now living in Brazil, a free man with nowhere to go because no other country will allow him entry. And he was only allowed to stay in Brazil because he fathered a child to a local half-Indian girl named Raimunda. His wife and family are still in Australia where they fled after he escaped.

As 'the one that got away', it could be argued that Biggs has made robbery pay. It is not true. He is broke, virtually penniless, making his living as a carpenter. All his £140,000 went in bribing people to assist his escape, expensive plastic surgery in Paris, the purchasing of false passports and giving 'friends' huge sums to keep their mouths shut.

The more senior of his partners in crime are still in prison and are likely to remain there for a long time yet, despite some genuine public sympathy for their plight. There is little doubt that the train robbers would have been accorded some hero status but for their one big mistake—battering Jack Mills. In the eyes of many people, stealing the money was fair game, after all the banks could afford the loss. But someone was injured, seriously hurt, and it is for this unnecessarily savage attack that the robbers will not be easily forgiven.

One rather interesting facet of that particular robbery is what fully happened to some of those who were connected with it. Jack Mills never fully recovered from the attack and, after struggling through sickness for several years, died. His young co-driver, David Whitby, a bachelor, died suddenly of a heart attack at the age of thirty-four. Frank Dewhurst, the Post Office man in charge of the cash on the train, also died from a heart attack at the age of fifty-one. Tommy Butler, the dedicated policeman, died suddenly at the age of fifty-seven, only a few months after the last of the robbers was safely behind bars.

Of the robbers themselves. William Boal, sentenced to seven years, died in prison, an officer at his bedside. John Wheater, a lawyer with a large practice, spent two years in gaol for handling the purchase of the farm hideout and ruined his career. His managing clerk, Brian Field, lost his beautiful German wife, Karen, who ran off and later married a German journalist after her young baby, born four months prematurely while Field was awaiting trial, died. Thomas Wisbey, one of the 30-year men, was taken in handcuffs to see his 16-year-old daughter, Lorraine, before she died from injuries received in a car accident. He was refused permission to attend her funeral. Biggs, is now virtually a prisoner in Rio de Janeiro, struggling to make ends meet and having already lost one son in Australia through a car smash. He was too frightened to attend the funeral because police were constantly watching for him. As for the rest, they are behind bars, the master criminals—Charles Wilson, Bruce Reynolds, Robert Welch, Douglas Goody, Roy James and James Hussey. So much for the perfect robbery.

Although the success of the police investigation into the train robbery put a large number of London's best criminals behind bars, there were still enough of them free to carry on the robbery business on a grand scale. Supermarkets, stores, post offices and banks were still their prime targets, the places where large sums of ready and untraceable cash were available to men of daring and skill. One of the key figures in possibly the most proficient gang of bank robbers in Britain was Bruce Brown, property developer, golf club captain, charmer extraordinary.

He featured prominently in the country's biggest-ever bank robbery trial at the Old Bailey in the summer of 1974 after police had completed their investigations into fifty-nine major robberies which had taken place in the south-east of England between 1968 and 1972. At the end of the trial, twenty-two men were sentenced to a total of 309 years imprisonment for their part in the robberies which, at the time, netted them a total of over £1 million and, possibly, nearer £2 million. The final figure may never be known.

All of the men were not involved in every robbery but some of the jobs the gang 'pulled' were at Barclays Bank in Ilford which yielded £236,000, another branch of Barclays at Wembley in which they got £138,000, a lucrative raid in Hatton Garden, London's diamond centre, and several security van hold-ups.

Brown was a leading figure in some of these raids and, like many other professional criminals, led a double life. On the surface he was a perfectly respectable businessman, buying properties and selling them for profit. He was a devoted father to his two young children and a loving husband to his attractive wife Glynis. He was a proficient golfer and one-time captain of an exclusive golf club in Middlesex.

He was also known as a good conversationalist, a steady but not extravagant buyer of drinks at the club bar and generally 'a jolly good sort of chap'. Brown was considered a truthful and trustworthy person. So much so that one of Scotland Yard's senior detectives—who was eventually a leading figure in solving the spate of robberies—was a personal friend. Their families enjoyed a holiday a holiday together in Germany and wined and dined together. They were even members of the same golf club and played together regularly. Brown was invited to the detective's promotion parties and the annual divisional dinner.

But the other side of Brown's double life was as a ruthless bank robber, an organiser of crimes, the 'brains' behind some of the most daring robberies ever carried out in Britain. Eventually, like his colleagues, he was caught and brought to justice. Their subsequent conviction was a classic example of the old mis-quotation: 'There is no honour among thieves.' For, the man who pointed the condemning finger at them and provided police with masses of damning evidence was one of the gang who agreed to turn Queen's Evidence in exchange for his own freedom—Derek Creighton 'Bertie' Smalls, who himself was accused of three bank and jewel robberies involving £170,000. The charges against Smalls, described by detectives as the 'biggest grass (informer) of all time' were dropped and he appeared in the witness box day after day describing in detail the many robberies various members of the gang had taken part in and, in some cases, even saying where the money had gone.

Strangely, but perhaps not surprisingly in the circumstances, Smalls hid his share of the robberies under a tree in a park because he did not trust banks! But the price he was forced to pay for his freedom was high. Even when he first appeared in court at the Old Bailey to hear the charges against him dropped on the advice of the Director of Public Prosecutions, he stood in the dock with a five-man police guard. Furthermore, the case was not listed in the ordinary manner and was heard, virtually in secret, half an hour before the normal court starting time. The reason: there were genuine fears for Smalls's life after many threats and strong rumours—taken very seriously by the police—that an underworld 'contract' had been put out. Clearly, the criminals, some of whom were sentenced to more than twenty years in prison, wanted Smalls out of the way, preferably dead before he could give his crippling evidence against them. The police, on the other hand, had the job of keeping him alive and safe from harm—at least until after the case was finished. This also meant placing a twenty-four hour guard on his wife and children at their home near Croydon, Surrey, for fear they might be kidnapped and used as a bargaining lever to silence him.

But Smalls gave his evidence and his former colleagues were eventually sentenced. Police continued their guard over him and his family for some months after the end of the trial and even provided them with a £25 weekly income out of public funds. Eventually, after several months, police protection was withdrawn along with the weekly 'wage'. Smalls was on his own, broke, and having to face the daily possibility of an assassin's gun. He has moved house, changed his family name, even adopted various disguises. But he will live in fear for the rest of his life.

Apart from bank robberies, Britain's detectives have been long worried about the growth of other kinds of theft. Hijacking, for instance, of vans and lorries containing easily sold items such as cigarettes, spirits and drugs. For the criminal, hijackings of this sort are largely a 'seasonal' trade, many of the larger hauls coming just before Christmas when huge amounts of stocks are on the move. By and large, lorry drivers are totally unprotected against gangs operating this kind of robbery, sometimes using considerable violence but often merely coshing the unfortunate driver over the head, tying him up and dumping him at the roadside.

Hijacking operations are usually well planned. There are very few recorded cases of vehicles being stopped where their cargo was valueless. Again, as in bank robberies, it is often important for the thieves to have 'inside' knowledge of the vehicle's route, timing, destination and cargo value. It is certainly not unknown for drivers to be in league with the gang. In fact, in most cases, he is the number one suspect in any subsequent police inquiry. But the driver is by no means always to blame. Even a number of the large haulage firms, familiar with carrying valuable loads, stick to routes and timetables that make it just too easy for a gang of hijackers. Furthermore, drivers themselves have favourite cafés and stopping places where they become regular customers. All hijackers have to do is be patient and keep the busier transport cafés under surveillance. Within a few weeks they will have picked out a 'customer'. The only thing left for them is to simply wait for the driver to leave the café and hold him up at gunpoint, or stage a fake road accident at some lonely spot. The gangs know full well that professional drivers have their own code of ethics and would never ignore a fellow driver in difficulty with his vehicle or what appeared to be an accident. Once he has stopped, the rest is easy for the gang.

Thefts of antiques and paintings have become such big business in the criminal world that Scotland Yard has established a special squad for dealing with it. Some robberies of this kind—such as the theft of the Goya some years ago—are done either by cranks or for some political motive. But some private collectors are still prepared to pay good money for a stolen Old Master and some dealers will not ask too many awkward questions if offered a valuable piece at a reasonable price. Galleries, museums and antique shops usually have a number of clever forgeries or items of dubious origin and even experts often have difficulty in telling the genuine article from the fake. An art dealer, therefore, who buys a stolen painting can always—and often does—plead ignorance about its authenticity and claim he believed it to be a clever copy of the valuable original. One Scotland Yard expert commented:

> This form of crime is certainly growing and is likely to grow even further. The more money people have to spend, either through growing affluence or in what they believe to be a hedge against galloping inflation, the more stolen paintings and antiques will come on the market and be snapped up. Most people do not know anything about paintings or antiques. So if an item is offered in a shop or gallery at, say, £250 they are likely to believe the dealer is asking the current market price and that, with present trends, it would appreciate over the years. In fact, they might easily have a more valuable painting, possibily worth up to ten times what they paid for it—but stolen. Its true background may not come to light for many years, possibly, generations. By that time, the thief could be dead or just totally untraceable.

So, while security is a growing industry, so is theft. In a sense, the two walk hand in hand, side by side, the one dependent on the other. If there was no theft, there would be no need for security: if there was no security, theft would become endemic: the tighter the security, the greater the guile of the thieves trying to beat the latest system.

Mr Carter has argued that it would possibly be uneconomic to stop all theft because the cost to the nation, in real terms, would be too great. Economically speaking, Mr Carter is no doubt right. But he is, after all an economist and takes no consideration of the moral degeneration that results from the youngster taking part in a lark that leads to petty theft. If a youngster can successfully get away with stealing a pencil from school, he might next try to steal one from a store. If that succeeds, he might try his hand thieving from someone's house. Only this time he might be caught—and that could easily lead to violence, even murder. It is a progressive pattern, well known to criminologists, if not to economists. Mr Carter and others of the same opinion are merely considering such matters in straight financial terms. But this is a narrow view, although it should be said that Mr Carter never pretended to look at it any other way.

It is, however, a view that no compassionate society could realistically accept. Theft cannot become an acceptable face of society, no matter what the economic arguments in favour of it may be. Rather, thieves should be taught a salutary lesson from the start. It is more likely that, in that way, they will not become professional robbers who, in many cases, turn their hands to violence; a naughty boy who draws on the wall is not likely to do it again if his father makes his displeasure perfectly clear.

However, security of personnel, property or equipment, should never be allowed to restrict the freedom of the individual. And this is always the danger. Restrictions of one type or another, of movement, access, availability, could easily be reinforced to cramp freedom of travel. This in turn could result in the loss of all sorts of other freedoms we now take for granted. Whilst security may be necessary, the authorities should ensure that the restrictions it imposes should not bring the predictions of George Orwell any the nearer. In other words, security should not necessarily mean we should be, or indeed need be, protected from ourselves.

chapter seven

Smuggling, vice and drugs

The hapless immigrant   Pornography and the call girl racket   Drugs and the
fight against the pedlars   The half-crown smuggling venture

For at least two centuries smuggling has been recognised as one of the traditional, even glamorous and romantic, crimes of the British Isles. Colourful stories of battles with the Revenue men have become an integral part of history. Almost alone, the smuggler, of all criminal classes, was hardly ever a figure to be despised, hated or ridiculed. In fact he was often considered as the maritime Robin Hood, though never a man who passed his illegal booty on to the poor of the day. Even today those engaged in slipping crates of spirits, cigarettes and perfume through the Customs security net are regarded with some admiration and even a degree of awe by the public at large. Time has not tarnished their image but their ranks have been swelled by a new breed whose activities are far more sinister. These are the men—and women—who peddle in drugs, vice and pornography. Their motive is the same as their predecessors—profit. But the implications of their trade have wider and more evil results: drug addiction, especially by the young, gang warfare, prostitution, protection rackets and corruption on an enormous scale. They have even started what amounts to a form of latter day slave traffic by shipping, often in horrifying conditions, wretched coloured illegal immigrants from India and Pakistan into quiet and lonely coves along the south and east coast of England.

These people, mostly illiterate and ignorant of conditions in the West are often left shivering with cold and terrified of what awaits them. But, almost without exception, their 'fare' for the trip cost them more than a first class air ticket. In a sense, those who finish up on the deserted beaches are the lucky ones. Many of their fellow countrymen who attempt the cross-Channel journey, police feel, are deliberately drowned by boat owners who 'pull out the plug' in panic when they suspect they are being tailed by Customs or immigration men at sea.

Although it is impossible to give exact figures of how many immigrants enter

Britain in this way each year, the authorities suspect they could run into many hundreds and the problem has become so acute that police forces in many southern counties have now adopted special alert procedures with their counterparts on the continent. For the smugglers, usually owners of small leaking vessels, it is a lucrative living which can net them between £6,000 and £10,000 a trip, depending on the size of their craft and the number of people they can squeeze aboard, mostly without regard to safety and certainly without any effort to provide comfort.

For the unfortunate would-be immigrants, the very high price of emigration from their native villages usually starts when some unscrupulous local businessman fleeces them for several hundred pounds before packing them off on a rickety bus or coach for the arduous and often hazardous overland journey to continental ports. In recent years several cities have become noted staging posts for the illegal immigrant traffic. In Munich, for instance, many of the Indians and Pakistanis who find themselves homeless and penniless are exploited by local employers who pay them starvation wages for long hours of work in restaurants and cafés. From there these miserable migrants, who have often starved themselves in order to pay for the remainder of their journey, move on to the North Sea ports, usually Ostend in Belgium, Hamburg in Germany, or the small fishing ports along the Northern French coast. Once again they swell the cheap labour market until, possibly having waited for several months, they board the vessel that will bring them to their final destination should they manage to evade detection and capture.

Scores have been rounded up wandering lost, cold and hungry along dark and wet roads while the smugglers slip quietly away to their home port to await another human cargo. Those who are found are then incarcerated in prison and eventually flown home. Those who slip through the net are still not out of trouble. Even among their own people in Bradford, Birmingham, London and Wolverhampton, the major centres of immigrant population, they have been known to be blackmailed, threatened with exposure to the authorities unless they pay what amounts to protection money.

There is another form of human cargo which regularly ferries itself between Britain and the continent. In this case while their journeys are not in themselves illegal or criminal their objectives certainly are. For these are members of a growing band of international vice racketeers and pedlars in pornography, dealers in sex for profit. For the smuggling of filth in and out of Britain has become a thriving international business, often accompanied by a considerable measure of violence aimed at protecting these growing empires. It is no longer unusual for businessmen, Government officials, potentates from the Middle East to have 'expense account' sex orgies in London's leading hotels and clubs. They are easy to arrange through hotel and club staffs who receive commission from the highly organised group of international 'Madams' who daily fly their beautiful and accommodating call girls between European capitals almost on a commuter basis. These girls, who live in high style in expensive flats and houses are often well-groomed and educated young women who work on a contract basis and can command as much as £300 or £400 for a weekend's sex.

In some European countries, with Government-approved brothels, these girls operate quite legally. But in Britain, where brothel-keeping and living off immoral earnings is still an offence, their operations need to be conducted in a clandestine manner. The law, however, provides few obstacles to the sexual requirements of the wealthy in Britain and abroad. The network of 'Madams', who seem to have no difficulty in recruiting sophisticated girls for their business, centre their activities around London, Amsterdam, Paris and Rome. In Germany they have several bases including Frankfurt, Hamburg and Berlin. For these women there are no dark and dingy rooms with a furtive few pound notes changing hands. For them, it is the high-life all the way and one of their girls would cost £100 a day or even more. The location of the rendezvous is always the best hotel suite money can buy and often payment is made by cheque or even credit card. In these cases the cheque is always made out in the name of a club, usually merely a business name used by the 'Madam' to conceal her real activities and save the client from unnecessary embarrassment. One senior Metropolitan policeman commented:

> This business has become so big and such a fact of everyday life in the best hotels and luxury flats that it is rather like ordering a meal from the head waiter. But often the service is more attentive. Instead of caviar and champagne you get the girl or girls of your choice and you can even specify the size and colour so long as you have the money to pay for them. Furthermore you can ask for and get any nationality of girls who specialise in particular forms of deviation. You get Japanese businessmen coming to London, for instance, whose one ambition is to make love to an English girl. This is arranged without any problem merely by dialling a telephone number. On the other hand it appears that visiting Arabs often enjoy group sex and it is not unusual for them to order six or eight girls at a time.

Despite the dangers of their way of life most of the call-girls in this class of business are uncommonly loyal to the woman who arranges their appointments. Hardly ever do they entertain men for money without her knowledge. One woman in London claims to have nearly 200 call-girls on her books and insists that her friends on the Continent, in some cases, have even more. In Britain, at least, these businesses, for that is exactly what they are, show almost a total profit: vice is not a taxable commodity in this country though prostitutes in some parts of Europe are legal and pay income tax just like anyone else. Prostitutes who operate at this high society level often become rich in their own right and it is not unknown for some to even marry their regular customers. In most cases the girls set themselves a financial target to be achieved while they are still young. One told us:

> I came to London when I was eighteen and told my parents that a friend had fixed me up with a job with a West End model agency. In fact, in those early days I did do some modelling and showed my parents the magazines in which

my pictures appeared. They immediately stopped worrying about me but I soon discovered there was more money for an attractive girl who was prepared to sleep with men. Any girl knows that this sort of life cannot go on forever and most want eventually to settle down and have a family of their own. I am no exception. I made up my mind that I would have enough money to be independent by the time I was twenty-five. And I did, too. Now I have a regular boyfriend who knows nothing about my past. I have my own luxury flat in the West End, my own car, plenty of clothes and a part-time model job. We are getting married soon and we are buying a splendid old house in the country. Many girls have done this before me and are now happy and successful housewives. A few of them, I am not going to tell you who they are, have even married men with titles. Others, of course, don't plan for the future and spend every penny they get on all sorts of stupid things. Some go on drugs and you can see them going steadily downhill. These either finish up in the gutter as £5-a-night prostitutes, drug addicts, cheap strippers or get themselves mixed up with nasty crooks. Some, of course, just drift back home again, marry some local boy and become average suburban housewives and mothers with all the problems of mortgages and having enough money for next week's housekeeping.

Some of the less successful prostitutes who fail to make a living in the call girl racket turn to posing and modelling for pornographic magazines and 'acting' in indecent films. It is in this area of vice that the unfortunate young women are more likely to find themselves under the influence of vicious and violent men who would not hesitate to maim, disfigure or even kill if their orders were not strictly obeyed.

These, of course, are the most tragic cases of all, the young and frightened girls, often 'hooked' on drugs, who face a degenerating future with no prospect of finding a better life. In a way, these are the victims of an increasingly permissive society, of an age where the harmless saucy seaside postcard has been replaced by a huge trade in explicit sex, pandering to the morally weak and immature as well as the deviationists and perverts. It is an ever-growing industry, with every conceivable taste − or more accurately, lack of taste − being catered for. While much of the pornography now freely available in Britain might, with some justification, be said to be harmless to the level-headed and intelligent adult, there is, equally, little doubt that some is capable of corrupting and those most likely to be affected are the young. It was with this possibility very much in mind that Parliament decided to legislate against the pornography business and introduced the Cinematograph and Indecent Displays Act. The effect of this was to ban nudes from the covers of magazines and books, stop the 'what the butler saw' seaside peep shows and the posting of unsolicited indecent mail. Furthermore, 'blue film shows' came under much stricter control and 'drag' and strip-tease shows in certain public places were also prohibited. Offenders are now liable to up to three months in prison and fines of up to £400 on conviction by magistrates. Those sent to higher courts can now be sentenced to gaol terms of up to two years.

However, much of the pornographic material distributed in this country originates abroad, particularly from Germany and Scandinavia. As there are no laws curbing its manufacture there, it is likely to remain the primary source of supply. This has opened up yet another avenue for the professional smuggler who is prepared to risk his liberty in the hope of making an easy profit. Much of the material is not allowed into Britain by law and smuggling is the only way of getting it into the country.

But without doubt the smugglers' biggest source of income is drugs. This is now an international industry on a massive and unprecedented scale. It is controlled by teams of ruthless gangsters who resort to fantastic lengths to make sure that addicts throughout the world receive their regular supply of dope. In Britain the problem of drug addiction is becoming increasingly grave and some authorities have suggested it may soon reach epidemic proportions. Customs investigations officers at seaports and airports and the 28-man Drugs Squad at Scotland Yard, along with their colleagues in provincial forces, are now involved in a desperate battle against the growing army of illegal drug importers. In 1973 Customs men alone captured more than nine tons of cannabis worth more than £8 million to the pedlars, and the Scotland Yard Squad arrested more than seven hundred wholesalers and middlemen in London. A further five hundred arrests were made by the Customs men and the total escalated past the 2,000 mark, thanks to vigilance by drugs squads in the rest of Britain. Police say, however, that although their success rate is high it has helped to increase the price of drugs and this increased profit margin will in the long run only mean that more smugglers will come forward to take the place of those they have arrested. In turn this has led to an increase in crime, especially theft and robbery, mainly by the young who need more funds to meet the higher prices being charged. For cannabis, valued at between £100 and £350 a pound weight, depending on quality, is now fetching more than £500 in the back streets. The same money would buy only one ounce of cocaine or heroin. Although the illegal importing of hard drugs continues to increase, the backbone of the market is still cannabis and Customs investigators have discovered that a new type of the drug has begun appearing in Britain.

This is known as 'Hash oil' a liquid produced by distilling resin into a black sticky fluid which can be easily hidden in baggage, plastic cosmetic bottle, airspray container and even tooth-paste tubes. It is at least twenty times more powerful than resin and sells for about £7,000 a pound to illegal wholesalers. These people then dilute it to the consistency of water before retailing to pedlars and addicts. Main centres for its production are in Morocco and Afghanistan but its manufacture can be a dangerous business. Customs officers in London have been told that a number of stills have exploded in both countries, killing several people. Some indication of the increase in drug smuggling can be obtained from the seizure figures for 1972 and 1973. In 1972 there were 1,200 kilogrammes of herbal cannabis and 4,712 kilogrammes of resin found by police and customs officers. The following year Customs men alone accounted for 3,623 kilogrammes of herbal cannabis and 5,358 kilogrammes of resin and 32 kilogrammes of liquid cannabis.

Most of the big hauls discovered entering Britain have been made on car ferries from Morocco. The smugglers, often posing as carefree holiday-makers and tourists, have adopted some ingenious methods to evade detection. One of the most frequent employed involves the use of caravans, where anything up to £500,000 worth of drugs can be concealed behind false floors, roofs and wall linings. The port of Southampton has become one of the main clearing centres for Britain's illegal drugs traffic as smugglers arrive on the ferry from Tangier. Customs men and agents working for the United States Bureau of Narcotics frequently travel the route and, although successful in many cases, it is estimated that they probably only discover a small percentage of the total smuggled.

Crew members are often used as couriers by the big drugs syndicates. These men have little difficulty in carrying shipments aboard and have ample opportunity to conceal their consignment during the crossing. With Morocco fast becoming the prime supply point of drugs for Britain, the Government there has tried to control the drugs market, although 'kif smoking' is part of the social life. Propaganda, warning of the health hazards involved, has appeared on television and in advertisements. But, at the moment, it seems to have had little effect on the illegal trade in drugs, although a co-ordinated attempt has now been made to stem the flow into Britain. From an office on the Albert Embankment in London, the Central Drugs Intelligence Unit is building up a nationwide filing system on all known drug smugglers, pedlars and addicts. Now, about 300,000 names are included on their lists and, despite their major successes, the figure is still increasing. First head of the unit, established in the spring of 1973, was Detective Chief Superintendent Martin White, who said soon after he moved into his new office: 'Either you just scratch at the surface or you try to get at the meat'. His meaning was quite clear: his new unit was going to make a determined effort, not to concentrate solely on catching the pathetic young addicts, but to use them as magnets to draw the 'cannabis kings' into the police net. Mr White and his colleagues assessed the drugs situation in Britain and quickly realised that the problem could not be tackled piecemeal. The first and most urgent task was to attempt to stop the drugs coming into the country. If this could be controlled, the second priority—catching the pedlars—would be that much easier.

But the men of CDIU have no illusions about the size of the problem. They fully realise that, possibly for some years, they may be unable to even keep the drugs traffic within containable bounds. This would almost certainly require international agreements from manufacturing and exporting countries— including Morocco, Jamaica, Pakistan, Nigeria, Lebanon, Afghanistan, India and Kenya among others—to deal ruthlessly with the problem from inside their own areas. Moves have already been made by Interpol to pressure these governments into taking tougher action. The international police organisation's chief officer, M. Jean Nepote, is emphatic that no mercy should be shown to those who deal and traffic in drugs. He has already told many governments that he thinks they are too soft with drug syndicates and he has insisted that only the severest of sentences will help reduce the flow. He summed up his attitude like this: 'If the sentence is ten years or twenty years, then they should serve ten years or twenty years. No parole, no time off for good behaviour. These pushers are no ordinary people. They are hard men and they only understand hard measures.' Interpol has already had considerable success in this field and drugs rings in Germany, Italy, Britain, France, the USA, Canada and Holland have been infiltrated and smashed by international police co-operation. Part of this success has been undoubtedly due to the 'early warning' system established by the Paris-based organisation which monitors and plots the movements and activities of the international drugs trade. Some of the biggest hauls have been made by undercover agents, working through Interpol, who have tracked pushers across two and three continents before pouncing.

Britain has certainly heeded the growing international demand for tough action against both drug addicts and the sinister men who 'push' them. Mr Robert Carr, as Home Secretary and guest of the British Pharmaceutical Conference in London in September 1973, made the Government's position quite clear:

> We cannot but feel compassion, not only for those caught in the toils of addiction, but also for their parents who find themselves powerless to prevent the seemingly inevitable self-destruction of their children. We know what a potent source of violent crime drug abuse can be if it gets out of control. That is not a situation we can tolerate developing in this country. Compassion is not enough. There can be no relaxation in the fight against drug abuse.

The Home Secretary was echoing the view of the judiciary which had been outlined by Lord Justice Roskill in the Court of Appeal only a month earlier. Without frills he warned in the sternest possible terms that anyone importing drugs illegally into Britain 'inevitably and inexorably' faced prison sentences. In such cases, he added, the court would not yield to sentiment. But drugs, illegal immigrants, international vice and pornography are not the only commodities handled by smugglers. Many of them are prepared to deal in almost anything, including diamonds, currency, bullion, arms and ammunition, art treasures and valuable antiques. In fact, their slide rule calculation is simple: if there is a profit at the end of a trip, the journey and the risk is worthwhile.

Even the introduction of decimal currency into Britain created yet another outlet for the smugglers' activities. The operation was so cleverly planned that most of its early stages were conducted entirely within the law. But it was becoming so successful that the Government of the day was forced to step in with restrictive measures to stop the national exchequer being 'milked' of millions of pounds.

Moreover, the people behind the scheme were not criminals in the accepted sense of the word. They regarded themselves as shrewd businessmen with an eye to profit. The plan was simple in its concept: all pre-1947 half crowns and florins were being called in by the Treasury as Britain prepared to switch to decimalisation. On the surface it was a straightforward financial exercise. But in fact the silver content of these coins made them worth more than their face value—when they were melted down. The Government had already prepared plans for the extraction of the silver which would then become bullion and be sold on the official silver market, with the profit going into the national purse. A lot of this money, however, found its way into the pockets of a small group of men who moved faster than the Government was able to recall the old coins. It was an operation of such fascinating dimensions that we followed its every move in detail from a plush suite of West End offices to a lonely border farm in the west of Ireland, through Dublin airport, to smelting plants in Belgium and Germany.

Initially the scheme was to export as many half-crowns and florins as possible to European smelting firms. There the coins would be melted, their silver abstracted, with the exporters pocketing the vast profits. The attraction, of course, was the silver. For example, half-crowns, florins and sixpenny pieces struck before 1920 had a 92½ per cent fine silver content and those minted between 1920 and 1946 contained 50 per cent silver. This made a pre-1920 half-crown worth more than double its face value with the later silver coins bringing a profit margin of about 20 per cent. All the businessmen had to do was to collect large quantities of these denominations, export them to smelters in Europe and collect the profits.

Originally there was no offence in exporting any amount abroad. The only possible offence in Britain would have been melting down the coins without official permission and this most certainly would not have been forthcoming. Even to the businessmen behind the scheme this loophole in the law seemed almost unbelievable and they sought advice from the Customs and Excise authorities, the Treasury itself and took counsel's opinion. But the situation was clear, there was no restriction and they could go ahead quite legally. A small commercial bank in London's West End agreed to finance the operation and advertisements in magazines and newspapers brought hundreds of parcels of coins daily through the post. The bank was offering 10 per cent above face value and this attracted the small entrepreneurs, particularly bus conductors and launderette operators, in fact anyone who had dealings with small change. Even bank staffs decided to cash in and syndicates of clerks were doubling and even trebling their salaries by sorting customers' money and retrieving the wanted coins. But the London businessmen decided to make the task easier for themselves and went straight to a major bank in the City of London and arranged for £1,000 of mixed silver coins to be picked up each day on their behalf by a security company. This was then sorted and the pre-1947 coins extracted. On average they scooped up £300 in 'useful' coins every week. The sorting still meant a vast amount of effort by the group but the clerks at the City bank solved their problem and offered to separate the coins themselves at a 10 per cent commission. Within a short time the pre-1947 coins were rolling into the group's offices at the rate of more than £4,000 a week. From there they were packaged and exported to Paris where they ended up in a refinery for smelting.

One of the group, a London solicitor, decided to take about £4,500 worth in the boot of his car and deliver it to the refinery himself. He drove to Southend airport and flew with his vehicle to France. Although he had no trouble with the British Customs officers at any time their French counterparts decided there must be something wrong with the venture and decided to impose what they called a 20 per cent 'uplift tax'. This would have made the venture uneconomic so the syndicate decided to avoid France on future trips and, instead, arranged for future refining to be done at a Brussels firm which is owned by a leading Hatton Garden refining and assaying company. All went smoothly for a time. The right coins were rolling in from all over Britain, being sorted and exported within a matter of days. Profits were being made as the refined silver was sold on the open market and members of the group were feeling decidedly happy.

Then came a further, much more serious snag which threatened the entire operation. Mr Harold Lever, then Financial Secretary to the Treasury, announced the introduction of a Control Order aimed specifically at stopping the mass export of silver coins. An official Treasury statement announced: 'There is evidence that current UK silver coins have been bought at a premium and shipped abroad for melting down.' A Government official commented: 'The object of the order is to stop this trade in silver coins so that the profits from melting down should go to the State and not individuals.' The Order was to come into effect within five days and this meant some high speed action to get as many coins abroad as possible before the deadline. They were, as one member of the group put it, 'going out by the planeload'. In addition to using scheduled airlines, at least six planes belonging to a flying taxi service took off from a small airfield just outside London. In this way, about £24,000 worth of coins were rushed to Ostend airport before the introduction of the Order which made the entire operation, as it then stood, illegal.

Officially, reputable refineries do not melt down the coinage of another country without official permission. It is regarded within the trade as 'an unfriendly act'. But business ethics played little part in the operation of using money to make money and the coins were being melted down by the thousand. Those responsible were not back street traders anxious for a quick profit. They were large international companies with solid reputations to protect. They thought they were safe and that nobody would find out what was going on. But they were wrong.

Customs investigators, who had been standing by, helpless until the Control Order came into force, were now in a position to act should any attempts be made to shift more consignments across the English Channel. By the time the new restriction had come into force it is estimated that silver coins worth £3 million at face value had been shipped out of Britain. The speculators were in a dilemma. The coins continued to pour in but the market had been dried up on them. Then they began to hoard the coins and puzzled how to recoup their capital outlay. Unless they shifted them quickly they stood to lose thousands of pounds. Their problem was simply how to get the coins out of the country without breaking the law. Eventually they found the route they wanted, through Northern Ireland, and it was this part of the operation which started one of the most fascinating smuggling rackets ever uncovered by Customs special investigators, who spent more than a year tracking down the men responsible and discovering the final destination of the silver coins.

The London-based group had found a ridiculously easy way of parting with their hoarded cash. All they had to do was sell the coins to dealers in Northern Ireland who would then take them across the winding border with Eire where no similar restrictive legislation existed. Once inside the Irish Republic the coins were 'legal' again and could be shipped openly to the continent. The only illegal part of the operation was the actual border crossing. For the Customs men, trying to catch the smugglers during this phase of the operation was a virtual impossibility. The border is riddled with dirt track roads, quiet paths and lonely farms. Patrolling it is totally impossible, as the British army later found during the IRA terrorist campaign.

Moving the coins to Northern Ireland was in itself, a sensitive business. While in no way contravening the law, the group did not want to alert the authorities by advertising their consignments which were flown from London, Manchester and Glasgow. So the batches of coins were crated in large wooden chests labelled 'Machine Tools' or 'Glass with Care'. Once at Belfast's Aldergrove Airport they were picked up by a small band of dealers and the London end of the operation was completed. From that point on, how the Ulstermen ensured that the coins were transported safely across the border was their responsibility. The people on the mainland just did not want to know. However, after dozens of consignments, usually valued at about £3,000 each, had been flown to Belfast one of the chests 'unexpectedly' broke open at Aldergrove. Instead of machine tools, out poured thousands of silver coins. The Customs investigators were convinced the breakage was no accident and suspected that someone 'had not been squared'. With the Customs officers now fully alerted to what was going on, the people in Northern Ireland advised their London colleagues to use other routes and within a short time car loads of coins were arriving in Ulster on British Railways steamer services which run between Liverpool and Belfast, Stranraer and Larne.

Even here there was always a risk that Customs men at the ports might suddenly discover what was happening and the London group thought long and hard before doing yet another switch and finally settling on one of the simplest but most ingenious ways of making sure the coins arrived intact in Ireland but out of sight of the Customs men. Once again they hired the air taxi firm but this time the planes flew, not to the continent, which would have been illegal, but to a small disused airfield called St Angelo, just outside Enniskillen—and only a few miles from the Eire border. The £90-a-flight service ran as often as twice a week to the single runway airfield just off the main Enniskillen-Strabane road. From the point of view of the men responsible for the Northern Ireland end of the operation, the arrangement could not have been better. The airfield was in a lonely spot, totally without Customs, air traffic control or any of the normal formalities found at larger airports. The only ground check on an aircraft having visited there at all was made by an old man who lived in a near-by bungalow. He occasionally appeared and asked pilots to sign a book registering their arrival. On many occasions he failed to appear at all and so the flight went unrecorded. Once in Northern Ireland it was a simple matter to slip boxes of coins across the border into Eire where they were taken to a firm at Dublin Airport and flown out for smelting on the continent. Customs officers estimate that at least £4 million left the country in this way, thereby robbing the Exchequer of a profit of about £3.5 million. It was a brilliantly conceived operation, virtually flawless in its execution—and, like most smuggling enterprises, highly profitable.

chapter eight

Terrorism

Rise and fall of the Angry Brigade   A jury cross-examined by a judge   Explosion blasts Old Bailey   Irish sign terror contract with Arabs   Sky-jack with a toy gun   British pubs become bombers' targets.

Until the beginning of the 1970s terrorism, in the eyes of most Britons at least, was a form of criminal activity exclusively the preserve of 'foreigners'. One expected fanaticism in Latin America and some European and African countries with repressive regimes, but even the thought of such a thing was so alien to the British way of life it was generally believed that it could never happen here. It was a widely held view that we had grown out of the adolescence of revolution and had matured after two bloody world wars—democracy had been fought for and so firmly established that sweet reason was, perhaps, the most potent and only weapon left for a changing society. Being an island probably did as much as anything to foster and nurture this sense of immunity. The seas around our coasts have for nearly a thousand years acted as an impenetrable shield keeping out those who wish us harm. Entering Britain, even for the law-abiding visitor, has never been an easy task; leaving the country after the commission of a crime is even more formidable, requiring minute planning and close attention to detail. Terrorists, like rabid dogs, were actively discouraged.

This cosy feeling of isolation, however, was soon to be shattered, not by terrorists infiltrating from abroad, but by home-grown British urban guerrillas—the Angry Brigade, a gang of highly intelligent and dangerous young men and women pledged, in their own words, to 'smash society'. Such an ambition is frequently publicly aired in many parts of Britain and, in fact, is regularly the topic for debate by soap box orators at Speakers' Corner in Hyde Park. But the Angry Brigade, although they too, talked much about revolution, also adopted violent measures, using guns and bombs to demonstrate their serious intentions. Fortunately, and due mainly to fine police work, they were rounded up before they caused death but not before they had carved a place in criminal history as one of the most cunning groups of urban guerrillas in the world.

In the space of less than a year they planted no less than twenty-five bombs, most of them in London, and after each explosion, they issued a communiqué claiming responsibility and explaining their actions. Although their acts of violence were alarming enough in themselves, there was an even more frightening 'spin off' as a result. They proved that terrorism was possible in Britain and their success gave positive encouragement and stimulus to other extremist groups, both within the United Kingdom and abroad, who previously had looked upon Britain as impregnable. Prominent among those who followed the Angry Brigade were the IRA and assassination squads from the Middle East.

By 1973, just three years after the Angry Brigade launched its campaign of violence, London had become the hiding place and breeding ground of some of the most dangerous political fanatics anywhere. Their activities are still causing grave concern to the police who face the dilemma of waging war against a completely new type of criminal. By comparison, the traditional British criminal who kills or maims for material gain, is a brute whose motives are understandable. Often he is of low intelligence and given time, patience and manpower, he will be caught by the police. But groups of university-educated fanatics, wise in psychology and aware of their legal rights, whose aims are nothing more avaricious than to capture the headlines with their outrages and propaganda, are men and women whose philosophy of life almost defy understanding. Few detectives, through no fault of their own, are equipped to comprehend their motives, making their eventual detection a long and laborious task.

There are set procedures in detecting crime, in the same way the criminals have a set formula to work to. Both sides have a shrewd knowledge of how the other works, so that to a point, rather like a game of chess, they can get inside each other's minds. By and large, the professional criminal plays according to the rules of the 'game' as understood by both sides. But with the new breed of young terrorist this type of quasi-sportsmanship does not exist. Never has one been heard to say when arrested: 'OK Guv, it's a fair cop.' The most an arresting officer can expect to hear is a curt demand to see a solicitor. More often he faces a blank face and a complete refusal to speak. It is only when the case comes for trial that the words spill out, accusing the police of planting evidence and 'verbals'—untrue statements manufactured by the police. If this ploy is not adopted or fails, the judge himself is usually attacked for holding a political trial, that is if he is granted the 'honour' of being recognised by the defendants.

The Angry Brigade, although they pioneered post-war terrorism in Britain, also inadvertently made a rod for the backs of those who followed them. Because of their success at evading capture and the grave concern being expressed by the Cabinet and Members of Parliament on both sides of the House, the Commissioner decided to set up the Bomb Squad at Scotland Yard. The man chosen to lead the team of hand picked detectives, Detective Chief Superintendent Roy Habershon, and his deputy, Detective Chief Inspector

George Mould, two highly experienced and shrewd detectives, were a thorn in the side of terrorists and their imitators and succeeded in breaking through the intellectual barrier which many were confident would protect them from detection and arrest.

Early in January 1971 Mr Habershon was posted to Barnet, the northern-most point of the Metropolitan police area, as the divisional CID chief. By West End standards this was considered by many at the Yard to be a 'quiet patch' where violent crime was the exception rather than the rule. For several days he spent much of his time feeling his way, getting to know his junior officers and generally settling in. Then on 12 January two explosions rocked the home of Mr Robert Carr, then Secretary of State for Employment, about a mile from Barnet police station at Hadley Green. Mr Carr, his wife and 13-year-old daughter, Virginia, were at home at the time. Describing the incident later he said:

> We were all three in the sitting room when, at about 10.5pm, I heard a loud explosion. My first reaction was that there was exploding gas coming from my boiler in the cellar. I told my wife and daughter to get down on the floor. I crawled to the sitting room door and peered round it into the hall. The front door was wide open and smoke was billowing in from outside. We went into the morning room at the back of the house to telephone the police but found my telephone was out of order. I saw my next door neighbour, Mr Millward, coming through the front gate towards my front door. We asked to go next door. As I left my house with my wife and daughter, my wife pointed out to me a black shiny plastic bag lying up against the front of the house just under the hall window. I did not suspect that it was a second explosive device but imagined that it was a relic of the one that had already gone off. We went next door and telephoned the police and I returned to the house. I began to have suspicions of the black plastic bag against the front door. I started to tell a police constable about this when I noticed Miss Harris, my housekeeper, walking along the pavement towards my house after her day out. I told her not to go into the house. I was just about to tell the police when I heard a sizzling noise and saw a flare of yellow light coming from near the front door and presumably from the bag. I was just at that moment standing outside my front gate and I rushed towards the Millward's front door and banged to be let in. As Mr Millward opened the door I heard a second loud explosion which I would guess was about fifteen minutes after the first.

Four months later when Mr Carr recounted the incident at Barnet Magistrates Court, he added calmly:

> With regard to the possible motives behind this outrage, I can say that I have not received any threatening or personal abusive letters or 'phone calls. In view of the fact that yesterday (the day before the explosion) was a day of demonstrations against the Government's Industrial Relations Bill, of which I am the responsible minister, I can only conclude that these explosions at my home were intended as part of the protest, but I am unable to indicate any particular faction which might have been responsible.

In one of its earliest communiqués, posted in Barnet probably the same night as the explosion at Mr Carr's home, the Angry Brigade claimed full responsibility. 'We are getting closer', it said menacingly. In a later communiqué they also admitted placing bombs outside the homes of Sir Peter Rawlinson QC, then Attorney General, and Sir John Waldron, who at that time was the Commissioner of the Metropolitan Police. Both were minor explosions which caused only superficial damage and no one was harmed. But until this time, 27 January 1971, Scotland Yard had been able to keep both incidents secret, hushed up deliberately to allay public alarm.

Only three groups of people knew of these two bombings; the victims, the police and the Angry Brigade. The revelation contained in Communiqué No. 5, not only caused great embarrassment at Scotland Yard, but its publication also had a marked effect on the public who, for the first time, realised that the Angry Brigade was a serious force to be reckoned with and not just a bunch of amateur tearaways out for kicks.

This 'scoop' was something of a master stoke in their propaganda campaign and established their 'bona fides' beyond all doubt with the British Press which until then was somewhat sceptical of their very existence. It dangled the bait under the noses of Fleet Street's news editors and they became hooked. They ignored at their professional peril future communiqués. In fact, the Angry Brigade had manipulated them into a position where they were forced to print practically every word. In time Fleet Street was to reprint in full the Brigade's whole philosophy, including what many considered outrageous and blasphemous attacks on the police and the Government. For example, in Communiqué No. 5 they said:

> We are not mercenaries. We attack property, not people. Carr, Rawlinson, Waldron, would have all been dead if we had wished. Fascists and Governments agents are the only ones who attack the public—the fire bombing of the West Indian party in South London, the West End cinema bomb. [These were two serious bomb explosions which injured many, and which the Angry Brigade claimed the police knew much more about than they were prepared to divulge.] British democracy is based on more blood, terror, and exploitation than any empire in history. It has a brutal police force whose crimes against the people the media will not report. Now its Government has declared vicious class war. Carr's Industrial Relations Bill aims to make it a one-sided war. We have started the fight back, and the war will be won by the organised working class with bombs.

This threatening letter, received by *The Times*, the Press Association and the underground newspaper IT, was written in block capitals, probably with the aid of a ruler, and was regarded as a direct answer to a speech Sir Peter Rawlinson had made to the Society of Conservative Lawyers, not long before his house was bombed.

In that speech Sir Peter spelled out in no uncertain terms the Government's policy on law and order, a platform which helped the Conservatives win the election. He said:

> No free society can tolerate a minority, often a minute minority unable to
> persuade or convince by argument, to bludgeon or terrorise the majority into
> acceptance of social or political demands. The assassins, the kidnappers, the
> terrorists, the rioters, all in different degrees are seeking to impose by force
> their will on the majority. Whether nation or individual, whether in the name
> of Fascism or Maoism, it is the application of the doctrine 'might is right'. The
> State cannot tolerate or refuse to prosecute the offender who robs, who
> burns, who invades, who terrorises, merely because that offender is
> motivated by intense political or social passions.

For a month after the bombing of Mr Carr's home there was a lull. Perhaps,
many thought, the Angry Brigade was only a flash in the pan after all. Then on
18 February of that year Communiqué No. 6 arrived at the offices of *The Times*
in Printing House Square. This time it was typewritten and, to demonstrate their
confidence perhaps, it was popped through the office letter box instead of being
sent through the mail. This was a more wordy document and gave a clearer
insight into the manner of men and women the police were working night and
day to trace. It said:

> We have sat quietly and suffered the violence of the system for too long. We
> are being attacked daily. Violence does not only exist in the army, the police
> and the prisons. It exists in the shoddy, alienating culture pushed out by TV,
> films and magazines; it exists in the ugly sterility of urban life. It exists in the
> daily exploitation of our labour, which gives big bosses the power to control
> our lives and run the system for their own ends. How many Rolls Royces . . .
> How many Northern Irelands . . . how many anti-Trade Union bills will it
> take to demonstrate that in a crisis of capitalism the ruling class can only react
> by attacking the people politically? But the system will never collapse or
> capitulate by itself. More and more workers now realise this and are
> transforming trade union consciousness into offensive political militancy. In
> one week a million workers were on strike . . . Fords . . . Post Office . . .
> BEA . . . Oil delivery workers . . . Our rule is to deepen the political
> contradictions at every level. We will not achieve this by concentrating on
> 'issues' or by using watered-down socialist platitudes. In Northern Ireland the
> British army and its minions has (sic) found a practice range: the CS gas and
> bullets in Belfast will be in Derby and Dagenham tomorrow. Our attack is
> violent. Our violence is organised. The question is not whether the revolution
> will be violent. Organised militant struggle and organised terrorism go side by
> side. These are the tactics of the revolutionary class movement. Where two or
> three revolutionaries use organised violence to attack the class
> system—there—is the Angry Brigade. Revolutionaries all over England are
> already using the name to publicise their attacks on the system. No revolution
> was ever won without violence. Just as the structures and programmes of a
> new revolutionary society must be incorporated into every organised base at
> every point in the struggle, so must organised violence accompany every
> point of the struggle, until, armed, the revolutionary working class

London, 8 March 1973. The Scene at Great Scotland Yard

Roy Jenkins, the Home Secretary, visiting the Horse & Groom pub, Guildford, after the bomb explosion, 6 October 1974. On his right is Mr Pat Matthews, Chief Constable of Surrey

overthrow the capitalist system.

Like all the communiqués it was signed 'The Angry Brigade' made into a stamp from a child's John Bull printing outfit. As if endeavouring to give the police and the jittery public time to comprehend and digest this verbal onslaught there was another month-long pause. During that time two men were arrested and charged with being involved in some of the bombings. One was later sent to prison for fifteen years and the other was acquitted. The nerve-racking silence was shattered on 19 March when a large bomb exploded outside the Ford Motor Company's offices in Gants Hill, Essex. Again no one was hurt, and again the Angry Brigade issued its usual cryptic communiqué admitting responsibility. This time, however, the author showed maniacal tendencies, letting his thoughts, his fears and his hatred spill over two foolscap pages. They would win their struggle, he claimed, even if it meant 'some of the Pigs will lose their lives'. The word 'Pig' referred to the police, who for the whole of that winter and spring had been intensely active in rounding up suspects. In a final defiant gesture, the writer ranted in capital letters:

'WE ARE READY TO GIVE OUR LIVES FOR OUR LIBERATION.
POWER TO THE PEOPLE.'

The coming summer was to prove the most spectacular in the Angry Brigade's short but violent career. It also brought their downfall and eventual capture. Between May and August they planted six more bombs, each at prestige targets. The first, however, was a strange choice—Biba's Boutique in Kensington High Street. It was a busy Saturday morning and about 500 people were milling about the store. The telephone rang in the managing director's office. The caller, who said he was speaking on behalf of the Angry Brigade, simply said 'You have only five minutes before the bomb goes off'. As the store was being cleared and searched, the bomb, hidden in a basement, exploded, slightly injuring one man and causing extensive damage to fixtures and clothing. As expected, *The Times* received Communiqué No. 8. Under the Brigade's 'official' stamp were the words typewritten in capitals: SPECIAL MAY DAY PRESENT. The text of the single sheet crammed with capital letters and double-underlining seemed to be a message for the very staff and young customers who had been attacked the previous day. Almost deliriously it said:

If you are not busy being born you're busy buying. All the salesgirls in the flash boutiques are made to dress the same, have the same make-up, 'representing' the 1940s. In fashion, as in everything else the capitalists can only go backwards—they've got nowhere to go—they're dead. The future is ours. Life is so boring there's nothing to do except spend all our wages on the latest skirt or shirt. Brothers—Sisters, what are your real desires? Sit in the drug store, look distant, empty, bored, drinking some tasteless coffee? . . . or perhaps blow it up or burn it down. The only thing you can do with modern slave houses—called boutiques—is wreck them. You can't reform profit, capitalism and inhumanity. Just kick it until it breaks. Revolution.

Needless to say this call to arms received little sympathy or support from the youngsters whom the Angry Brigade felt disposed to protect and lead. The credibility of the Angry Brigade was beginning to wear thin in the minds of many unless, of course, this was meant to be a 'fun' gesture to show that they also had a sense of humour. Whatever the motive they quickly changed their tack to show that they were as serious and fanatical as ever. Within the next three months they planted five more bombs with frightening ease, which made politicians and public alike wonder how efficient the tight security precautions being taken by the police really were. The targets were: Tintagel House; Blackmore House, near Ongar, Essex, the home of Mr William Batty, managing director of Ford's; an electricity sub-station in Chequers Lane, which supplies his Dagenham plant; a flat in Rivermead Court, Fulham, the home of Mr John Davies, who was then the Secretary of State for Trade and Industry; and a Territorial Army Drill Hall in Parkhurst Road, Holloway. This was their last bomb.

On 20 August police raided a flat in Amhurst Road, Stoke Newington, North London, shared by Miss Anna Mendleson, then aged twenty-three, Miss Hilary Anne Creek, twenty-two, James Greenfield, twenty-three, and John Barker, twenty-three. After a search detectives found 2 sub-machine guns, an automatic pistol, 81 rounds of ammunition and 33 cartridges of explosives. All four were arrested and charged and after being committed for trial by magistrates appeared at the Central Criminal Court on 31 May 1972.

At their trial the judge, Mr Justice James, took an unusual course of action in what was to be a long and unusual case—he questioned potential jurors about their politics. Were they, he asked, subscribing members of the Conservative Party? Were they a friend or relation or a constituent of either Mr Robert Carr, Mr John Davies, Sir Peter Rawlinson, Sir John Eden, MP, or Mr Woodrow Wyatt, a former Labour MP? Were they friends or relations of Mr Batty or Sir John Waldron? Were they members of the Territorial Army, or had they relations or close friends likely to serve in the armed forces in Northern Ireland? Were they relations or friends of members of the police or Securicor? By now the potential jurymen must have wondered whether they were to try the case or indeed if they were on trial themselves. But there were still more questions to come from the judge which must have absolutely flabbergasted them. Had they any connection with the United States or Spanish embassies in London, or the banks of Spain and Bilbao, Iberian Airways or any Italian government office in the United Kingdom?

Mr Justice James then asked them:

Have you formed any impression in your mind that the accused are members of an anarchist organisation, of the Angry Brigade, and if so are you capable of putting that impression out of your minds? If you have formed an impression, is it so deep-seated that you feel you are not a suitable person to serve on a jury? If that is the case please say so.

Finally, as if to plug any possible loophole, he asked if they were friends or relations of any members of the judiciary. The process took a little under three hours before twelve men were eventually sworn in. Nineteen potential jurors were excused on the grounds that they were biased, thirty-nine others were challenged before they took the oath and two others were released. This extraordinary procedure was adopted by the judge after two of the defendants had claimed that the case would develop into a political trial and they would get an unfair hearing because of the adverse press publicity prior to their appearance in court. After such a unique and lengthy inquisition of the jury no one could ever accuse the judge of not being fair to the defendants. Many, however, with considerable justification, felt he was very unfair on the prosecution, having eliminated a huge section of the community from performing their civic duty as jurors. If this method of empanelling a jury ever becomes an established practice it will be virtually impossible ever to get a conviction in a criminal court. By the standards adopted in this case should mothers and fathers be barred from sitting as jurors in cases of sexual assaults against children? Should the wealthy pass judgment on tax evaders or the poor on shoplifters? The possibilities and permutations are limitless and frightening.

A number of senior detectives at Scotland Yard found it difficult to conceal their irritation both during and after the trial. Those who had close contact with them during many trying months could easily appreciate their feelings. Tracking down the Angry Brigade was an immensely complicated piece of detection. It was not, as a casual observer might have thought, just a question of hunting for a small group of uniformly dressed revolutionaries wearing black cloaks and carrying ticking bombs, with shoulder flashes marked Angry Brigade. There was nothing conventional about them, a factor which allowed them to elude arrest for so long.

After the bombing at Mr Carr's home and several other explosions in the following spring in other parts of London Mr Habershon had an interview with the Commissioner. There were obvious similarities but the investigation was being left to senior detectives in the divisions where they occurred. A joint and concerted attack was needed and the Commissioner agreed to the setting up of the Bomb Squad under Mr Haberson, giving him overall responsibility for the inquiry. In another part of Scotland Yard Mr Mould was working with a small team of detectives trying to track down a gang which was amassing a large quantity of cash from audacious frauds using stolen credit cards and cheque books. The names of some of those suspected of being behind the frauds also cropped up several times in the files of the Special Branch, who by this time were also working closely with Mr Habershon. Their files dated back to August 1967 when the United States embassy in Grosvenor Square was machine-gunned. The following year there were two explosions at the Spanish Embassy and the American Forces Columbia Club in Lancaster Gate.

Twelve months later two unexploded bombs were found at the Bank of Spain and the Bank of Bilbao in London, These were quickly followed by explosions at the Bank of Spain in Liverpool and the Bank of Bilbao in King Street,

London. All these incidents were followed by the publication of communiqués issued by a group calling itself the First of May Revolutionary Solidarity Movement. There is evidence that some members of this organisation broke away to form the Angry Brigade early in 1970. It soon became clear to Mr Habershon, Mr Mould and their Special Branch colleagues that the cheque book and credit card frauds were a major part of the conspiracy, providing ready money to buy explosives and weapons and travel to France and Italy where the London 'cell' of revolutionaries learned modern techniques in urban guerrilla warfare. Having drawn up a list of suspects, the police then had the dangerous task of infiltrating the scores of extremist political groups which at that time proliferated in communes set up in houses and flats in North London. Young detectives, men and women, and all volunteers, set about passing themselves off in the hippy community where drugs and revolution were their daily diet. Long untidy hair and scruffy dress was only a small part of their disguise. They also had to swot up on the jargon and philosophy of these weird rebels. They were aware that they could easily give themselves away and put their lives at risk as much by saying the wrong thing as being seen reading the *Police Gazette*. This undercover squad combined with the laborious routine investigation carried out by more than one hundred other detectives working on the case finally led to the arrest of some of the prominent members of the Angry Brigade.

A few slipped the police net but were so stunned at being outwitted by the men they contemptuously called 'Pigs' that they could summon only enough courage to issue one more communiqué. This one, No. 14, arrived at *The Times* offices the day after their leaders were sent to prison. Claiming that they were innocent it proclaimed: 'Sooner or later they will be freed. Sooner or later you will hear from us again.' Police feared that the ten-year sentences might result in the formation of an even angrier brigade, but their fears were unfounded. The Angry Brigade had written their last communiqué.

Scotland Yard now found itself in a somewhat refreshing dilemma – what should happen to the Bomb Squad? There were still about thirty highly skilled detectives attached to the squad under Mr Habershon and it seemed to many that having succeeded in smashing the Angry Brigade their task was completed. Ironically, it was the IRA who convinced the commissioner that the Bomb Squad should remain intact. For as the Angry Brigade trial was drawing to its close a massive bomb exploded near the top of the 620 feet high Post Office Tower in London, causing widespread damage. Responsibility was quickly claimed by a man with an Irish accent who telephoned the Press Association in Fleet Street. He said he represented the Kilburn battalion of the IRA, although both the Official and Provisional wings of the IRA in Dublin were quick to deny knowledge of the incident. Evidence later discovered by the Bomb Squad gave a clear identification of the man responsible who is known to have escaped to Eire soon after the explosion. Delving into his background, police also found that he was a close associate of the Angry Brigade. One theory, still believed by some senior detectives, is that the man who planted the bomb, with the assistance of a woman accomplice, did so on a freelance basis as a gesture of solidarity with the

Angry Brigade.

Only the IRA can say whether, in fact, they had forewarning of the explosion but the Provisionals cannot deny that just twelve months later they held a secret meeting in County Monaghan where they decided to extend their campaign of violence in Northern Ireland to the streets of London.

On 8 March 1973 they attacked with a ferocity not experienced in London since the Blitz of the Second World War. Their mission accomplished, they fled to London Airport straight into the arms of the Special Branch. Behind them lay 238 injured, many disfigured and maimed for life. This was the culmination of three months intensive planning and training in Eire and Northern Ireland. The only detail they overlooked was their escape.

The date chosen for the attack was significant—it was the day the citizens of Northern Ireland went to the polls to vote on the border plebiscite. The Belfast IRA high command were totally opposed to the vote taking place and as early as January began to draw up plans to demonstrate this violently to the Westminster Government. The leader of Belfast's Provisionals, Mr Seamus Twoomey, appointed Dolours Price, a 22-year-old student teacher, to take charge of the expedition to bomb London. Miss Price, attractive, highly intelligent and ruthless; had been a prominent member of the IRA since her school days and was believed by many to have been the 'brains' behind many violent acts of terrorism in Ulster. It was left to her to pick her squad and train them with the help of technical experts in the south. Her first selection was her 19-year-old sister, Marian, also a student teacher, whose skill with the rifle had earned her the nickname the 'Armalite widow' by troops serving in the province.

The third member of her headquarters staff was Hugh Feeney, aged twenty-one, also studying to become a teacher. He and Dolours had been friends for many years and active members of the People's Democracy, a student organisation familiar with violence to achieve its end. He was appointed the squad's quartermaster, being responsible for the disposal of £350 which was appropriated by the IRA to finance the mission. The 'foot soldiers', as the other seven members of the group were called, were selected with slightly less care, resulting in one of them later confessing his involvement and betraying the others. Once formed they set about putting their plan into action. On four separate days between 16 and 21 February they hijacked four cars at gun point in Belfast and drove them to a hide-out in the Republic where the vehicles were re-sprayed and given false registration plates. Two days before the attack the four cars, loaded with a total of 600lbs of gelignite, were ferried from Dublin to Liverpool and then driven to London. Soon after dawn on 8 March the four cars were parked, bombs primed and set to explode at 3pm. Their four targets had been carefully selected. One was left outside the Central Criminal Court in Old Bailey, another outside New Scotland Yard in Victoria, the third was outside the British Forces Broadcasting Services premises in Dean Stanley Street, Westminster, and the fourth at the Central London Recruiting Depot in Great Scotland Yard, off Whitehall. Casually they made their way to West London Air Terminal in Gloucester Road, where they boarded buses for Heathrow, where with airline tickets they had bought the previous day, they planned to fly to Dublin.

Police in Belfast and London, however, were not idle. The Royal Ulster Constabulary had warned Scotland Yard to expect trouble that day, although they were unable to give any clear indication of how it would arise. Forewarned, the Metropolitan Police were out in force. Not only were they prepared for a spectacular demonstration from the IRA, they were also preoccupied with traffic chaos caused by a rail strike. Parking restrictions had been waived to allow people to get to work by car. The Special Branch at London airport (in fact at all airports throughout the country) had been on a full-scale alert since 7am that day. The police had not the faintest inkling of what to expect until two sharp-eyed members of the Special Patrol Group spotted something suspicious about a car parked on a meter outside Scotland Yard. The registration number on the car, a Ford Corsair, did not tally with its year of manufacture. Detectives were called and searched the car. They found a package of 170 lbs of gelignite hidden under the rear passenger seats. Explosives experts defused the bomb within an hour, rendering it harmless. This was obviously the 'trouble' the RUC had warned the Yard about—but were there more bombs still undiscovered? A massive needle-in-the-haystack search was mounted by the police scouring thousands of streets and car parks for vehicles with similar give-away characteristics. Working on the basis that the one discovered bomb was set to explode at 3pm, it was fair to assume that if there were others they had been set to explode at the same time.

Nearly five hours after the car bomb was found outside the Yard a man with a strong Irish accent telephoned *The Times* giving the descriptions, registration numbers and locations of three more car bombs. The police were told immediately and a frantic search began. The car bomb in Dean Stanley Street was quickly found and defused but the other two, outside the Old Bailey and the recruiting office, went off before they could be tackled by the explosives experts. The police still do not know the identity of the telephone caller, although they suspect he was one of the original raiding party who panicked before going into hiding.

Meanwhile the tension at Heathrow was close to breaking point. Seven men and three women, including the Price sisters and Feeney, had been taken into custody for questioning and to be searched. Each one of them gave a false name and address and gave untrue answers when asked what they had been doing in London. These lies sealed their fate. Other legitimate passengers bound for Dublin had been open and honest when asked the same questions and police had no reason to suspect them or detain them. But when the members of the IRA squad's answers were checked, a relatively simple and speedy operation, their falsity gave rise to immediate suspicion. Some of them carried airline tickets with consecutive serial numbers, indicating that they had been bought at the same place and at the same time, and yet they denied knowing each other. A coincidence, perhaps in the case of two of them, but surely not ten? Detective Chief Inspector Mould had arrived at Heathrow by this time. He knew that a bomb had been defused just outside his office at the Yard earlier and he knew the time it had been set to explode.

He knew nothing of the call to *The Times*. The publicity which followed the discovery of the first bomb brought a deluge of hoax calls from trouble-makers and the near mad. As far as he was concerned there could still be more bombs—somewhere. Everything pointed to the ten detained being responsible. Minutes seemed to tick by like seconds. At 2pm Dolours Price and her team were still lying, denying and arrogantly demanding their rights and release. At a quarter past two Mr Mould, without doubt one of the finest exponents in the art of interrogation at Scotland Yard, decided to make one last attempt. He called Marian Price into his tiny makeshift office near the departure lounge. Puffing gently on his pipe and adopting his best 'Uncle George' approach, he put his cards on the table. He assumed that other bombs had been planted and pleaded with her to reveal their locations. Many innocent people could be in danger, and anyway, he reasoned, the IRA always, even in Belfast, gave a warning to clear the area before bombs went off. The IRA would not now, at this late stage, criticise her if she told him. But during the next thirty-five minutes, as the two faced each other across a table, all Marian would say was: 'I do not intend to tell you anything. You have no right to keep me here.' Her continuing silence and her subsequent actions proved beyond all doubt that she was guilty. Through all Mr Mould's pleadings she sat staring fixedly at the corner of the table, biting on a crucifix pendant hanging around her neck. From his long experience Mr Mould realised that she had undergone instruction in anti-interrogation techniques and was in fact neither hearing—nor listening to anything he was saying.

Then, as if she had suddenly snapped out of a trance, she slowly and deliberately raised her left hand until it was almost under Mr Mould's nose and looked hard and long at her watch. It was 2.50pm and she smiled. The significance of this dramatic piece of mime was not lost on the detective. 'Am I intended to gather that the timing of the other bombs has just expired?' said Mr Mould as he left the room to make a hasty telephone call to the Yard. A minute later he returned. Marian was still smiling. His fists clenched, the nails biting into the palms of his hands, he looked down at the pretty auburn haired girl and said: 'Other bombs have exploded and from what I am told there are many people injured, perhaps dead.' Marian grinned broadly and the detective, displaying remarkable self-control, merely said: 'I have no further questions for you at the present'. He nodded and a policewoman led her off to Ealing police station.

All ten were later charged with conspiracy to cause explosions and their trial was held at Winchester Crown Court six months later. This quaint and historic Hampshire city was chosen on security grounds following a series of threats by the IRA to either 'spring' the defendants or take hostages in return for their release. Special cells were equipped at Winchester prison which is only a hundred yards from the Castle where the trial took place. Troops from an adjoining barracks were on twenty-four hour alert in case of attack and more than a hundred uniformed and plain clothes police from the Metropolitan force, many armed with rifles and revolvers, were drafted into the area.

During the ten-week-long trial the usual allegations of planting evidence were made against the police, all of which were rejected by the all-male jury. The judge, Mr Justice Sebag Shaw, the jurors and some of the senior detectives in the case were all guarded night and day by armed police. So tight was security in Winchester that holiday-makers and tourists boycotted the city in their thousands, much to the cost and chagrin of the local tradesmen and hoteliers. Everyone entering the court building was thoroughly searched, lawyers, reporters, police, members of the public, even a nun.

The Price sisters, Feeney, and five of their 'footsoldiers' were all found guilty and sent to prison for life. Mr Justice Sebag Shaw, who ignored many of the insults hurled at him from both the dock and the public gallery, described their actions as wicked and evil. Had they been able to 'sneak' back to Dublin they would have undoubtedly gloated over their achievements, he told them. When Dolours Price heard the life sentence she shouted, 'That's a death sentence'. Her sister, arrogant to the end, looked long and hard at the judge and commented: 'It is all right. We absolve you.' This generous act of absolution, however, was not granted to William McLarnon, aged nineteen, and Miss Roisin McNearney, aged eighteen, who earlier had stood in the dock with the other eight. McLarnon, described by the judge as the 'weak member' of the gang, had confessed to his part in the bombings and had implicated the others when questioned by police soon after the explosions. He pleaded guilty to the charges and was sent to prison for fifteen years. Miss McNearney, who claimed she was a recruit to the women's section of the IRA, was acquitted. She said she went to London for 'fun' not knowing the purpose of the trip.

After her arrest she helped police considerably, pointing out hotels where the gang stayed in London and car parks where the car bombs had been left before being positioned outside their targets. Both the jury and the prosecution took pity on her, the youngest of the party, knowing that her life would forever be in danger from the IRA for her betrayal. She has since left Britain and is living abroad with her parents. Both she and McLarnon have been told that they will be shot if caught by the IRA.

The Provisional IRA was furious over the sentences and stepped up their campaign of violence which had started even before the Winchester trial began. By the time the Bomb Squad had left that city more than sixty parcel and letter bombs had been planted in London and the Midlands. An army bomb disposal officer was killed in the Midlands when a parcel bomb exploded, a girl secretary received serious facial injuries when a letter bomb exploded in her hands at the Stock Exchange in London. Tragically, a postal messenger, employed by the BBC at the time, committed suicide by cutting his throat. As he was carried to an ambulance medical staff heard him mumbling 'Letter Bomb. Letter Bomb.' The words were still on his lips when he died.

By December of 1973 the IRA increased the ferocity of their attacks and reverted to the use of car bombs. One, containing at least 80 lbs of explosives injured fifty-two people, most of them women, when it went off outside a Home Office building in Westminster. A second, on the same day, injured two policemen who found the car parked outside Pentonville Prison. From the many clues found by detectives and forensic scientists who examined minutely the debris after each explosion it was obvious that the IRA were adopting new tactics.

Instead of shipping 'special service units', as they liked to describe them, across from Eire and Northern Ireland, they had set up a series of bases in the London area. Cars used in explosions were being stolen from the streets of the capital and it was evident that the bombs in both cars, letters and parcels, were being manufactured somewhere close at hand. Again, women were thought to be playing an equal part in the attacks, making detection that much more difficult. A young couple walking arm-in-arm carrying a shopping bag don't immediately strike even the suspicious as two terrorists carrying a bomb. Their escape routes had been changed too, since the disastrous day when ten were arrested together at London airport. Close ties had been established with sympathisers in France, Belgium and Holland where IRA men on the run could hide before returning to Dublin.

More frightening information was passed to Scotland Yard on the first day of 1974 when the IRA announced that they had entered into a pact with Palestinian guerrillas to carry out joint acts of terrorism in Britain. It had been known for some time that the two factions had been strengthening their ties with each other, with several Middle Eastern guerrillas receiving training in terrorism from some of the IRA's top instructors. The Special Branch and the Bomb Squad regarded the news with special significance, coming as it did only a few days after the attempt to assassinate Mr J. Edward Sieff, the president of the huge Marks and Spencer store empire. Mr Sieff, an active supporter of the Zionist Federation of Great Britain and Ireland, was shot at point blank range in the head by a masked man who burst into his St John's Wood, London, home.

Amazingly the 9 mm calibre bullet ricocheted off his teeth, lodging in the back of his neck and missing an artery by the merest fraction of an inch. He quickly recovered and in a televised hospital interview from his bedside, defiantly announced that this attempt on his life would not diminish his support for the Jewish cause. The Popular Front for the Liberation of Palestine, a ruthless terrorist organisation with world-wide contacts, claimed responsibility for the shooting and alleged that Mr Sieff had 'poured millions of pounds' into Israel, funds to help finance the Middle East war of 1973.

Many other prominent Jews living in Britain had been the victim of terrorist attacks, mainly, until that time, as recipients of letter bombs. Black September, another Middle East terrorist group had pioneered this form of violence two years earlier, posting their lethal packages all over the world. One opened at the Israeli embassy in London killed the Agricultural Attaché in 1972. These innocent-looking letters have in recent years been perfected and streamlined after the first wave sent by Black September failed to explode. Their construction was simple. The bomb, made with a plastic explosive connected to a minute detonator and a trigger mechanism, was sandwiched between the hollowed out pages of a book the size of an ordinary paperback. The earliest type of letter bomb simply fizzled and flared when the envelope was ripped open. But later ones received in London were more sophisticated, only exploding when the curious took the book from the envelope and opened the pages. The two ounces of plastic explosives secreted inside is capable of blowing a man in half at close range.

With terrorism on a global scale, Interpol, the police intelligence network spanning 114 non-communist countries, might have played, and indeed, many felt should have played, a much more prominent role in plotting the activities and movements of known militant organisations, giving early warnings to affiliated countries that violent fanatics were on the move.

But Interpol, which celebrated the 50th anniversary of its founding in September 1973, is a much misunderstood organisation, due mainly, perhaps, to sensational and inaccurate television films. Many could be forgiven for believing that it has squads of go-anywhere 'super-cops' of the James Bond and Maigret ilk. In fact, it is nothing more glamorous than a message receiving and transmitting 'machine'. Interpol, with its headquarters in Paris, and staff of about 130, is a clearing house for information about international criminals and is only as efficient as it is allowed to be by the affiliated members. In its glass-fronted office block headquarters are housed more than 700,000 files on wanted international criminals containing full descriptions and all relevant facts supplied from the 'victim' nation, anxious to trace a man known to have fled their country. These files are regularly up-dated and circulated to police forces around the world. And this, basically, is where Interpol shows its true value, it keeps tabs on criminals who feel confident they are safe once abroad. But in many ways, Interpol, has failed to wake up to the needs of the police in the 1970s. It refuses to change its constitution which lays down that it must not interfere in crimes which have political, racial or religious characteristics. Practically every act of terrorism in recent years could easily be classified in at least one of those three 'untouchable' crimes.

If ever there was a time in criminal history when international co-operation was needed to wage war on the do-or-die assassin and ruthless bomber it is now. Unless Interpol shakes off its ostrich-like attitude and concedes that the motives behind a crime are of secondary importance to its commission, it could soon lose its reputation and credibility as a crime-fighting auxiliary. This would be sad, for it has had a fine record over the years and still does a first class job, especially in the fields of international fraud and drug smuggling. But there are clear signs that the Western European police forces need much stronger ties than those that bind them through Interpol. Political crimes apart, many chief constables of forces in counties facing the English Channel and the North Sea, have already started to by-pass Interpol and deal direct with their counterparts on the continent for crimes which the Paris headquarters could and would handle if asked. Some forces in Britain have started sending their officers on language courses so that investigations can be undertaken abroad. This is also true of many European forces, especially the French, German, Dutch and Belgians, who regularly have detectives working in Britain. Closer links are also being forged between Scotland Yard and the Federal Bureau of Investigations in the USA. In fact it was following a tip off from the FBI that the Yard was able to thwart an attempt to assassinate Mr Adbellah Chorfi, the Moroccan Ambassador in London. A young American girl, carrying five pistols and 150 rounds of ammunition, and her two confederates, a Moroccan and a Pakistani, were arrested at London airport by Special Branch detectives soon after the Yard had received the tip from the FBI.

Hardly was 1974 a week old when the terror campaign launched by Arab extremists took a dramatic and frightening turn. Police in Brussels discovered that Palestinian guerrillas had succeeded in smuggling three Russian-made Sam 7 missiles into Belgium and planned to attack undisclosed airports in Europe, one believed to be Heathrow. Troops with tanks, armoured cars and machine guns were immediately drafted into the area and, assisted by police, ringed the vast perimeter of the airport. From a terrorist point of view the Sam 7 missile is an ideal weapon, being small, light and capable of being fired by one man from the shoulder. Its infra-red heat-seeking warhead locks onto the hot vapour trail of jet aircraft and has a range of up to three miles with deadly accuracy.

It was with this very much in mind that by the end of July 1974 the Government had rushed through legislation transferring Heathrow to the jurisdiction of the Metropolitan police so far as security and policing was concerned. The officers of the former British Airports Authority police were invited to stay on in the new force and over 90 per cent agreed to do so. This was a tense period in the world of aviation with the threat of hijacking by terrorists ever present, and regularly accomplished. A British aircraft, however, had never been hijacked (or skyjacked as some newspapers described it) on or over British soil, but the climate was such that summer that it seemed only a matter of time before it happened.

In fact, it was nearly six months after the Yard had moved into the airport that a timid looking Iranian, on an internal flight from Manchester to London, waited for all the passengers to disembark before he pulled a toy gun on a stewardess and told her to tell the captain to fly him to Paris.

He wanted to avenge his brother who had been killed in France, he said. His toy gun and grenade (an empty canister) looked real enough to the five members of the crew who for the next nine hours became his hostages. The French authorities had refused the plane permission to land so he then demanded £100,000 in bank notes to be put aboard. This done, he was flown to Stansted airport, Essex, where he was told a car would be waiting to drive him to Dover so that he could continue his journey to France. As the British Airways One-Eleven came to rest at Stansted, he ordered a steward to accompany him to the car. Mr Alan Bond, the steward, aged thirty-five, father of two, said later:

When we opened the door I was pushed out as hostage carrying the £100,000. He had the gun in my back. Suddenly a big police light flashed onto us. I saw my chance and hit him as hard as I could over the head with my torch. He went down on his knees with his hands in the air.

While a police dog snarled and stood guard over the crumpled, pathetic form of the would-be-hijacker one of his kennel mates bit Mr Bond on the backside, so rounding off a successful joint police and army security operation. In many ways they were lucky that their first experience of a hijacking was carried out by a young 'mixed up' foreigner and not a fully committed terrorist determined to succeed at all costs.

This form of dedicated ruthlessness, however, was much in evidence in the streets of London and many of the major provincial centres, where the IRA turned 1974 into what many dubbed 'The Year of the Bomb'. Where in the previous year the bombs had been comparatively small and the targets mainly property, the IRA suddenly switched tactics and started to bomb innocent children as well as men and women. Their new onslaught began on New Year's Day and went on with only a few brief pauses until Christmas.

In January alone there were bomb incidents of varying types on eight separate days. A warehouse in Birmingham was the first to come under fire bomb attack with a Royal Navy Recruiting Office near-by running it a close second. Then there was a four-day lull before the bombers moved to the London area. The home of Major-General Philip Ward was badly damaged by an explosion only minutes before bombs were found at the Boat Show and Madam Tussaud's. The following day a 30 lb gelignite bomb exploded at the Chelsea home of General Sir Cecil Blacker. After a number of incendiary bomb attacks on London stores the terrorists turned their attentions to a series of book bomb attacks. One was disguised in a bible and sent to the Roman Catholic Bishop to the Forces and another to an Old Bailey judge. On the first day of February, Mr Reginald Maudling, a former Home Secretary, was slightly hurt when a letter bomb exploded at his home.

Three days later the worst single act of terrorism to have been committed in Britain shocked and angered the by now bomb-weary country—twelve people, men, women and children, were blown to pieces and fourteen others were seriously injured when a coach was ripped apart by an explosion. The bomb had been placed in the luggage boot of a coach which did a shuttle run between Manchester and Yorkshire for servicemen and their families returning to camp after week-end leave. As it travelled along the M62 road at Birkenshaw, Yorkshire, with many of the passengers dozing, the time-bomb detonated, tearing the vehicle in two.

The following week a 20 lb gelignite bomb rocked the National Defence College at Latimer, Buckinghamshire, injuring ten people. After the carnage caused by the coach bomb it is almost impossible to believe that the person responsible would have the stomach to plant another, yet she did. At Wakefield Crown Court six months later Judith Ward, aged twenty-five, was found guilty on twelve counts of murder—her victims on the coach—and also to causing the explosion at the College. The jury also found her guilty of causing an explosion at Euston railway station the previous year in which eight people were injured. She was sent to prison for life for the coach murders, 20 years for causing the explosion on the coach, 10 years for the college bombing and 5 years for the attack at Euston station. Passing sentence Mr Justice Waller commented: 'These offences are so heinous that no figure could be put on what would be appropriate to their gravity.'

While Judith Ward was safely locked away the bombing campaign continued unabated. During the spring of 1974 there was a wave of attacks on army installations in Yorkshire and offices up and down the country, causing few injuries but considerable damage. Then in the middle of July there was a large explosion at the north end of the Houses of Parliament in which eleven people were injured. Exactly a month later a woman died and thirty-five were hurt when a bomb exploded at the Tower of London while hundreds of visitors, many from abroad, were in the immediate vicinity.

The time was fast approaching when the British public would not stand idly by, waiting and wondering where the next bomb would explode. Members of Parliament, not always the most attentive to public opinion, were becoming alarmed not only at the increasing toll of the dead and injured but the audacious way the IRA were thumbing their noses at all attempts to tighten security.

One example of their supreme confidence came on 23 July when police discovered a parcel bomb on board a British Airways Trident flying between Belfast and London. The fact that the IRA had been able to smuggle the bomb aboard at all was embarrassing enough for the security forces but when it was realised that one of the passengers was Mr Jamie Flanagan, the Commissioner of the RUC, red faces went white at the thought of what might have happened if the bomb had exploded.

Car bombs and incendiaries continued to explode in London and the provinces throughout the summer and autumn, and then on 5 October two public houses in Guildford, Surrey, became targets for the bombers. Teenage girls stationed at the WRAC training centre just outside the town, and recruits to the Guards at Pirbright, made regular Saturday night visits to the pubs, the Horse and Groom in North Street and the Seven Stars, just fifty yards away. A group of London-based IRA men and women, carrying shopping bags full of explosives, mingled with the laughing youngsters, who in many cases were tasting their first night of 'freedom' since joining the army. The shopping bags, or time bombs as they were, were left hidden under the furniture in the two pubs. Both exploded within a few minutes of each other. Five people were killed, two of them young WRAC girls, and sixty-eight others were hurt by the blast, some disfigured and maimed.

Out of the chaos and confusion Surrey police conducted a brilliant piece of text-book deduction. Needless to say, the bombers disappeared into the night after spending only a short time in the two pubs, which had been open about three hours at the time of the explosions.

By a process of elimination a team of a hundred detectives then set about the formidable task of tracing everyone who had been in either pub at any time during that evening. The operation was led by Mr Christopher Rowe, Assistant Chief Constable of Surrey and his CID chief, Detective Chief Superintendent Walter Simmons, who soon realised that the memories of many of the pubs' customers would need jogging after their terrifying experience. They hit on the idea of using Polaroid cameras to photograph every witness they found, full face and side view. After a month of day and night inquiries their team had traced more than 400 men and women who had been in either the Horse and Groom or the Seven Stars that night. So thorough was the investigation that eventually they knew exactly the time each customer entered the two pubs, where they stood or sat and to whom they spoke. By considerable skill and exemplary devotion to detail they were able to sketch into their giant jig-saw the faces of several men and women who were eventually traced. Army Intelligence officers from Northern Ireland were sent to Guildford to help with the investigation. Their expertise proved invaluable.

For the rest of October that year there was no respite from the bombers. Two military clubs in London were blasted by explosions and two waiters were injured at a third. Then the attacks switched to Birmingham. Two magistrates living in the city found their cars had been booby-trapped with sticks of gelignite fixed to the underside of their vehicles. Fortunately they were rendered harmless. But on 28 October, Mrs Brenda Howell, wife of the Sports Minister, Mr Denis Howell, and their son, David, had a lucky escape when a similar bomb fell from under their car and exploded in the drive. Neither was hurt.

In London the IRA again turned their attention to the pubs, this time bombing the King's Arms, Woolwich, killing two and injuring thirty five people, many of them service personnel from a nearby barracks. Then on the night of 21 November the IRA struck their most devastating blow—they bombed two crowded Birmingham city-centre pubs, killing twenty-two people and wounding another 183.

That was enough. Parliament rushed through the Prevention of Terrorism Act and it was law within ten days of the Birmingham outrages. The IRA, both Provisional and Official wings, was made an illegal organisation in Britain. Membership and support of it also became an offence with the maximum penalty on conviction on indictment of five years and an unlimited fine. The Act also ruled that it was an offence to wear clothes or display articles demonstrating support in public for the IRA. Penalty on conviction would be three months or £200 fine.

One of the most valuable features of the new Act was the introduction of Exclusion Orders. These could be made against people who were concerned in the commission, preparation or instigation of acts of terrorism, or who attempt or may attempt to enter mainland Britain for the purpose of committing acts of terrorism. This was a tremendous help to the police, for it meant that they could ship back to Ireland people they were convinced were up to their necks in terrorism but about whom they had insufficient evidence to go to court and prove it to the satisfaction of a judge and jury. As a result of this clause several men were given a 'one way ticket' out of Britain. There was a right of appeal against the exclusion orders. One even took his case to the House of Lords without success. Anyone deported from Britain under such an order who attempted to return without permission could be sent to prison for five years. The same penalty applied to anyone who helped or harboured.

The Act also gave the police powers of arrest without warrant in certain circumstances. In particular, it empowered them to arrest people they 'reasonably suspected' of being concerned with either the commission, preparation or instigation of terrorist acts. Anyone arrested under this provision could be held for forty-eight hours and then the Home Secretary could order that he be detained for a further five days before being brought to a court or released. The measures, described by Mr Roy Jenkins, the Home Secretary, as 'draconian' when he introduced them, were to last, in the first instance, for six months only, and then to be re-examined to see whether they should be extended.

The new Act was generally welcomed although a few doubts were expressed in an editorial in the monthly magazine, *Police*, the official organ of the Police Federation. Under the headline, 'Will it work?' the article said:

> Some of this world's many totalitarian rulers must have smiled wryly on reading of the Government's 'draconian' measures to combat the IRA. To British democrats, the spectacle of our liberal country being forced to confront the menace of terrorism is unpleasant. No doubt the perverted minds behind the bombings will gain satisfaction and a feeling of triumph in having forced the British Government to impose the widest restrictions on individual liberties since the wartime Defence Regulations. The Prevention of Terrorism Act is our society's instant reaction to the horror of the Birmingham explosions. The death roll there was terrible, yet it must be asked why we waited until a tragedy of these proportions had occurred. Only in the number of deaths did the Birmingham bombings differ from the atrocities at Guildford, Woolwich, the Tower of London and in the case of the servicemen's leave coach. If the Government can be criticised for its tardiness, however, Parliament cannot be faulted for the speed and near unanimity with which it approved the long overdue legislation. Not for the first time public opinion has proved a powerful goad to the politicians.

Mr Jenkins, in fact, was left in no doubt that there was strong feeling in the House for the return of capital punishment for murder by terrorist acts and there was a very real chance that the 'hard-liners' would delay his new legislation and insist that hanging be written in as the ultimate punishment for this type of crime. He skilfully avoided this confrontation by offering the House another day for a full debate on the subject, thereby side-stepping the opposition to his new Bill.

On the night of 11 December a crowded House filed into the lobbies on a free vote and, as expected, the abolitionists won. After a debate in which a number of remarkably fine and sincere speeches were made the final vote was: Against hanging 369. For 217. Majority 152. A powerful speech by Mr Jenkins did much to destroy the case for the return of the scaffold. He said that having looked at the matter afresh he had come to the conclusion that the re-introduction of the death penalty would not merely secure no improvement but would in all likelihood make matters worse. It would lead to a still greater threat of violence than would otherwise exist and would mean death warrants for innocent and as yet unidentified persons.

He did much to reassure the many MPs who were worried that those convicted of terrorist acts would only serve short terms of their prison sentences. This idea was 'wholly false', he said. He saw no prospect for amnesties for those who had committed cold-blooded and indiscriminate murder or maimings. Neither, he said, did he recognise political excuses for crimes of that order.

During the debate, Mr Jenkins revealed that Sir Robert Mark, the Commissioner of the Metropolitan Police, had sent him a statement, freely volunteered and in the context of the debate, in which he said that of his six most senior officers five were opposed to the return of capital punishment. Mr Jenkins told MPs:

> I should add . . . that in reaching this conclusion the Commissioner has been greatly influenced by his own view of effective deterrents. This he regards as the likelihood of detection followed by, for the guilty, the near certainty of conviction. He thinks that this process would be weakened by capital punishment. He fears that majority verdicts, which at present result in one out of nine convictions, including a number relating to terrorists recently, will have to go.

The Home Secretary explained that being the author of the measure to introduce majority verdicts he did not think that such verdicts could remain for capital offences and once it was said that a verdict was good enough for one form of offence and one form of punishment, it became difficult to defend it for others. Mr Jenkins also agreed with Sir Robert's view that, majority verdicts apart, juries would in general be more hesitant to convict with a capital sentence.

The views of Mr William Whitelaw, the former Minister responsible for Northern Ireland, were already well known, for when moving the abolition of the death penalty in Northern Ireland he had said:

> I am therefore absolutely convinced . . . that in the days immediately before and after any proposed execution the police and the soldiers would be at an increased risk. As a result, the effort to protect the lives of policemen and soldiers by making an example in the case of a death which cannot be reprieved, would be likely to provoke more shooting and more risk of death than to reduce it.

Forced to anticipate the debate because of its early publication date, the *Police* journal carried a strong editorial which left MPs in no doubt how the Police Federation felt on the subject of capital punishment. It said, in part:

The whole subject has been revived because public opinion feels helpless in the face of a small group of fanatics to whom murder is not only a necessary incidental risk but a quite deliberate means to an end. Sentences of thirty years imprisonment, already imposed on some persons convicted of terrorism, appear unreal in the light of possible future changes in the political situation. The argument that hanging might create martyrs and even be welcomed by those who seek such a status, has to be weighed carefully against the realisation that the only martyrs so far have been on one side, and all of them innocent.

In the Lords the day after the Commons debate, Lord Hailsham said that the public must accept that if the death penalty were restored for terrorist crimes one could expect an escalation of terrorism in the immediate aftermath. Hostages might be taken and murdered in revenge. Prominent people, perhaps members of the Royal family, might be threatened or actually attacked. But by depriving the courts of the death penalty, he said, Parliament had put a premium on killing. The one argument against the death penalty which weighed with him was that it was a horrible and degrading thing. But, he felt, it was the lesser of two evils. The indiscriminate slaughter of innocent victims for political ends must stop, he said, and nothing could exercise a more powerful influence in the minds of potential criminals than the death penalty. They had not 'scrupled' to inflict it on some of their defeated enemies, war criminals of the last war, sometimes for crimes less serious than those at present troubling Parliament. Before resuming his seat he said quietly, but none the less dramatically, that the previous evening one of his daughters was in a club in London when it was the victim of a bomb attack. 'Mercifully, she was unharmed, otherwise I would have been among the parents mourning their children', he said. (It is timely to note here that in January 1975 police revealed an IRA plan to kidnap Prince Charles and hold him hostage. The scheme was shelved, however, because the IRA felt they could not penetrate the security guard surrounding the Prince.)

Lord Widgery, the Lord Chief Justice, was firmly of the opinion that capital punishment could act as a deterrent in regard to murder, terrorist or otherwise. He said it seemed that there had been a marked difference since the abolition of hanging in the grievous nature and the degree of violence used by certain criminals, mainly robbers, against innocent people who got in their way. Formerly, he said, professional criminals planning to rob a bank by violence would always insist on firearms being left at home. The reason was that in those days if one of them in panic fired and killed all would hang.

The deterrent effect of those circumstances on the more responsible members of the gang must have been enormous. Now, not a Friday passed without a wage snatch, bank robbery or something of the kind, and firearms, particularly the sawn-off shotgun, were exceedingly common. This 'appalling change' in the degree of violence used must be in some way related to the fact that the game was now worth the candle whereas previously it was not. For serious premeditated crime, such as acts of terrorism, he said, the only real way to restore the value of human life was to return to capital punishment.

When the most senior judge in the land makes a considered judgment such as that, the country's legislators ignore him at their peril. But, as was seen during the debates in both Houses, there were as many eminent men, and women, who just as sincerely, held opposing views believing them to be the right answer. It must also be conceded that without the return of capital punishment for a trial period of several years it is impossible to prove that hanging would reduce the present increasing rise in murder by terrorism. On the other hand, it is possible to disprove the theory that the certainty of arrest and conviction is a greater deterrent. The capture of Judith Ward for the M62 coach bombing did not deter those responsible for the attacks on the Guildford pubs. The arrest of men and women for those murders did not prevent the carnage in Birmingham. And, when the West Midlands police arrested the men responsible for those attacks, there were still more IRA men ready and willing to come forward to continue the campaign of terror. It seems that the only people likely to reflect at any length on the certainty of arrest and conviction are those who have been caught and face a long spell in prison.

chapter nine

Royal Ulster Constabulary

Violent way of life   The barricades go up   IRA's own rough justice   Yard
help RUC to investigate murders   The bravery of the young policemen   The
mounting death toll   Silence defends the guilty   Churchmen win a peace
pause   The rising cost of Ulster

It would be futile, in terms of the United Kingdom, to talk about violence
without referring to the situation in Northern Ireland which, by virtually any
world standard, has proved to be the most virile hotbed of personal antagonism
in recent years. For it is in this tiny province of only 1,500,000 people that more
than 1,000 have died and countless more have been wounded, bombed or
terrorised in a manner which most people in the United Kingdom cannot believe
or begin to comprehend.

There are for instance, entire communities in districts of Belfast who have not
had a genuine full night's sleep since August 1968. Their slumbers have been
consistently broken either by the activities (sometimes almost unbelievably
gruesome) of the IRA terrorists, or house-to-house searches (sometimes with
the minimum of diplomacy) by soldiers of the British army conducting checks
for hidden weapons and explosives. It would not be untrue to say the people of
Ulster's six counties have grown to accept violence as a perfectly normal way of
life.

Perhaps the most startling example is that there are now children of school
age who were born to the sound of gunfire and the blast of bombs, who have
always known the proximity of gunmen, soldiers crouching guardedly on front
door steps, the daily toll of death and destruction. To these children violence is
not some form of frightening and unaccustomed terror; it is their mode of life,
something they have always known and grown to expect. Equally significantly,
most of their parents were products of a similar environment. Bombs, bullets
and dead bodies are nothing new; the only remarkable thing is that the majority
of people have remained sane enough to realise the evil of it.

The province of Ulster once enveloped nine counties but was reduced to the present six on the Partition of Ireland in 1921. Its separation from the other twenty-six counties was a move born of violence, which had been endemic within the nation for centuries. Briefly, the Protestant majority in the north formed its own Government and held uninterrupted power until 1972, when the Stormont Parliament was disbanded by Westminster.

Moves for a unified Ireland came from the predominantly Catholic south, supported by their religious brethren in the north. On the other hand, the three-to-one Protestant majority in Ulster always regarded the Province as a Protestant state and fervently endeavoured to keep it that way. Given this situation, suspicion has always been rife on both sides. The Protestants, particularly those belonging to the powerful Orange Order, have always been wary of the motives of their Catholic neighbours, who, they believed, were committed to the disruption and eventual annihilation of Ulster separatism.

The Catholics, however, were firmly of the opinion that the Protestants regarded and treated them as second class citizens, depriving them of homes, jobs and an equal stake in their society. The result was that religious and political feelings became, in effect, one and the same thing. In simple terms, Protestants voted Unionist and Catholics voted Nationalist, though both were right wing in their outlook and their supporters were mainly drawn from working-class homes where hot water was, until recently, a luxury and outside toilets commonplace.

There is no doubt that discrimination existed, particularly in jobs and housing. But perhaps the most glaring example of the way discrimination operated in Ulster, was in Londonderry where more than 70 per cent of the resident population was Catholic, yet the then City Council was controlled by Protestants. This anomaly resulted from the simple fact that ratepayers could not vote. As most of the Catholics lived in council-owned properties they were automatically disqualified at the ballot box. It was gerrymandering in its worst form and provided the base hate for the Civil Rights marches in the late 1960s.

It was from these demonstrations that the two communities, who had appeared to be healing their long-standing wounds under the guidance of Captain Terence O'Neill, by far the most liberal of Ulster's Prime Ministers, polarised their positions. The Protestants saw their supremacy position threatened and the Catholics an unprecedented opportunity of making inroads into the society from which they felt they had been prohibited. The situation became increasingly worse and erupted in August 1968, despite the promise of civil rights equality for the Catholic population and official recognition that their grievances had some substance.

There will doubtless be disagreement for centuries about who first sparked off the campaign of violence, but the result was that both sides eventually attacked each other. There can be little worse—as history has taught us—than violence born of sectarianism. But the results were devastating when on 19 August the following year, after months of tension, threats and intimidation, billows of black smoke poured skywards from several areas of Belfast and long tongues of flame licked their way through the darkness. Catholics and Protestants alike were literally burning each other's homes, whole streets where there had once been friendly neighbours. Gun-fire rattled through the night as people with burning torches rampaged through the Ardoyne area, once one of the few districts where 'both sides' had lived peacefully together. The madness manifested itself primarily in the Farringdon Gardens area where terraces burned for days. The police were helpless, along with the army which had moved into Northern Ireland only a few months earlier in an effort to contain what was obviously about to become a potential civil war situation.

The scene was set. 'Defence organisations' sprang up in Catholic areas where people feared attack from extremist Protestant groups. Within a short time law and order crumbled as old IRA hands, many of them veterans of internment and previous campaigns, once more saw an opportunity to revive the militant Republican cause. The IRA was soon re-born and with it came the terror, the murder, the senseless brutality, that the Province has now come to accept as part of its daily diet.

It should be remembered that the police, for long regarded by the Catholics as a para-military arm of the Stormont Government, was as a body genuinely mistrusted by them. Any attempts to move into Catholic areas to protect the local population from attack were totally rebuffed by gunmen who manned street barricades and became the nucleus of the IRA fighting force. The men behind the makeshift 'defences' established their own law and order situation and became the *de facto* police force. They also emerged as judge, and jury, and in some cases executioner, meting out tougher justice for misdemeanours than any legal police authority, even in a totalitarian state.

Their unofficial writ ran completely, as authorised police officers ventured into the areas hardly at all. To have taken the risk would have meant almost certain death from a sniper's bullet. Ironically the 'second class citizens' (and there was justice in their claims) found themselves under a much tighter rein than before. Whereas a petty thieving offence might have warranted a fine or a ticking off from the local magistrate, the new regime, governed by gunlaw, became a latter day Star Chamber where petty offences were punished with medieval severity. Tarring and feathering, a traditional IRA punishment for petty offenders, who were left chained to a public lamp post for all to see and denigrate, again became commonplace. Sex offenders, and there were still a few in the early stages, were quite likely to be crippled for life by either being severely beaten up or shot through the knee caps. Traitors to the cause were usually hooded and summarily executed with a bullet through the back of the head. Their bodies were invariably left in the open as a dire warning to anyone with similar ideas of 'betrayal'.

Faced with this complete break-down of established law and order, the bewildered Royal Ulster Constabulary soon discovered that accepted police methods were totally ineffective. For a start, the terrorists established a number of 'No Go' areas, entire districts totally prohibited to not only the police but the armed forces. Murder either by bombing or shooting was not only an everyday occurrence but so utterly commonplace that it became merely a statistic on an RUC crime graph. Investigation became a virtual impossibility although police officers in many cases knew the identity of those responsible for the violent deaths of innocent people. They knew not only their names, but their addresses and even telephone numbers. Arresting them was a different matter for they lived behind the impenetrable barricades of the IRA strongholds.

The murder rate increased with such alarming rapidity that Scotland Yard's Murder Squad, led by Detective Chief Superintendent Eric Payton, moved into Ulster believing that an outside team of investigators would be more acceptable to the local population than the RUC. In fact the London men were on a hiding to nothing before they even left Heathrow Airport. After months of inquiries the Yard team uncovered several murders and were able to name several murderers—but the guilty men had all skipped across the border into Eire and to safety.

The men from London, used to going anywhere, seeing anyone without fear, suddenly found themselves in a situation they had never encountered before. 'Let's go and see . . .' was always answered by his RUC counterpart with 'You must be joking! You are putting your head in a noose. They will shoot you without any compunction and probably shoot you twice if they see you with us.'

This was the greatest problem the Yard men found when they arrived in Northern Ireland. In fact, as they embarked at the heavily guarded Aldergrove airport they were placed under police protection—hardly the most encouraging way to start a murder inquiry! But this was Northern Ireland, not London, the place where men died daily because they went to the wrong church; the province where violence touched every family; where even to go to work on a bus was putting life and limb at considerable risk, buses being prime hijacking material for the numerous barricades around the city and perfect booby-traps for unsuspecting police and soldiers who ventured to clear the roads.

For without argument, the barricades, the hijackings, the bombings, and of course, the murders, were all criminal acts no matter their guise or pretensions of patriotism. The IRA saw themselves as the equivalent of the war-time French Resistance and considered their methods as nothing more nor less than 'acts of liberation'.

Ever since the troubles began, newspapers throughout the world have been packed with horrifying accounts of the death and destruction which has swept across Northern Ireland. Most people are now aware of what happens when a bomb goes off without any warning, as it did for example in the Abercorn Restaurant in Belfast. In this incident alone two young girls lost their lives, two attractive sisters—having a break after shopping for a wedding dress—had their legs blown off, and another 150 received injuries, many of them serious.

What is not so well known is the fantastic strain this mindless violence has put on the police. Apart from living at close quarters with the bombers and gunmen, the RUC itself has been one of the prime targets. The force has a full-time strength of only about 4,500 (about 1,000 under establishment) and, of these, more than half have been injured in one incident or another, several on more than one occasion.

A classic example is the case of Constable Gerry Clyde, still only in his mid-20s, who has been involved in no less than eight hair-raising encounters. He has twice been blown up and injured and escaped unhurt on six other occasions. Once a Land rover in which he was travelling with another officer came under fire from the IRA and his colleague was shot in the head. Another time he was charged by about 400 rioters including some who were throwing petrol bombs, when he had only a dustbin lid for protection. Once he was in the Springfield Road Police Station in Belfast standing next to Sergeant Michael Willets of the Parachute Regiment when a terrorist threw a large bomb over the wall. The sergeant was killed while protecting civilians with his body and was posthumously awarded the George Cross. Constable Clyde was badly injured. He explained:

I had twenty eight stitches in my face and my back was badly scarred. I had only just returned to work after a couple of months when I heard something falling in the station yard. I went out to see what it was and—boom! It was another bomb. I caught the full blast and finished up in the street with more injuries. I was off work for another two months. Being involved in eight explosions is a bit unnerving, especially when you get shot at as well. Everyone calls me Jonah and some of the lads say they would not go on patrol with me for a gold clock.

In a way Constable Clyde is fortunate because he can still continue his chosen career as a fully-active policeman. Detective Constable Ronald Mack, is not so lucky. His hearing has been partly destroyed after a 20lb bomb exploded only five feet from him. But, he said, philosophically:

I am the luckiest man alive, really. I got out of my car and saw the bomb on the pavement next to the passenger door. Before I could do anything it went off and most of the blast went over my head. My car was totally wrecked and so was a furniture store twenty yards away. An army bomb expert told me later that I would have been blown to bits if I had been two or three feet further away. . .

One man who virtually came back from the dead was Sergeant Eddie Kelly. He was so badly injured that even surgeons nearly gave up hope of saving him on the day an IRA Death Squad called at his home in Newry, Co. Down, only a few miles from the Eire border. Sergeant Kelly told the dramatic story himself:

It was shortly before 9am when I was opening the doors of my garage and my daughter Mary, who was only five at the time, was opening the garden gates. I had forgotten something and was going back into the house when I saw a man get out of a car and aim a revolver at my face. I thought: 'My God, I am going to be shot', and ran back towards the garage to take cover behind the doors. He fired as I turned and the first shot hit me behind the ear and came out through the bridge of my nose. A couple more hit me in the right side of my chest and another lodged at the top of my right lung. I was hit five times altogether and one bullet narrowly missed my heart. I was lying behind the garage doors by this time.

Then another man in the car—there were four in all—fired a whole magazine into the doors of the garage obviously hoping to finish me off. Then they drove away. I never lost consciousness and I never thought I was going to die. The only thing that worried me was the loss of so much blood.

The entire incident lasted only fifteen seconds. It was witnessed by Mary, the eldest of Sergeant Kelly's five children, who was in the direct line of fire, and his panic-stricken wife who was watching from the front door. These are just some of the many nightmare stories that members of the RUC can tell. But, few of them, even those who escape death by a whisker, feel any animosity towards their attackers. Their attitude was perhaps best described by Constable Mack whose career was almost wrecked by the blast of a bomb:

Injuries of this sort are part of the job in this country, I suppose. I had interviewed between fifty and a hundred IRA men before this happened and I have no hatred for them. I just wish they would stop.

A senior officer in the RUC commented:

It always amazes me that these men who have been shot and bombed feel no bitterness towards the people who did it. But this sort of adversity has resulted in a fantastic 'esprit de corps'. Even so, after all these attacks and a series of others on policemen's homes while they have been sleeping with their families, I am astonished, not that the Force still functions so well, but that it functions at all.

A glance at statistics for just one year—1972—perhaps explains his amazement: there were no less than 3,000 separate attacks on policemen; 269 attacks on police stations, including more than 200 when bombs, rockets and guns were used; 745 members of the force were injured on duty; and a staggering number of 17 policemen were murdered by terrorists while on duty.

Just before he retired as Chief Constable of the RUC in 1973, Sir Graham Shillington commented:

These figures reflect an unprecedented campaign of violence against police personnel and police buildings. I am proud of the courage and devotion to duty of officers in all ranks who have endeavoured to provide a service to the public in face of these appalling conditions.

The escalation of violence in the province resulted, not unnaturally, in a mammoth 16·4 per cent increase in indictable crime. The official figure—for 1972 alone—was 35,884 known major crimes, nearly 100 a day in a total population of only 1,500,000. As if dealing with the ghastly results of terrorism was not enough, robberies increased by the 'colossal' figure of almost 261 per cent! But the most frightening of all the official statistics for Northern Ireland was announced by Sir Graham in one short paragraph in his final report:

> The number of murders and attempted murders reached an unprecedented level. Of 479 deaths in violent circumstances during 1972–376 have been recorded as murder. Corresponding figures for 1971 and 1970 were 123 and 14 respectively and this, I feel, is indicative of the loss of respect for humanity in the province in recent years. Attempted murders totalled 1,210 compared with 298 in 1971 and 12 in 1970.

Apart from these figures, which would send any chief constable elsewhere in Britain insane, there was one further total which would ensure he qualified immediately for a protective straitjacket–1,495 explosions. London went into a state of near panic when a few letter bombs began arriving through the post and two IRA bombs exploded at the Old Bailey and Great Scotland Yard near the British Forces Broadcasting headquarters.

But the people of Ulster have lived with an average of nearly five bombs a day, every single day, for several years. This is a measure of the madness which has gripped the tiny community. Add the nauseating fact that more than 200 British soldiers have lost their lives in this undeclared war and the full truth of the carnage begins to dawn.

But, faced with these almost unbelievable crime figures, the police still attempt to find the culprits. However, their difficulties are far greater than those encountered by any other force in Britain. For a start, the RUC is still mistrusted by some sections of the community, mostly the poorer Catholics whose ghetto areas are virtually 'out of bounds' to outsiders. Furthermore, people will not talk, privately or publicly, about most terrorist crimes for one very simple reason: any hint that they have been assisting the police–or the army for that matter–will almost certainly have one result. Their execution. Such is the fear of the gunman's bullet that even large cash rewards remain uncollected. One man summed it up: 'There is not much point in being a rich dead man. Most people prefer to remain poor and live happily on their old age pension.'

Sir Graham, who under normal circumstances would have been justifiably angry with his 450 detectives for clearing up only 21 per cent of indictable crimes, lamented:

> The continuing violence and utter disregard for the law coupled with an understandable fear on the part of some sections of the public to co-operate with the police made the investigation of crimes extremely difficult and in many cases well-nigh impossible.

Imagine any chief constable on the British mainland speaking in such apparently defeatist terms. Such language as 'well-nigh impossible' is tantamount to throwing in the towel. But Sir Graham was in no way being defeatist. He was merely expressing what has become a fact of life in an area where fear of retribution is a more potent weapon than the proverbial long arm of the law. Although he did not spell it out, what the hard pressed Sir Graham was saying was simply this: We know in many cases the identities of the culprits and we can arrest them. Bringing them to trial is an entirely different matter. Where do we get witnesses?

There are countless instances where the RUC are not only aware of the identity of murderers but have cast iron evidence to prove their guilt. Detectives have spent many arduous and dangerous months tracking down the people responsible for bombings and shooting only to find one insurmountable barrier: the 'witnesses' have flatly refused to stand in a public court of law and point the finger at those they know to be guilty.

But RUC detectives at one time faced a further frustration. Even if they had succeeded in bringing an accused person to trial, finding a jury that would be totally objective was sometimes impossible. In theory, the problem should not have arisen. Any 'twelve good men and true' would have been enough. In practice it was not so simple. How, for instance, was a jury, largely composed of rate-paying Protestants, expected to give a reasonable and unbiased verdict in a trial involving an ardent and committed Republican Catholic?

Equally, the situation could well have been reversed if an acknowledged member of the extremist Protestant Ulster Volunteer Force (UVF) stood in the dock before a jury which was predominantly Catholic? In both situations the juries would be likely to bring a 'guilty' verdict. Conversely, a Republican before a Catholic jury or a UVF man before a Protestant jury could be reasonably confident of acquittal. In these circumstances it was surely fair to ask: How was it possible for justice to operate? The answer was simple—it did not. Considering all these odds, the only remarkable thing, to paraphrase the RUC spokesman, was that anyone was brought to justice at all. Further, given these enormous difficulties, a crime detection rate of 21 per cent must be considered as a near miracle.

The problem of securing witnesses and information, given the unique circumstances of Ulster, is well recognised by the police. So much so that they have a publicly advertised telephone number, widely displayed on buses, in shops and bars throughout the country which people can use to provide information anonymously. It has, without doubt, been a great success and a number of convictions have resulted from it. The scheme, of course, has had its critics, mainly those who feel it reeks of Gestapo tactics. Maybe in the traditions of good old British fair play, where everyone should stand up and be counted, they have a point. But Northern Ireland is not like that.

With politics and religion so inextricably and dangerously intertwined, where the two main platforms of public opinion are so diametrically opposed, the man at the next desk in the office can secretly be your biggest enemy. You, for instance, might be a sniper of the IRA and he could easily do similar work for the UVF—and neither need know. If, however, one discovered what the other was doing during the night hours, he could make a quick telephone call on the 'anonymity line' and alert the police without anyone being the wiser. It is a far from satisfactory situation but, in the absence of anything better, information received in this clandestine way is a marked improvement on no information at all.

It is this sort of situation, whereby the overworked police have lots of information and evidence without being in a position—for one reason or another—to bring the suspect before a court, which has led to a number of men being incarcerated in the internment camp at Long Kesh, only a few miles outside Belfast. Under the Northern Ireland Special Powers Act, they may be held there, without trial, for an indefinite period. Here again, it is a situation not found anywhere else in the United Kingdom.

Long Kesh, or the Maze Prison to give it the official title, is a top security prison camp. The number of internees and detainees held there has varied widely, from over 1,000 at the height of the violence to below 500. The internees, mostly Catholics, who are either known or suspected of being members of the IRA and prepared to use all kinds of violence to achieve their political ambitions, live in huts, often cold, damp and draughty. They have recreation rooms, wash-houses and a cinema and their day is controlled by prison officers who administer internal discipline and security. Outside, the high wire perimeter fence, floodlit by night, army patrols are constantly on duty to discourage any escape attempts.

So far, nobody has succeeded in breaking out and remaining free, but all sorts of methods have been tried, including tunnelling, snipping the wire, posing as visitors and even being disguised as soldiers. It is a strange and frustrating environment for men who have been neither charged nor convicted of any offence. Some were plucked from their beds by the security forces on the night of 19 August 1970, after Mr Faulkner, then Prime Minister under the old Stormont Parliamentary system, signed the order to begin internment. It was an old method of dealing with the IRA and had been used successfully during previous campaigns. But Republican veterans claimed that 'this time it was different'. In the first place, more men were interned than ever before. Second the decision, when finally taken, came unexpectedly. Further, the move itself created a massive outburst of violence as Republican strongholds of Andersonstown, Ballymurphy, New Barnsley, all in Belfast, and the Bogside and Creggan districts of Londonderry, erupted in protest.

Finally, and here it must be emphasised that nobody has emerged with a shred of proof to support the theory, some people in these areas are convinced that a significant number of men were interned by the Protestant-dominated executive, merely to settle old scores and ensure that personal enemies were locked safely behind bars. Those chiefly responsible for this situation, it was alleged, were the hated 'B' Specials, the part-time policemen with a tradition of shooting first and asking questions later. It was the men of this force, say the protesters, who put in 'I'm sure so-and-so's a member of the IRA' reports to their superiors which in themselves were virtually sufficient to ensure a man's detention.

Although nobody has yet successfully escaped from Maze Prison and remained free the same cannot be said about Belfast's Crumlin Road prison. In fact, just before Christmas 1971, twenty-two prisoners, many awaiting trial on charges concerning terrorism, were playing football on one of the recreation grounds. Suddenly a rope ladder was flung over the wall and nine members of the IRA climbed to freedom before guards had time to consider what was happening. About the same time, 'Dutch' Docherty and Martin Meehan, two of Belfast's most notorious IRA leaders, staged one of the most audacious escapes from Crumlin Road. Their disappearance was noticed at the nightly roll call and within minutes the entire centre of Belfast was surrounded by road blocks in an attempt to cut off all possible escape routes. In Andersonstown and other Catholic areas, celebration bonfires were lit and people danced in the streets, overjoyed that two of 'the boys' had fooled the guards and escaped to freedom. For two days massive searches were made around the city, the homes of hundreds of known IRA sympathisers were meticulously combed in a concentrated effort to find the men. Finally, security chiefs, convinced the pair had somehow slipped the net and made their way to the then safety of Eire, called off the search. But, it was discovered later, it was only then that Docherty and Meehan climbed over the wall to freedom. They had been hiding in the prison all the time!

It should be remembered that, in those days, authorities in the South of Ireland were not as co-operative with their Northern counterparts as they are today. Most known IRA killers and bombers could appear on television, write in the Press and walk the streets south of the border with complete immunity. The reason: they had not committed any offence in Eire (though being a member of the IRA was always an offence there) and so were free to come and go as they wished.

Many of them congregated in Dundalk, a small town just south of the Ulster border. Not surprisingly it soon became known as Dodge City, the haven of the law-breaker. From there the IRA gangs would ambush British army patrols on border duty, drive a few miles inside Ulster to execute some policeman (always a 'legitimate target') or plant a bomb. The RUC and British army were helpless. Officially, there was a degree of co-operation with the Republic's army and police. In practice it amounted to very little and there was more antagonism, rather than goodwill, between the security forces on both sides. But it should be remembered that the Eire authorities faced a very real problem when dealing with men they knew full well were responsible for much of the violence and death across the border. Which jury in Dublin, or elsewhere in the south for that matter, would convict a man for whose cause they felt much genuine sympathy? Any such trial, they argued with some justification, would be a complete mockery and achieve nothing. In any realistic terms, extradition was also a non-starter at that time. Few, if any, Irish judges would sign such an order once the man before him had pleaded that the allegations against him were purely political. Since then, co-operation has improved greatly, mainly since the Eire government realised the IRA posed as much a threat to their own authority as they did to that in the North.

So the position in Ireland, where violent men are murderers or heroes remembered in song, according to your point of view, where 'death for the cause' is a glorious thing, is still unresolved. Further, it is likely to remain unresolved for many years to come. For the new generation, born to violence and reared under the muzzles of guns, will be ripe for shouldering arms when their fathers are ready to exchange their para-military uniforms for a comfortable pair of fireside slippers.

This is a crucial problem already exercising the minds of senior planning officers in the RUC, educationalists and sociologists throughout Northern Ireland. They fear the incessant bombings, shootings, mindless lynch-law justice, could well have long term effects on the emotional stability of the province's younger generation.

No chief constable in England is in the least envious of Mr James Flanagan—who replaced Sir Graham Shillington and became Ulster's first-ever Catholic police supremo—in the enormous task that lies ahead. But even Mr Flanagan himself will not have to face those problems when they arise. He has asked that his appointment be terminated at the end of 1975. The police authority agreed, if reluctantly, 'because of the onerous nature of the duties involved.'

But for a short time in early January 1975 it looked as though Mr Flanagan might still be in office at an historic turning point in Ulster's stormy political history. For on 20 December 1974 the Provisional IRA's ruling Army Council, at a meeting in Dublin, announced an eleven-day ceasefire to operate over Christmas and New Year. The suspension of 'operations' would run from midnight 22 December until midnight 2 January 1975 and was in response to pleas from a group of Protestant churchmen who had earlier held secret talks with IRA leaders in the tiny west coast village of Feakle, in Co. Clare. The actions of the Ulster church leaders had been 'courageous and positive' and their approach 'frank and constructive' at all times. The statement said:

As a result of the meeting in Feakle, Co.Clare with Protestant churchmen, the leadership of the Republican movement have ordered the suspension of offensive military action in Britain and Ireland over the Christmas period. A number of points for a ceasefire were presented by the church representatives to Republican leaders at this meeting. These points were considered at length by the Army Council. Written observations on the points were made and a set of counter-proposals drafted embodying the three basic demands of the Republican movement. These have been forwarded to the British Government. . .

One of the aims of calling the truce was to give the British Government an opportunity to consider the IRA's proposals for a permanent ceasefire. The three main demands were: an end to internment, the withdrawal to barracks of all British troops and British recognition of the right of Irish people to govern themselves. Until these points had been agreed, there was no possibility of ordering a permanent halt to the campaign of violence. The statement later continued:

> We have noted the statement from Mr Rees (Mr Merlyn Rees, the Ulster Secretary), and we expect a cessation of aggressive military action by Crown forces and an end to all raids, arrests and harassment and no re-introduction of RUC personnel in uniform or plain clothes into areas where they are not acceptable. Any breach of these terms will be considered as a refusal to accept the eleven days cessation and appropriate action will be taken to protect our people. We also trust that the British Government will avail itself of this opportunity for bringing to an end the evil of internment. The leadership of the Republican movement awaits a reply from the British Government to the proposals for a total ceasefire. If there is not a satisfactory reply by midnight, 2 January, then the IRA will have no option but to resume hostilities.

There was never any chance that Mr Rees would, or indeed could, agree to such sweeping peace terms and the IRA leadership must have known this all along. Why then, did they agree to a temporary ceasefire at all? Was it really a gesture of goodwill, a genuine response to the efforts made by the Protestant churchmen? Or was it a ploy in order to regroup their hard-pressed forces and re-stock ammunition dumps? Certainly senior army officers and RUC experts were thinking along these lines. They, more than anyone, knew the IRA was losing ground, militarily and politically and were a weaker force than at any time since 1969.

But at least the unusual quiet which settled over Belfast, Londonderry and other 'target' towns gave tired and weary RUC officers a few days to recuperate and equally exhausted troops a chance to rest. It also gave the statisticians at police headquarters a chance to bring their 'incident board' up to date. This is the chart, hung in the RUC Press Office, which coldly logs every spine-chilling event and makes grim reading. For as 1974 ran out, the board showed that, since 1968 no less than 2,514 policeman had been injured on duty—more than half the total force of around 4,500. In addition fifty full-time policeman and nine reservists had been killed during the same period. Terrorists had also exploded 4,334 bombs and made off with £2,241,952 in 4,909 robberies to finance their war of terror. Further, 807 civilians had lost their lives and more than 10,000 injured, many having lost limbs and suffered permanent damage. The army death toll stood at 232 regular soldiers and forty-six part-timers of the Ulster Defence Regiment.

In cold print the figures mean little. In terms of human suffering and misery, they mean that virtually every family in the province has been affected, either directly or indirectly, by a terrorist bomb or bullet—friends and relatives shot or injured, bombed out of their homes or jobs. In these circumstances it is not difficult to see that forgiving and forgetting will take years, possibly even generations.

However, the search for peace had to go on and, not for the first time, senior Whitehall civil servants made unofficial contact with Republican leaders in the hope of securing some settlement. But the hardline Protestant organisations protested loudly at any such moves. How could any British Government, they argued, engage in face-to-face talks with terrorists and murderers? Some, like the Reverend Ian Paisley, paraphrased Churchill and demanded the tools to finish the job. But Mr Rees, anxious to succeed where politicians throughout the ages had failed, was quite happy to hold out carrots in the faint but fervent hope that the IRA donkey would keep travelling along the road to peace. He spoke of 'a genuine and sustained cessation of violence' creating 'a new situation'. In other words, if the terrorists really wanted a settlement, they should continue the eleven-day ceasefire for an indefinite period. In return, hinted Mr Rees, the British Government would release detainees from Maze Prison, a few at a time, on a progressive basis: the longer the ceasefire, the more men would be freed. Further, the army would operate fewer street patrols and raids on houses, and, therefore, be less in evidence. In fact, the number of soldiers stationed in Ulster had been declining throughout 1974. By the end of the year there were 15,000 stationed throughout the province—compared with nearly 18,000 at the height of the troubles.

But the unofficial talks between the IRA leadership, the Protestant churchmen and the bowler hat brigade from Whitehall, failed. After a long and difficult meeting in Dublin on 16 January 1975, Republican leaders decided by a narrow 4-3 margin to continue the violence. The bombers were back in business.

The 'hawks', led by Seamus Twomey and Joe O'Hagan—two of the three IRA leaders who made a spectacular escape by helicopter from Mountjoy Prison, Dublin, in 1973—had just won the day against the 'doves' led by David O'Connell, the political 'brains' behind the organisation. But, by the cruellest of ironies, Joe O'Hagan, the IRA quartermaster and allegedly number three in the hierarchy, was arrested by Dublin Special Branch officers only hours after the fateful talks had been completed. Had he been captured only twenty-four hours earlier, the vote would have been deadlock and peace might have been given a chance in Ireland.

The fact that the IRA had extended its ceasefire for two weeks had, in itself, given the war-weary people of Ulster a remote hope that something positive was about to emerge. The news from the IRA Army Council shocked everyone, including Mr Gerry Fitt, leader of the mainly Catholic Social Democratic and Labour Party. He said: 'It will be an absolutely insane, mad person who will order a resumption of hostilities. And they will certainly have no support from Catholics or anyone else in the North.'

Mr Rees announced:

I share the feeling of outrage and disappointment of the people of Northern Ireland, that the provisional IRA have today shown a total lack of concern for the people's clear call for an end to violence. I will not be influenced by any views which are backed with threats of the bomb and the bullet.

For their part, the IRA complained of 'a lack of response' from the British

Government and, therefore, 'could not in all conscience renew the ceasefire'. Church leaders expressed their shock and disappointment and Mr Paisley adopted an 'I told you so' attitude.

So, was Northern Ireland back to square one? Was there now no chance of peace and was it going to be a bitter no-holds-barred struggle to the end? In the early weeks of 1975 nobody knew the answers, though the level of IRA activity certainly declined. One of the big worries to the British Government, though nobody in Whitehall would admit it in such terms, was that the IRA might escalate its campaign in mainland Britain, hoping to raise enough panic that public opinion would demand the immediate return of all troops from Ulster. Given that situation, the RUC and its reservists, along with the Ulster Defence Regiment, would be the only security forces protecting the province from the terrorists. More realistically, it would almost certainly result in a bloodbath between Catholics and Protestants, an open civil war situation. And nobody dare allow that to happen.

Meanwhile, the cost of defending Ulster from the bomb and the bullet was rising all the time. Although no firm estimates were available, it was widely understood to be hovering around the £1 million a day mark. With inflation bouncing along at an annual 20 per cent, it would not be long before it topped £500 million a year.

Further, to this had to be added claims for compensation, decided by the Ulster Criminal Injuries Compensation Board. At the end of 1974 these stood at a remarkable £123 million.

No less than £110 million of this money was for damage to property, houses, shops, hotels, buses and cars which had become the debris of war in Northern Ireland. The remaining £13 million was for compensation to relatives of those killed (including British soldiers) and to people injured by the violence.

The amounts paid out often appear to have been anomalous, £60,000 to a Belfast man whose spine was broken by a bullet, but only £500 to the widow of a British private soldier killed in an explosion. The dependants of the thirteen killed by British soldiers in Londonderry on the famous 'Bloody Sunday' in January 1972, received between them £42,000. Not surprisingly this caused an outcry among the Protestant population who claimed all those who died were either IRA men or had been breaking the law anyway by taking part in a banned procession. In fact, there was no evidence produced to the tribunal, led by Lord Widgery, the Lord Chief Justice, that any of those who died had belonged to any organisation. What did emerge, perhaps significantly, was that a number of them had not been handling guns or explosives. Forensic tests on some others, however, had proved positive. How could it happen, the arguments ran, that relatives of suspected men, shot in the line of duty by British soldiers, received more compensation money than the widow of a dead soldier? Where was the justice?

The matter is totally in the hands of the Northern Ireland Criminal Compensation Board which assesses, in the case of a married man, how much he gave his family, his regular earnings and his job promotion prospects. On this basis a sum is agreed. But dependants of anyone killed in Northern Ireland can claim a lump sum for burial costs and another for 'loss of dependency'.

Given this sort of financial drain on Britain's already over-burdened resources, it is hardly surprising that, if for no other reason, the British Government wants a quick end to the violence. Apart from the distressing cost in lives and personal injuries, it is also far too heavy for the Exchequer to carry indefinitely.

chapter ten

Forensic science and the Home Office

New aids to detect criminals   Case history of how scientists trapped a girl's killer   Scotland Yard's 'eye in the sky'   How insects may be trained to find buried murder victims   The problems of the forensic pathologist   The National Police College and university successes

When moors murderers Ian Brady and Myra Hindley buried the bodies of their victims in the deserted moorlands on the Lancashire-Yorkshire-Cheshire boundary, one of the most difficult tasks facing investigating detectives was finding them. They spent days probing around the likely areas, prodding sticks into the ground in the hope of finding something. But forensic science, probably one of the most progressive technologies in the world, has come a long way since those days of 1965. If the same search had to be done now, it is almost certain the bodies would be discovered much more quickly, thanks to new scientific aids developed in forensic laboratories. For a start, police could call on the invaluable assistance of, surprisingly, flies! Or even the Sexton Beetle, or perhaps even a trained fox. For experiments at Home Office laboratories have shown that all three are able to detect human remains buried underground. Experiments started by burying some dead pigs and at the same time cultivating the phoridae fly and setting swarms of them free. It was found the flies clustered most heavily over the pigs' graves.

Delighted at this success, scientists then put some of the flies in a box and, using a highly sensitive detector in the hope of picking up their excited buzz, they carried the box over the ground. But this failed and, at the same time, the scientists discovered the flies were no use in winter anyway. Still, further tests are now going on in the hope of perfecting a technique where these flies can be used in murder inquiries where the location of the corpse could otherwise be near impossible. At the same time—on the advice of the British Museum—the scientists began experimenting with the Sexton Beetle, having trapped some by using a dead mouse as bait. It is said the beetle will travel several miles to find a carcass in which to lay its eggs. Again the difficulty was finding a detector sensitive enough to pick up the beetle's sound of excited success—when it rubs its back legs together. Once this handicap has been overcome—'we are still working on it', said one of the experts taking part in the experiments—the fly and the beetle could become important allies for the police in their fight against crime.

At the Home Office Research Station at St Albans, other experiments are going on with a fox the scientists have called Fred. Foxes are reputed to be good at detecting buried remains. But Fred, at the moment, is not proving such a great success. Although he has a keener nose than dogs, he is less obedient and does not cover the ground so thoroughly. Still, the experts are persevering in the hope that Fred might eventually prove useful. Meanwhile, on the advice of the Royal Veterinary College, scientifically planned dog trials have taken place, using Alsatians and Border Collies, to see whether they can be trained to detect, initially, dead pigs. If these turn out to be successful, scientists believe there is every hope they may be used to detect the buried bodies of murder victims.

The whole idea of using animals and insects for this type of work came from the Home Office's Scientific Advisory Council. The Council discovered that infra-red detectors which show chlorophyll variations in plants are a not too reliable guide. Seismic tests have also been tried and thermal cameras which can detect differences in the heat absorption when soil has been disturbed have also been used. But the Atomic Energy Authority is now analysing gases from pigs carcasses in the hope that a detector device can be developed.

These are just a few of the developments which are happening in forensic science and new discoveries are taking place every day. Often it is a case of trial and error and some techniques may take years to develop. But research, under the auspices of the Home Office, is unceasing. Private enterprise, too, plays its part and manufacturers of all kinds and types of devices are constantly knocking on the Home Office's door in the hope of selling their products to the police. For the Home Secretary has direct overall responsibility for the police in Britain, the prisons and their inmates, Borstal institutions, approved schools, the probation service, immigration and aliens departments. As a result, it is one of the biggest and most complex of Government departments with a vast annual budget, some of which is channelled into the development of forensic science, now an invaluable factor in solving thousands of crimes every year.

The growth rate of research to assist the police can be calculated from the greatly increased expenditure. In 1970, the Police Scientific Development Branch of the Home Office had an annual budget of only £280,000. In the 1973-4 financial year, this figure jumped to more than £1 million. This emphasis on research indicates the Home Office policy is one of using all possible technical assistance to help the police in the hope that this will increase the crime detection rate and, in addition, save officers tasks that could be done more easily and more efficiently by machines.

Just how valuable the aids of forensic science can be to the police were highlighted by just one case which was investigated by the Lancashire county police working in conjunction with scientists at the Home Office Forensic

Science Laboratory at Chorley, only a few miles from the police headquarters at Hutton. The body of a 17-year-old Sunday school teacher was found, partly concealed behind a hawthorn hedge, near some fields at Brying Lane, Wrea Gree, Kirkham. Home Office pathologist, Dr. B. B. Beeson, said death had been due to asphyxia, due to pressure on the neck. Several scratches on the body could have been caused either by barbed wire or the prickly hedge. Although only one shoe was found near the body, the remains of another and charred remnants of clothing similar to those missing, were found in a field seven miles away. Both the shoe and the clothing had been burned, quite innocently, by the person who found them. But the ashes were examined by the Chorley scientists and they told detectives they contained metal components similar to those found in the shoe near the body. Scientists also made a close examination of the girl's clothing and reached the conclusion that her attacker was a blood Group B secretor. They also decided that, because there was no soil either on her tights or shoe, her body had been taken in a vehicle, then carried to the spot where it was found.

The probable use of a car led to police making a close examination of all tyre tracks near the scene. The rear width of the most likely car (its tyre marks were the freshest) indicated it could be an Austin A60. The tread shape of the tyres gave police another vital clue—those on the rear were a common Dunlop type, but the Fisk Premium cross-plies on the front were relatively rare. Further, swabs taken from the dead girl's clothing—indicating a blood Group B attacker—sent officers away to take 10,000 saliva samples. Of these 5.9 per cent were found to be of the right blood group. More forensic tests discovered thirty dark red fibres on five of the girl's clothes. Some of these had microscopic amounts of black rubber at one end and scientists concluded they had probably come from a non-woven red car carpet with a black rubber backing. Armed with this latest scientific probability, detectives went away again—this time to discover who made such carpets, and for which particular cars. Checks with Crossley Carpets of Halifax came up with the right answer. Crossleys checked the forensic laboratory samples with similar car carpets they had made and found the ones which matched best were those manufactured for the Austin A60 range, 1962 series. But the scientists were by no means finished. They told police of the two tiny fragments of leather with a pale blue painted surface which had been found clinging to the dead girl's jumper. Furthermore, a small flake of red paint had been discovered in the fibres of her skirt. Although the flake of paint was only one square mm in surface, the boffins reported that it contained three distinct layers of paint, two shades of red on a cream undercoat. Even more news: small particles of grey material, possibly body filler, were clinging to the cream undercoating.

So the police now had narrowed their inquiries. The tiny specks of blue-painted leather, possibly from a car, indicated the vehicle they were searching for was of the older type. Modern mass production cars do not have leather seats. And it appeared from the red flake of paint that the car could have been completely, or partly resprayed. So the police now had at least some idea of what they were searching for: an old car which had probably been resprayed, which had flaking blue leather seats and red carpet of the type used in the Old Austin A60—and Fisk Premium tyres. Determined detectives searched all over Lancashire, sending samples from likely vehicles to the forensic science laboratory for tests to be made. Finally, by sheer diligence, they discovered a battered 1960 MG Magnette in a scrap yard at Poulton-le-Fylde near Blackpool. It had been partly painted over black on top of red, had blue leather seats and dark red carpets. The tyres were missing but three of the four were recovered. Laboratory samples taken from the girl's clothing matched exactly those taken from the MG. And the tyre tracks taken in the field where the body was found, matched exactly with those which had been used on the vehicle, even down to an impression of a repair plug! Finally, probably the best piece of evidence—an 8in.-long hair was found on the red carpet and this was identical to the dead girl's. The last owner of the car was traced and a saliva sample showed him to be blood Group B. He was charged with the girl's murder nearly four months after her body had been found. Eventually he was found guilty of manslaughter and admitted being in the car with the girl when she died. But he insisted he had never intended to kill her, only quieten her when she began screaming.

Only a few years ago, that sort of investigation would have been impossible. The man now serving ten years' imprisonment would very probably still be at large but for the joint skills of the scientists and the police. It is common knowledge that millions of sets of fingerprints are kept by police and more than one serving prisoner has been convicted on such tell-tale evidence. But a Liverpool detective, Sgt L. V. Alexander, has come up with a new idea—palm prints. He thought of it while lying awake in bed having seen, after nineteen years in the fingerprint department in the Merseyside Criminal Records Office, many perfectly clear palm prints go to waste because nobody had bothered to classify them. So Sergeant Alexander began many years of experimentation and research into devising a method of coding, searching and filing, and finally came up with a system which is now fully operational in Merseyside. It has been successful, too. More than 400 identifications have resulted and now a manual has been published which contains all aspects of the system. It shows that the practice of palm-printing is equally reliable and in some cases superior to finger-printing. However, until the system becomes widely accepted, finger-printing will still be used by the world's police, although variations on the theme are now being tried, particularly in the USA.

There, experiments have taken place with what has become known as hand geometry, an idea evolved from measuring American air force pilots for gloves. For the discovery was made that the hand has measurable characteristics which are unique to the individual. The whole concept has now been incorporated into a machine, the Identimat 2000—now marketed in Britain—which could well replace security locks and even keys in the future.

The machine works like this: each person is given a card on which is coded certain characteristics of their hand; the length of the fingers, the translucency of the web between them, pressure of the muscles, the splayed position of each finger bone. The card is then slotted into the machine and the right hand placed in grooved slots on the machine. If they match, the machine will automatically open a door, a safe or whatever. If the holder loses his card, a thief could not use it—because his 'hand characteristics' would not match. The door or safe would stay shut.

Along with the development of fingerprint and palm-print techniques has come another forensic aid to the police—a device to locate footprints which would otherwise be invisible to the naked eye. The detection system was developed by the Cotton, Silk and Man-Made Fibres Association, working under contract to the police. It began when it was discovered that people walking across carpets or hard floor coverings left a trail of electro-static footprints, an effect particularly noticeable in centrally-heated buildings where the air tends to be dry. Scientists found that, by sprinkling polystyrene beads on the floor where someone had walked, they stuck because of the electrical 'charge' left by the person's feet. Those sprinkled on areas where nobody had walked were easily blown away. Apparently, such footprints can be detected for many hours and police researchers, who have been experimenting with the system, are certain the technique will eventually prove useful for 'scene of crime' officers, particularly to indicate where the intruder has walked, thereby locating where extensive forensic examination and fingerprinting should best be concentrated. Further, the 'magnetised' beads could well indicate the size, shape and pattern of the person's shoes. Research is now going ahead to see whether a more sensitive device can be found to detect footprints over a longer period.

All these scientific aids can prove invaluable in the never-ending fight against crime, but they cannot beat eye-witness accounts of events, particularly if the eye-witness happens to be a policeman! Senior officers at Scotland Yard realised this and in the summer of 1973 they began using a £35-an-hour helicopter as a sort of permanent eye in the sky. The helicopter—code named 'India 99'—tours the skies above London at a height of 500 feet all day, every day. It has a range of over 800 miles and logs an impressive one hundred incidents a month. Scotland Yard chiefs believe the helicopter saves the work of one hundred men operating a search on the ground and has already scored several notable triumphs to prove the point. Its first coup was to foil a prison escape from Brixton. Several prisoners succeeded in clearing the prison wall but 'India 99' called from Lea Valley, spotted the escapers as they hid in back gardens. From that point it was a simple matter to call squad cars to the scene and direct them from the air. Not long afterwards, the helicopter found two Borstal escapees in Dagenham, spotted four suspects hiding in dense undergrowth in Plumstead Marshes and even surprised lead thieves stripping a roof. It has attended the scene of scores of bank and store raids, traced a source of pollution on the Thames and reported motorway fog. The helicopter is manned by a rota of thirty sergeants and constables specially trained at Scotland Yard and is directly linked with the control room and all wireless and Flying Squad vehicles on the ground.

While aids such as these and the increasing help given to the Home Office's

Police Scientific Development Branch is more than welcome, one branch of forensic science is in a state of near-collapse and will certainly fold up within the next few years unless the Government steps in to revitalise it. For, almost unbelievably, there are less than thirty forensic pathologists working full-time in the country today. This in itself is startling enough but the bald fact is that there are no young pathologists in training for forensic work. None at all. And, unless something is done—and quickly—Dr Bernard Knight, of the Welsh National School of Medicine, believes that: 'Some day soon, the police are going to end up, stranded alone with a body in a muddy field.' Since the beginning of 1972, this highly specialised branch of medicine has lost ten senior men; seven of them, including the famous Professor Francis Camps, have died. There are now only five professors on the active list in the whole of the United Kingdom and the youngest qualified forensic pathologist in service is now over thirty-five. In short, the speciality is in imminent danger of dying. The remaining thirty dedicated men represent only about a third of the number necessary to maintain an adequate medical detection service. Because of this, forensic pathologists are given far more work than they can reasonably be expected to handle—and over an alarmingly wide area. The result is that, if any of them are either ill or on holiday, the service is hopelessly overstretched. As an example, Dr Alan Usher, of Sheffield University, covers all south Yorkshire, all of Derbyshire, Nottinghamshire, Lincolnshire and part of Staffordshire. But he has been called away as far as Oxford. The South-East is covered from London. From Cardiff, Dr Knight has been on jobs as far apart as Torquay and the Midlands.

One reason, in England and Wales, anyway—Northern Ireland has its own State service—is that forensic pathology is based almost entirely at the universities and there are only five of these interested enough in the subject to maintain a forensic presence of sorts—London, Birmingham, Sheffield, Leeds and Newcastle. And, of these, three are one-man outfits and have to be virtually self-supporting because the general view is that forensic medicine should be a community-supported service, like public health.

Realising they are in the universities under sufferance, some forensic pathologists, anxious to pay their way, are forced to perform what has been described as 'a scandalous number' of coroners' post-mortems. Hardest pressed of all are the units attached to the five London teaching hospitals—St Thomas's, Guy's, the London, St George's and Charing Cross. According to published figures, each of the three or four pathologists on duty at the London Hospital averaged between 1,400 and 1,875 post-mortems each year in the years between 1963 and 1967. So, a job that should normally take four hours or more to do properly has to be done in about twenty minutes. Obviously, as forensic pathologists will freely admit, quite a few 'unnatural deaths' slip through the screening net. Moreover, in the autopsies carried out at the London Hospital, 263 of the cases had been suggested by coroners' report as 'natural deaths'. In fact they contained 174 poisonings, 48 injuries, 11 cases of accidental asphyxia, 1 hanging, a cut throat and an electrocution. In addition, there were 27 major crimes, including 1 murder, 17 battered babies and infanticides and 9 criminal

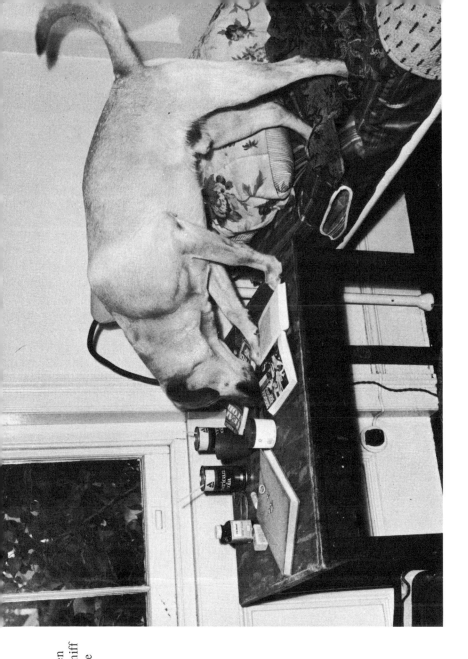

This labrador has been specially trained to sniff out drugs. Police have found them more successful than alsatians

A police frogman emerges from the murky depths of the River Thames with the vital clue in a murder hunt—an old Army rifle, dumped in panic by the killer

abortions. Dr Hugh Johnson, of St Thomas's Hospital in London, commented: 'These illustrate the point we try to make—that there is no such thing as an easy and straightforward case.'

Despite this, much police work and the vast percentage of coroners' work is done by general pathologists including some who have not the training to carry out forensic work. Even worse, some post-mortems ordered by coroners are still done by general practitioners with no pathological training at all. But the reason so many forensic pathologists, who each receive a £200-a-year retainer from the Home Office, do many coroner-requested post-mortems at £7.50p a time (the fee goes up to £12 if they have to attend the inquest) is to pay for the upkeep of their university department. However, many post-mortems have to be carried out under appalling conditions. Dr Usher, with more than a touch of bitterness, wrote a paper called 'The Smallest Room But One', in which he detailed the totally inadequate facilities at most small mortuaries. He said:

Next to public conveniences, to which many of them bear a curious and revealing architectural resemblance, they are usually the smallest buildings erected and maintained by the local authority, and one cannot help but feel that their size accurately reflects the interest taken in them.

It is, therefore, not surprising that, with so much work to do, so few adequate facilities in which to do it, forensic pathology is 'falling into disrepute'. However, the dwindling band of practitioners battle on, trapped, as they see it, between the Home Office, the Health Service and the universities. What they need, they say, is some form of real recognition and a stable financial structure in which they can work. This, in the end, would cost much less than £1 million paid out each year in coroners' fees.

It has been suggested that if about twelve centres were established throughout Britain (again excluding Northern Ireland), the country would have the sort of forensic pathology service it urgently requires. Further, there would be time for all-important research programmes to be undertaken and this, in the end, might elevate the speciality to the level of academic acceptability. Unless something of this sort is done quickly, the service is in real danger of grinding to a complete halt.

Meanwhile, with the alarming increase in terrorist activities—particularly by the IRA—in Britain, the Home Office Police Scientific Development Branch has been encouraging the introduction of new devices which may help trap would-be bombers as they arrive in this country, and infra-red equipment to detect any movement near vital installations which could become prime targets. Air travellers are now familiar with one of the most widely-used devices, an electronically-operated metal detector which is drawn across the body of each traveller. Any metal object, such as a cigarette case or lighter, will cause the machine to give off a loud buzzing noise. So will the presence of a gun, a knife, a grenade or any other object that might be used by, say, a hijacker. These devices save much time and the embarrassment many people feel at a physical body search. Moreover, baggage passing through Heathrow, the world's busiest airport, obviously cannot be individually inspected, piece by piece. It would take too long and it would be doubtful whether any passengers would actually get off the ground. So X-ray equipment has been installed, with the resulting images being examined by a low-light television camera developed by EMI Electronics. A gun, grenade, or a booby-trap bomb hidden in any suitcase can be spotted and identified immediately. The equipment has already proved a major success and police have made several arrests as a result. Now, the authorities, concerned with the possibility of car bombs going off in busy cities, are investigating the possible use of similar but more easily transportable equipment to aid detection.

However, no matter how much the Home Office and the ancillary branches encourage the use of all types of devices to improve criminal detection methods, and finance research programmes aimed at the same objective, its primary role is more important than all these: the recruitment and training of police officers. Recruitment, in recent years, has been stepped up through the increasing use of television and newspaper advertising and lectures to university students in the hope of encouraging the more academic to the service. This in itself has been successful, though students with 'O' and 'A' level qualifications are now more common than usual in the police force. In fact, some standard along these lines is usually required before young men are considered for acceptance. Training, initially, is usually at a fairly local level, each force running its own scheme where recruits learn the basics of police methods and the rudiments of law and court procedures.

But perhaps the biggest step in encouraging a high academic standard and the quest for promotion came in 1953, when the National Police College moved to the magnificent Bramshill House in Hampshire, a large Renaissance mansion set in 250-acre grounds and including an 18-acre lake. Earlier, it had been sited at Ryton-on-Dunsmore near Coventry and it was the success there that encouraged Whitehall to invest in the impressive 1612 house. It is here that higher professional and academic studies can be undertaken. In a sense, all the studies are professional in that they relate to police work, but the College already has an impressive record of its students moving to full-time university courses as a direct result of their achievements at Bramshill.

The first of these went in 1964 on Bramshill Scholarships and already more than 150 officers have won university places. Obviously, most of them were 'mature students' in that their ages ranged from 25 to 36 years, and there were initial fears they would be unable to compete with youngsters fresh from the sixth form, their minds already geared to concentrated academic study. But Mr Philip John Stead, Dean of Academic Studies at Bramshill explained: 'The reverse has proved to be true. The police officer's self-discipline, clear sense of purpose and Police College training have proved powerful academic assets.' The subjects they have studied include, not unnaturally, Law, Social Studies, Modern History, Modern Languages, Psychology and Economics. The results have already been impressive. One officer, without a single 'O' level, returned from university with a First Class in Law. Another, at the age of thirty-six, won a First Class Honours in History, and Second Class Honours is now considered the 'norm' for Bramshill men. They are now accepted by more than half of Britain's universities, including Oxford and Cambridge.

Some police forces actually run similar schemes themselves and these, along with the successes from Bramshill, have given the police service a significant cadre of university-trained officers. One of the real advantages of the college is that it gives the police officer a chance to sit back and think about principles as well as routine. It has been pointed out that policemen have little opportunity in normal circumstances for study or reflection. Again, while this is true of many occupations, it is particularly true of the police. For men are on duty on a shift basis, 365 days a year—and often with their leave and rest days cancelled. According to Mr Stead:

> It is not a holiday but a tonic change, making new demands on intellect and energy, and offering continuous challenge which always comes when the best people in a profession are brought together in a common task. In that situation, the students gain knowledge and understanding, including a better insight into himself as well as others.

Britain has always boasted it has the best police force in the world, and often this has been questioned, even ridiculed. But if Bramshill is anything of a guideline, the boast may well still be true. For the College has already, in only twenty-five years, won itself an international reputation. As an example, many of the College staff have taught and advised in Africa, Europe, Canada, the USA and the Caribbean. Further, its advice on higher police education is sought from all over the world. In fact, Bramshill has been such a terrific success that research is now going on into whether it would be possible to open a Police University where students would obtain degrees in Policemanship. The USA has a similar scheme in operation at the City University of New York which has incorporated the John Jay College of Criminal Justice—now enjoying close links with the activities of Bramshill.

chapter eleven

Courts, law and prisons

Lawyers who tell lies   Lord Goddard knew the five crooked barristers   Too
many acquittals   New oath to stop perjury   The confusion of conspiracy
Lord Chancellor supports lay magistrates   Bail hostels   Conflict on sentencing
Pensions to stay out of prison   'Life' for prison officers

British justice has for centuries been the envy of the world, the model and
foundation for many a developing society. The traditional sense of fair play has
always been synonymous with the British way of life, so much so, that any
cheap or under-hand act is automatically dubbed as 'not British'. Such universal
respect was not easily won and it is right that it should be preserved and
cherished. Would it be regarded, then, as unpatriotic, or even heresy, to suggest
that this whiter than white image is showing distinct signs of tarnish? Has fair
play not become gamesmanship? Does the blindfolded statue on top of the
Central Criminal Court at the Old Bailey symbolise our blind faith that right will
be done, or that we would rather not see what is being done in the name of
justice? There is little doubt that those who daily observe the machinery of the
law in all its components are concerned that the scales of justice are showing a
widening imbalance.

Probably the gravest aspect of the present trend in our 'let's-try-and-get-
away-with-it' society is the attitude of a growing group of lawyers. To watch and
listen to some of them propound wholly outrageous excuses and arguments for
their clients, in criminal trials especially, often makes the independent observer
wonder whether, in fact, these highly paid advocates should not be standing in
the dock themselves. Their seemingly careless regard for the truth, and their
enthusiasm for the half-truth, is distressing to witness.

One man, who is probably as well qualified to express this opinion as anyone
in Britain, is Sir Robert Mark, the Commissioner of the Metropolitan Police.
Late in 1973, when delivering the Dimbleby Lecture on BBC Television, he so
lambasted sections of the legal profession that some Members of Parliament
almost exploded with indignation, demanding his immediate resignation. The

lecture, delivered quietly and courageously, and watched by millions, caused a sensation. The legal profession, as many other groups do when under attack, immediately closed ranks, demanding that Sir Robert should name the guilty men. Prove it, was the almost unanimous cry accompanied by the advice that policemen should stick to catching criminals and not dabble in matters that do not concern them. A few, who shouted before thinking, suggested that instead of giving advice to the legal profession Sir Robert should put his own house in order first. This was a silly mistake. For it was at precisely this time that the Commissioner was completing one of the fiercest purges undertaken in any police force in the world. It was no secret that at the time Sir Robert took over the force it had rather more than its fair share of 'rotten apples'. But within a year he had ruthlessly rooted most of them out. With a clear conscience he could stand before the television cameras and say that his house was being put in order. He had not made himself popular among his men, but he had certainly gained their respect.

One of the many aspects of the legal system Sir Robert complained of was the increasing use by criminals and their lawyers of technicalities to secure an acquittal at any price. He said:

> Every effort is made to find some procedural mistake which will allow the wrong-doer to slip through the net. If the prosecution evidence is strong the defence frequently resorts to attacks on prosecution witnesses, particularly if they are policemen. They will be accused as a matter of routine of perjury, planting evidence, intimidation or violence. What other defence is there, when found in possession of drugs, explosives or firearms, than to say they were planted? Lies of this kind are a normal form of defence, but they are sure to be given extensive publicity.
>
> In many criminal trials the deciding factor is not the actual evidence but the contest between a skilled advocate and a policeman, or other witness, under this kind of attack, often what Lord Devlin calls 'the world of fantasy' created by a defence counsel at a loss for anything better to do on behalf of his client. The advocates for the defence are, for the most part, only doing their job. They are there to get their client off. In a hopeless or unpopular case this can be a distasteful task. To be a criminal lawyer needs professional knowledge, integrity and, when acting for the defence, moral courage. Whatever his personal feelings about the case the lawyer must devote himself to the cause of his client with all the persuasion and skill at his command. At the same time he also owes a duty to the cause of justice and the ethics of his profession.
>
> He must not put forward a defence which he knows to be false. It is not for a defence lawyer to judge his client's case. However unlikely his story may sound he is entitled to have it heard. But it is a different matter for an advocate to say things which he knows to be deliberate lies. To do this is not to take part in the administration of justice but to help to defeat it. Most lawyers observe very high standards. They manage to serve both their clients' and the public interest honourably and well. So much so that most of them tend to be frankly incredulous when it is suggested that there are some

lawyers who do not. The kind of behaviour I have in mind is often easy for the police to recognise but almost impossible to prove. We see the same lawyers producing, off the peg, the same kind of defence for different clients. Prosecution witnesses suddenly and inexplicably change their minds. Defences are concocted far beyond the intellectual capacity of the accused. False alibis are put forward. Extraneous issues damaging to police credibility are introduced. All these are part of the stock in trade of a small minority of criminal lawyers. The truth is, that some trials of deliberate crimes for profit—robbery, burglary and so on—involve a sordid, bitter struggle of wits and tactics between the detective and the lawyers. Public accusations of misconduct, however, have always been one-sided, with the result that the doubts about the criminal trial mostly centre upon police conduct, as if ti.e police alone had a motive for improper behaviour.

Let there be no doubt, that a minority of criminal lawyers do very well from the proceeds of crime. A reputation for success, achieved by persistent lack of scruple in the defence of the most disreputable, soon attracts other clients who see little hope of acquittal in any other way. Experienced and respected Metropolitan detectives can identify lawyers in criminal practice who are more harmful to society than the clients they represent. A conviction said to result from perjury or wrong-doing by police rightly causes a public outcry. Acquittal, no matter how blatantly perverse, never does, even if brought about by highly-paid forensic trickery.

Two examples demonstrating the lengths to which some lawyers are prepared to go to pull off an acquittal were cited by Sir Robert:

The first is a form of questioning to smear a member of the Flying Squad of unblemished character giving evidence in a strong case. 'Are you a member of the Flying Squad? And is it not a fact that four or more members of that Squad are presently suspended on suspicion of corruption?' Before the judge can intervene the damage is done. The jury is influenced by the smear in direct contravention of the principles governing the criminal trial. That kind of theme is played extensively and with infinite variations. The second example is what Conan Doyle would have called 'The Curious case of the Bingo Register'. This was a case in which a hardened criminal burgled a flat and wounded one of the elderly occupants very badly. He was identified, arrested, denied the offences and was remanded to prison. A month after committal for trial his solicitor disclosed an alibi defence which suggested that he was playing bingo at a club on the night of the offence and had signed the visitors' book. Enquiry showed that the prisoner had actually signed the book at the foot of the relevant page but that unfortunately for him the two preceding and the two following signatures were those of people with different surnames who had visited the club in one group and signed the book together. The signature could, therefore, have only been entered later and, it would seem, must have been written in prison. The prosecution notified the defence of their findings. Defence counsel thereupon withdrew from the case, as indeed, did the instructing solicitor. The prisoner, on the advice of his new solicitor and counsel, pleaded guilty and the matter rested there. It was not, of course, possible to prove who had taken the visitors' book to prison, although the prison authorities pointed out drily that only a visit by a lawyer or his clerk would be unsupervised and such visits had occurred. This was, in fact, a painstaking attempt to establish a false alibi for a dangerous persistent criminal.

It is interesting to compare this wholly dishonest and unethical act with a comment made by Earl Mountbatten of Burma who headed an investigation into prison security and escapes in 1966. In his report he wrote:

> The legal adviser of a prisoner who is party to any legal proceedings, whether civil or criminal, is allowed reasonable facilities for interviewing him in the sight of a prison officer, but out of his hearing. I have no doubt from my inquiries that on rare occasions, but those often the most serious, this facility is abused. I am also afraid that, very rarely, solicitors or their clerks have been used to convey information improperly to or from a prisoner.

Even in the early 1950s the Bar was deeply conscious of the black sheep in their midst. Mr Herbert Hannam, a former District Detective Chief Superintendent of the Metropolitan Police had his memory jogged by Sir Robert's television lecture as he recalled in a letter to *The Times:*

> In 1955 after months of investigation I gave evidence at the Central Criminal Court in a trial before Lord Goddard, who was then Lord Chief Justice. The defendants were a solicitor, a police officer and one other who were each sentenced to long terms of imprisonment for conspiracy to pervert the course of justice. On the day after sentence was passed, at four o'clock, on the direction of the then Commissioner, I attended the private chamber of Lord Goddard at the Law Courts. He had not risen and I was seated to await him. A few minutes later he entered the room, snatched off his wig, threw it on a table, looked at me and said; 'Ah! Hannam, I asked the Commissioner to let you call and see me.' He held out his hand, shook me warmly and continued, 'I wanted to tell you personally what a great service you have done to the community by catching that b . . . .' and he named the solicitor. We sat and had tea together and I was thrilled by his conversation. He mentioned by name five barristers and eleven solicitors and said, 'it is a pity we cannot get that lot as well. Every defence they put up is perjury and corruption is clear. It must break the heart of the police as well as shame their own profession. My brothers (fellow judges) know this as well as I.'

Defending the commissioner in a mounting storm of protest from lawyers, Mr Hannam added:

> That was eighteen years ago, the position is worse today and senior detective officers could still list the minority. The Bar Council and the Law Society know this but the sad feature is that while Sir Robert stressed that the police function is to ascertain the truth, leaders of the professions seem determined to cover up and by their current remarks even lead the public, whom they and the police serve, to conclude the Commissioner is biased and wrong and that

their members are pure.

As if anticipating the furore that was surely to follow, Sir Robert concluded his lecture unrepentant, demanding as of right to be able to express his views freely and unfettered.

> Some people cling to a curious, old fashioned belief that there is something vaguely improper in a policeman talking about the law, the courts and lawyers. No doubt the General Staff felt the same way about the infantryman on the Somme. But as Lord Devlin said, 'the police have a right to demand that the path that they must tread should be clearly designed to lead to a just result for the community for whom they act, as well as for the accused.' You simply cannot ask men to do one of the more difficult and sometimes dangerous jobs of our time and expect them not to reason why. Or if you do, you will be unlikely to get the kind of men you want. The policeman knows as much about crime and investigation as anyone. Of course his view should not necessarily prevail. But it should be heard. It may be the verdict of a minority, but our system of justice is too important to be left to any one section of society, lawyers or police.

Another telling observation Sir Robert made during his lecture, which was delivered in the presence of many eminent lawyers, concerned the law and those charged with the responsibility of framing new legislation.

> Once enacted, some laws are dumped like unwanted babies on the back door of the police station with little or no enquiry as to their eventual health. Some of them are found to be stillborn and others are dying for lack of teeth. Public criticism of their ineffectiveness is usually directed to the police rather than to the difficulties over which the police have no control, such as the process of trial.

Accepting that this was the 'policeman's lot', however, the Commissioner did not mince his words when it came to the frustrations felt by the police when cases came to court:

> Of all the people in England and Wales who plead not guilty and are tried by a jury, about half are acquitted. You may, perhaps, say to yourselves, 'Well, why not? Perhaps they really were innocent. How do the police know they were guilty?' But things are not quite so simple.
> For one thing, the English criminal trial never decides whether the accused is innocent. The only question is whether, in accordance with the rules of evidence, the prosecution has proved that he is guilty—and that is not at all the same thing. There may be all kinds of reasons why the jury does not think that the prosecution has proved guilt. They may think that he probably did it but that the defence has raised some reasonable doubt. Or sometimes a piece of evidence which would have put the matter beyond doubt is not available, or is excluded by the rules of evidence. Occasionally they are just taken in by a false but plausible, story, or by an exceptionally persuasive advocate. You must not, therefore, think that anyone who is acquitted must have been

innocent. There are many other possible explanations. But one thing is certain. Every acquittal is a case in which either a guilty man has been allowed to go free or an innocent citizen has been put to the trouble and expense of defending himself. There must be some rate of failure. We can't always expect to convict the guilty or never to prosecute the innocent. But in my opinion a failure rate of one in two is far too high. I doubt whether it would be tolerated in many other kinds of activity, so I certainly think it is something that needs looking into.

Sir Robert was undoubtedly right—there has never been a comprehensive investigation into the jury system and how it works. In fact, the very nature of the law as it is at present expressly forbids such an inquiry as jurors are not allowed to discuss with others their deliberations either during or after a trial.

For the purposes of research, however, it is difficult to see any objection to tape-recording all that is said in the jury's retiring room so that a fair analysis can be made of how they reached their verdict. The room could be secretly, but officially, 'bugged' so that at no time were the jurors conscious that their conversations were being overheard.

Some interesting research into the work of juries has been conducted by the Oxford Penal Research Unit which during one experiment installed 'shadow' jurors in courts to listen to evidence in twenty-eight criminal trials. The 'guinea pigs' were selected from the electoral roll and were a fair cross-section of all social classes. They were also paid the normal jury rate and when the 'real' jury retired they were also taken to a quiet room where they considered the evidence and recorded the verdict they would have brought in had they been trying the case. Short one-day trials were selected for the experiment; malicious wounding, larceny, assault on police and motoring and drug offences, and so on. At the end of the research period the 'shadow' jury, it was discovered, disagreed with the 'real' jury in seven cases out of twenty-eight. In five cases they were convinced of the defendants' guilt, although they were acquitted, and in the two other trials they felt the 'real' jury had returned guilty verdicts on innocent people. It is difficult to draw any hard and fast conclusions from these twenty-eight cases—after all, who is to say that the 'shadow' jury was more accurate than their 'real' colleagues—but it does indicate that here is a wide field in which more research is needed. Sir Robert took a somewhat similar view:

There is very little reliable information about how and why juries arrive at their verdicts because no one is allowed to listen to the discussions in the jury room. Lawyers obviously believe that public confidence in the jury would be undermined if this were allowed to happen. I find this curious. If exposing the truth about the jury would destroy the public's belief in its value, then surely it is high time that belief was destroyed. I cannot think of any other social institution which is protected from rational inquiry because investigation might show that it wasn't doing its job. My own view is that the proportion of those acquittals relating to those whom experienced police officers believe to be guilty is too high to be acceptable. I would not deny that sometimes commonsense and humanity produce an acquittal which could not be justified in law, but this kind of case is much rarer than you might suppose. Much more frequent are the cases in which the defects and uncertainties in the system are ruthlessly exploited by the knowledgeable criminal and his advisers.

After the dust had begun to settle and the Commissioner's views had been digested, the *Police Review,* a journal read by many thousands of policemen, and lawyers, commented drily: 'One thing you are not supposed to do when asked to deliver a foundation lecture, is to shake the foundations'. A few flaws in the foundations were discovered, however, by the Criminal Law Revision Committee, who in 1972 published a report following eight years' work by some of the leading lawyers in the country. Prefacing a number of recommended changes in criminal law they said:

There is now a large and increasing class of sophisticated professional criminals who are not only highly skilful in organising their crimes and in the steps they take to avoid detection, but are well aware of their legal rights and use every possible means to avoid conviction if caught. These include refusal to answer questions by the police and the elaborate manufacture of false evidence.

The committee felt that strict and formal rules of evidence, however illogically they may have worked in some cases in the past, may have been necessary in order to give the accused persons at least some protection against injustice. But with changed conditions, these safeguards were no longer serving a useful purpose, and in some cases were proving to be a hindrance rather than a help to justice. The committee were firmly of the view that the laws relating to evidence should be 'less tender to criminals'. Today, the innocent accused, reported the lawyers, has nothing to fear from a relaxing of many of the restrictions on admissibility of evidence, restrictions of which tend to be far too favourable to criminals. Throughout their long deliberations the committee was insistent that 'fairness' in criminal trials meant 'that the law should be such as will secure as far as possible that the result of the trial is the right one'. It also criticised the idea that a criminal trial was to be regarded as a kind of game played according to fixed rules in which a guilty person was entitled to acquittal if he could get the advantage of a legal technicality resulting from the rules.

The committee also spent a considerable time examining what is popularly called the 'accused's right of silence'. Under the present law, if the accused, when questioned or charged, fails to mention a fact on which he later relies in his defence, it is not permissible to draw an inference from his failure to mention the fact, that his evidence about that fact is false. This, decided the committee, was contrary to commonsense. An innocent person had nothing to fear from mentioning the facts which would exculpate him and would naturally be expected to do so, whereas the guilty, by delaying producing the false story until his trial, may prevent the prosecution from checking it and proving it false. It was proposed, therefore, that if the accused failed, when being interrogated by a police officer or anyone charged with the duty of investigating charges, to mention a fact which he afterwards relies on, the jury may draw such inferences as appear proper in determining the question before them, and the failure may be treated as corroborating any evidence given against the accused to which the failure is material.

There was a minority on the committee, however, that was nervous of this recommendation being implemented until the use of tape recorders at all police stations had become compulsory. A number of police stations have been issued with recorders, for experimental purposes only. A Home Office committee made up of lawyers, police and other interested parties is to make a careful detailed study before recommending to Parliament that the use of tape recorders during interviews should become statutory.

On the question of the police caution, a requirement in the judges' rules which states that at a certain stage in an investigation the police must tell a suspect that he is not obliged to say anything, the committee found that it should be abolished as it would be wholly inconsistent with their proposals concerning the right of silence. Instead it was recommended that the accused, when charged, should be handed a written notice advising him to mention any fact on which he intended to rely in his defence and warning him that if he held this fact back until his trial, it might have a bad effect on his case.

The committee also explored the knotty problem of unsworn statements, a device used by many experienced criminals to have their say in court before a jury without going into the witness box where they can be cross-examined by counsel. The committee considered that this aspect of the present law was far too favourable to the defendant. When a 'prima facie' case had been made out against him it should be incumbent on the accused to give evidence. This would effectively tear down the protective shield that many hide behind and force the accused to choose between either remaining silent or making a statement on oath in the witness box. Where he decided to remain silent the jury would be entitled to draw such inferences as were proper from his refusal to give evidence or answer questions. The judge, in his summing up, might also remind the jury that the accused's refusal may be considered as corroboration of the evidence given against him. In many ways this was one of the most controversial points of the Revision Committee's report, for it would give the jury discretion to arrive at a verdict not wholly based on the evidence they had heard. At the end of every trial the judge goes out of his way to tell the jury that they are the judges of the facts in the case and that they should rely only on the evidence they have heard in court. If this new recommendation is adopted it means that the jury will be entitled to give the prosecution the benefit of the doubt, if any—a complete reversal of the accepted basic principles of British justice that the accused is entitled to the benefit of the doubt, where it exists.

The oath, one of the very cornerstones of the legal system, also came under examination by the committee who recommended that it should be replaced with a less flowery and more direct promise to tell the truth. The centuries old oath—I swear by Almighty God that the evidence I shall give shall be the truth, the whole truth and nothing but the truth—is, it is considered by many practising in courts, to be something of an irrelevance in an age where religious principles and beliefs are nowhere near as universal as they were. The highly respected and influential legal commission, Justice, takes a similar view, feeling that the oath should be simplified and emphasising that if a person lied he would be liable to a criminal prosecution. A report by Justice said that the existing oath had 'lost its virtue' as the religious and moral outlook of society had changed down the years. The report added:

> There can be little doubt that a large proportion of wrong decisions in our civil and criminal courts result from perjury. There is equally little doubt that the incidence of perjury is widespread and that it is frequently committed without shame and without effective sanction.

The special committee set up to look into the whole question of the oath and perjury, under Mr Muir Hunter QC, made this proposal:

> After the conviction of a witness for perjury, a convicted person who has suffered any injury should be given an unfettered right of appeal with legal aid and the right to apply for a new trial. A tort of perjury should be established giving the victim a right to sue for damages. Alternatively, a judge should be given the power to award compensation and the Criminal Injuries Board should be allowed to pay compensation where the convicted perjurer has no means.

The committee proposed the new oath should be drawn up on the lines similar to: 'I solemnly declare and promise that I will tell the truth. I am aware that if I tell a lie I am liable to be prosecuted'. The last sentence may be rewritten to state: 'I am aware that if I tell a lie or wilfully mislead the court (or tribunal) I am liable to be prosecuted'. Explaining the need for a change in the oath, Mr Geoffrey Garrett, Chairman of the executive committee of Justice said:

> We are proposing that the threat of spiritual damnation be replaced by the threat of civil and legal sanction. We think that the warning of legal sanction will have more effect on a person's mind. It is a reflection of our society today. Religion is declining in significance and the sanction in the present oath is no longer so imposing.

It was also felt that instead of a witness reading the oath from a card or repeating it after a court official, it should be administered either by the judge or magistrate in the court. This would give the meaning of the oath far greater authority, solemnity and meaning, and would help focus the full attention of the witness on the consequence of telling an untruth. Under the present law a perjurer cannot be sued for damages, although, as Mr Garrett pointed out: 'A lie in court or before a tribunal can be as much a cause of personal injury as a theft, assault or dangerous driving'. After a three-year study into the whole question of perjury the committee estimated that only about forty or fifty convictions for perjury were secured each year, although it was common knowledge that false evidence was often given in court.

In the summer of 1973 the Law Commission published a report of their investigation into conspiracy, another thorny subject which has caused heated arguments between lawyers for decades. After skilfully threading their way through the labyrinth of case law, they proposed that the offence of conspiracy should be limited to cases of conspiracy to commit crime. This would place severe restrictions on the existing common law conspiracy which makes it an offence to conspire to commit any unlawful act. They were also aware that their new proposal could leave several gaps which might have to be plugged with creation of new offences. The Commission was undoubtedly mindful that only a few weeks before they published their report the House of Lords had decided that a conspiracy to trespass was a criminal act, although trespass itself was a civil matter. Lord Hailsham of Marylebone, then the Lord Chancellor, delivered the main part of the judgement in that case, and it was clear that he was strongly in favour of a wide interpretation of conspiracy. But if the new proposal is ever enacted by Parliament, conspiracy to trespass, for example, would no longer be an offence. Other, somewhat lesser offences involving sit-ins and demonstrations, which take on serious proportions when tagged with the word 'conspiracy', would also be dealt with in a less dramatic manner. Much of the anger caused by the bringing of some conspiracy charges can be directly attributed to the muddle-headed way legislators and lawyers have chosen to interpret the law relating to conspiracy. The Law Commission was sympathetically aware of some of the problems. Its report stated:

It seems to us not merely desirable, but obligatory, that legal rules imposing serious criminal sanctions should be stated with the maximum clarity which the imperfect medium of language can attain. The offence of conspiracy to do an unlawful act offends against that precept in two ways. First, it is impossible in some cases even to state the rules relating to the object of criminal agreements except in terms which are at best tautologous and unenlightening. Secondly, in those cases where at least a statement of the offence is possible, that statement covers such a wide range of conduct that it is impossible (assuming a set of facts established) to decide whether an offence has been committed or not. It seems, to us, therefore, that the offence of conspiracy to do an unlawful, though not criminal, act ought to have no place in a modern system of law.

The often criticised practice of including a count of a particular offence and another count of conspiracy to commit that offence on the same indictment, should continue but only in very limited circumstances, and the onus should be on the prosecution to decide at the outset which charge to proceed with, said the report. The Commission was also concerned with the penalties following conviction of conspiracy. At present anyone found guilty of conspiring to commit even a trivial offence can be sent to prison for life. Instead the commissioners proposed a two-tier system of penalties. Where the conspiracy involved the commission of one offence only, the maximum sentence would not be allowed to exceed the maximum which could be imposed for committing the substantive offence. Where, however, there was a conspiracy to commit a series of offences of the same kind, the penalty would be raised to twice the maximum for the substantive offence. It was proposed that a conspiracy to commit one summary offence, which can be tried by magistrates, should be no offence at all, but conspiracy to commit a series of summary offences of the same kind should become indictable and carry a maximum penalty of two years' imprisonment.

While conspiracy, perjury and many of the other more 'glamorous' headline-catching crimes continue to exercise the most eminent legal brains in the country, the very grass roots of the legal system—the lay magistrates—should not be ignored. Of all criminal cases brought before the courts each year 90 per cent are handled by magistrates, men and women whose only qualification for the awesome task of acting as judge and jury is their innate commonsense. They have many critics and are often the butt of jokes but the British legal system could not function without them. Their training and selection leaves much to be desired but few would question their honest application of the rules of fair play and humanity. It is undoubtedly true that they are slower than their professional counterpart, the stipendiary, but then many of them are untrained in the law. Neither do they receive an annual salary, like the full-time magistrate, of about £8,000. It is also a fact, although this is no fault of their own, that they, generally speaking, come from one section of the community—that section which can afford to give up a minimum of twenty-six half days a year to sit on the bench without financial hardship.

Soon after Lord Hailsham was appointed Lord Chancellor in 1971 he was quick to reveal himself as a champion of the part time justices. In a speech opening new courts in Blackpool he said:

> I would regard the abolition of the lay magistracy as a sheer disaster and
> politically as sheer lunacy—far more so, in a way, than the abolition of trial by
> jury. Admittedly, in a busy city centre a stipendiary magistrate is necessary to
> get through the mere volume of work—and very well indeed they discharge
> their difficult and responsible, though often distasteful work. For sheer
> competence, for getting through seventy cases or so in the course of a
> morning's work there is, of course nothing to touch them, and, as I say, there
> is no other practical way of coping when the work reaches a certain level. I
> also admit that a lay bench is considerably strengthened when it is thickened
> up by the addition of a professional lawyer or two working for nothing in his
> spare time. But the public do not like their case being dealt with summarily
> by a single man, however professional he may be. They do not like to feel that
> justice is administered like a production line in a factory. They like to see two
> or three magistrates on the bench and recognise them as respected local
> figures. And they are right. What they lose in professionalism they gain in
> local knowledge. What they lose in speed they gain in the added humanity of

having three quite differently constituted human beings putting their heads together.

A growing tendency among many lay magistrates, for which they can be quite properly criticised, is their reluctance to grant bail in many cases. Figures published at the end of 1973 showed that of 44,501 men and women charged with criminal offences and remanded in custody 2,186 were eventually acquitted and a further 15,648 were convicted but not given custodial sentences. These figures substantiate a long-held belief by many lawyers that some magistrates use remands in custody as a shock lesson to the accused in cases where they have no intention of finally passing a prison sentence.

The most comprehensive analysis of the bail system was carried out by the Cobden Trust, which concluded that bail was being refused to far too many people, and in some thousands of cases the question of bail was not even mentioned. Half the cases studied in the survey showed that magistrates made up their minds about the question of bail with no further information about the accused other than the charge he faced. In only about one-third of the cases did the magistrates have any information about the accused's family, employment and accommodation. By far the most important and persuasive influence on the decision finally taken by the justices comes from the police. There is nothing sinister in this as more often than not the police are the only people in court able to supply information about the accused, unless he is legally represented. When opposing a bail application the police usually rely on what have almost become stock objections; the man has a previous record, there is reason to believe he will abscond, he will interfere with witnesses, and there are further inquiries still to be made. Having heard that list, few magistrates would be prepared to grant bail. There is no doubt, however, that some magistrates are too timid and seem almost afraid to stand against the police. Often, ample sureties are available and willing to stand, with many defendants promising to report twice daily to the police, if necessary, to prove their good intentions. Apart from this apparent weakness on their part there are many flaws in the system which leave the magistrate practically powerless. The homeless and the drifters, for example, are often remanded in custody solely because they have nowhere else to go.

The Home Office, acutely aware of the position, is giving careful consideration to the establishment of bail hostels to alleviate this very situation, so that as well as keeping a man out of prison, thus saving the cost of his upkeep, a man could find employment proving, in the intervening period before his next appearance in court that given a chance he can be a useful member of society. Clearly there is a case for implementing a suggestion by the Law Society that all magistrates courts should have the free services of a 'duty solicitor', to ensure that anyone requiring legal advice gets it at the precise moment he needs it most. Also worthy of consideration is the attachment of an 'amicus curiae' to act as an independent 'friend of the court', assisting the bench on matters not directly affecting the charge but relevant to side issues, such as the question of bail, legal aid and domestic problems.

Some magistrates, unable to decide what to do with a defendant, adopt a somewhat cowardly attitude and make an order remanding the accused into custody for medical reports. Unless there is another and more serious reason for taking such a step this is obviously a wrong and weak decision. To keep a person in a remand prison costs between £35 and £40 a week and most remands for medical reports are of two weeks' duration, although some magistrates still insist on three weeks despite a Home Office circular suggesting that fourteen days was long enough. There is obviously a strong case for having medical and psychiatric reports on remand prisoners whose liberty is being taken away for other reasons but it seems indefensible to lock up a man or woman solely for a doctor's report. Any medical service provided in prison can be equally well supplied outside by the National Health Service. In fact, three prisons, at Durham, Risley and Brixton, operate an out-patient service, a service, incidentally which is poorly used by the courts.

It has been estimated that in Britain's prisons on any one day of the year there are about 4,700 men and women—all unconvicted. Ignoring the hardship, suffering and in some cases the blatant injustice of such a situation, it costs the taxpayer more than £8 million a year, money which could be well spent on providing bail hostels designed to keep people out of prison and in full-time employment. Many magistrates, especially in the London suburban area, would perhaps think twice about keeping people in custody if they spared the time to visit a remand prison such as Brixton, the largest in Britain. A penal institution as far back as 1819, the prison was originally designed to hold a maximum of 450 men. On any normal day now the number of inmates awaiting trial exceeds 800, with men sharing cells with one or two others. On fine days they are allowed one hour's exercise, but if it rains or is too cold they are cooped up in their cells, idly lying on their beds, for the day and night. Such an aimless existence can last anything from half-a-dozen weeks to as many months, boredom turning to frustration which often explodes into violence. The authorities try their best to segregate the first offenders—although, of course, they are still technically innocent—from the 'old lags', but sheer lack of accommodation often makes this impossible. To the genuinely innocent, and first offenders, it can be a nightmare experience and one that magistrates should seek to avoid when considering disposal of cases before them.

The need to ensure that the right people are kept out of prison has become as important as the necessity of incarcerating the worst kinds of public enemy. Some of the provisions under the Criminal Justice Act, 1972, were obviously tailored especially with those needs in mind and could, if allowed to work effectively, cut the present prison population of about 37,500 by half. The Act gave the courts four alternatives to sending people to prison. The first was the Community Service Order. This was a scheme run by the probation service in which offenders were offered the opportunity of undertaking up to 240 hours work in the community as a direct alternative to prison. The scheme started on an experimental basis in six areas—Nottinghamshire, Shropshire, Durham, Inner London, South-West Lancashire and Kent. Nottinghamshire was one of the first to become operational and by the end of 1973 a total of 130 people had received community service orders. Of these only seventeen defaulted and five of them were subsequently sent to prison. The remainder worked hard, grateful to be spared a prison sentence. Among the tasks undertaken by the offenders were clearing of disused canals and waterways, decorating and repairing the homes of the elderly and, in some cases, work with children.

Although the scheme is administered by the local probation service it was noticeable that many of the tasks provided came from outside voluntary organisations. Many probation officers are concerned that the whole system could break down at any time solely through lack of ideas for new and worthwhile work. Only one other country has tried a similar scheme, Poland, and it collapsed simply through lack of work and interest on the part of the community. Apart from the obvious social advantages of keeping people out of prison whenever possible, the economic side should not be ignored. To keep a person occupied for the full 240 hours costs about £140—to lock him up for nine months costs about £1,400.

Two other schemes under the Act, Day Training Centres and Adult Probation Hostels, although obviously more costly to implement and organise, could go a long way to cutting the prison population. The first four Day Training Centres were set up in London, Liverpool, Sheffield and Pontypridd, and half-way through 1974 there were signs that with time the scheme could become successful. The setting up of Adult Probation Hostels, considered by many concerned with penal reforms as a logical progression of the juvenile scheme, has been hindered in some areas by local communities objecting to the siting of the hostels near their homes. As early as 1971 the Government set itself a target of 110 hostels to be dotted about the country, providing 1,750 beds, and for once, it seemed there was no shortage of money to finance the buildings. The National Association for Care and Resettlement of Offenders, conscious that the whole scheme could be easily shelved if building plans continued to be obstructed by local objections, launched a national campaign of 'public education' in an attempt to dispel the fantasies that all offenders are violent sex maniacs. Slowly the message went home and the blockage on many hostel plans was grudgingly freed.

Another alternative to prison offered in the Act was the establishment of Detoxification Centres where offenders with drink problems could be treated. Increasingly now alcoholism is being regarded as a disease rather than a weakness of moral fibre. It is also becoming far too costly to use prisons as drying-out clinics for drunks, bearing in mind it would cost about £40 a week to keep them 'off the bottle'. In the year before the Act was introduced 3,261 people in England and Wales were sent to prison for simple drunkenness and of these 3,038 served sentences of less than a month. There is no doubt that drunks are a nuisance, occasionally offensive and abusive, often a danger to themselves and sometimes to others, but it has never been statistically proved that a spell in prison has ever helped to swell the membership of the Band of Hope!

In fact, the whole concept of judicial punishment is in dire need of review and revolution, and ironically, the poor financial state of Britain in the mid-1970s has now produced a climate where far more alternatives to prison must of necessity be found. Quite by accident the decade may prove to see greater penal reform than any this century. The Criminal Justice Act was a fine base for reform. Under Section 23, courts were given the power to seize and sell property used in connection with the commission of crime, thereby helping to compensate the victim. Although in itself this was not a revolutionary change in a law, it did help to involve the victim, often the one person overlooked. It is significant that in the early part of the 1970s an organisation was formed calling itself the National Victims Association, its main aims being to help victims of crime. They were quick to focus attention on one form of injustice which has caused anger for a long time. Its chairman, Alderman Charles Irving of Cheltenham, said soon after it was founded:

> Every year thousands of innocent people are being blackmailed into paying for crimes they did not commit—by Britain's two big power suppliers, the State-owned Gas and Electricity Boards. They are the consumers whose meters are broken open and robbed by thieves who are never caught. Under current gas and electricity supply agreements, customers are held responsible for all cash losses and damage. If they do not pay up they are cut off. The idea that poor people or pensioners who had already suffered the shock of a break-in, should actually pay for the privilege of being victims, could only have been conceived by a mindless bureaucracy like the Gas or Electricity Board.

It is certainly a fair point to make and obviously an ideal case where the offender, if caught, should be made to pay some form of compensation.

Whenever the question of punishment is debated the protagonists immediately fall into two camps, and rarely can reason shake the blind obstinacy of either side. They are as committed as the Protestants and the Catholics, the left-handed and the right-handed. One side, according to the other, is made up of the 'softies' and the 'do-gooders' while they argue with the 'hang-em-and-birch-em' brigade. Extremists from both sides constantly grab the headlines and the limelight, casting shadows over the many who try to tread the middle road of commonsense. When all the arguing is done, is it not a question with a simple alternative? Should courts impose penalties as punishments for past crimes or pay regard to the prevention of future crimes? Retribution or rehabilitation? One has only to delve into contemporary archives to discover that even some of the country's most eminent judges and lawyers cannot agree which should be paramount in their minds when it comes to sentencing offenders.

Lord Salmon, regarded by many at the Bar to be one of the wisest men ever to have graced the Bench, made his position clear in 1973 when he delivered the Riddell Lecture to the Institute of Legal Executives:

> There is no doubt that severe prison sentences do act as a deterrent. They are the only weapon Society has with which to defend itself. If we increase the

certainty of apprehension and then award the appropriate sentences, I feel confident that we shall conquer this wave of crime that now threatens to engulf us.

Short prison sentences, he added, were useless:

> That just gives the young man a cachet with his friends; but the idea of losing his liberty for a long time is a real deterrent; and it does not wring my withers that a man, even a young man, who has used his liberty to maltreat his fellow human beings, should be deprived of the opportunity of doing so for a long time to come.

He then dealt the so-called 'softies' a devastating blow:

> For them there is no such thing as a criminal responsibility or wickedness or fault or blame. According to their philosophy, the man who commits some cold-blooded, premeditated, brutally vicious attack on a fellow human-being is no more to be blamed than if he himself is suffering from a severe attack of chicken pox or German measles. Just as in one instance his spots are merely symptoms of the disease, so in the other instance his actions are merely symptoms of a maladjustment for which he cannot be blamed. The fault lies, according to this theory, solely with modern social conditions, the environment in which he has to live, and possibly heredity. It follows, because that man is not to be blamed, that it would be unjust for him to be punished as a criminal; he should be treated only as a patient. Can I be bold enough to say that, in my view, this is nonsense, and dangerous nonsense, too? It means that we might as well close the courts of criminal law and shut the prisons, which as far as I know, together with our police force, are the only weapons which society has for defending itself against crime.

Sir Brian MacKenna, a brother judge, and one with long experience of criminal law, took almost the opposite view when he lectured to a summer school organised by the Howard League for Penal Reform only a few weeks later. Had we not experimented too much in the past, he asked, and was it not now time to consider more moderate sentences for some serious crimes? He questioned whether exceptionally heavy sentences served any useful purpose and suspected that the range of even normal sentences was unnecessarily high:

> The material I have examined, so far as it goes, does not tell against the experiment I would make of lowering the level of penalties for some, at least, of the more serious offences, although I recognise that there are obstacles to the making of the experiment which are not easily overcome.

One of these, said Sir Brian, was the belief, which died hard, that the sentencer should have the retributive aim of punishing the offender, whatever might be the effects of the punishment. 'Perhaps our penal code, when it comes, will define the aims of criminal punishment and will exclude retribution once and for all', he commented.

That sort of attitude was just what was wrong with the present legal system, claimed a number of lawyers and magistrates who held a meeting in Accrington, Lancashire, to form a group known as the Crime Punishment Reformers. This group, lead by local solicitor, Mr George Pratt, who is also clerk to the bench, blamed what they called the 'do-gooders' who had infiltrated the system, causing it to deteriorate. Many of them, claimed the group, were sociologists associated with courts who were 'half baked and half trained'. They were helping to frustrate the magistrates who could not hand out the sort of punishments they felt appropriate. Mr Pratt told his group:

> A succession of do-gooding administrators and politicians had eroded an effective system of dealing with criminals and it was time the trend was reversed. Since the war punishment has become a dirty word. The avowed object is to achieve remedial treatment as if the average criminal was a person suffering from a disease and was to be treated as a patient. This was not true in one case in 100. Apart from the inadequate types, most criminals are bad; some are positively wicked. The attitude towards criminals has been largely determined by theoretical sociologists who, despite protests of judges, magistrates and leading police officers, have had a dire influence on successive governments.

It is fair to guess that the blood pressure of the staunch men of Accrington would have shot up several degrees had they read a report of remarks made by Judge Kingham. During a conference he called on employers to let people with criminal records 'jump the jobs queue' over people who had never appeared before a court. At the same time he also said he was going to urge his brother judges and magistrates to 'bend over backwards' to let petty criminals keep their freedom. Petty criminals make up a large percentage of the prison population, he said, mainly for offences against property.

> For such crimes, generally speaking, people should not be sent to prison even if they have a record of previous convictions. They do not benefit from going, and the public certainly do not benefit if, when they come out, they go and commit further offences. Prison is simply a place of incarceration and we are deluding ourselves if we think that it is anything other than that. I do not think retribution is consistent with humanity or with a moral sentence. I do not think that anyone can look at the figures and walk out into the street with their heads held high. I think it is a disastrous situation. The plain fact is that the present system of sentencing is not a success.

Read and re-read, Judge Kingham's words were not, in fact, so 'way out' as at first they may have seemed. As he explained, 70 per cent of all ex-Borstal boys commit further crime and 50 per cent of those held in detention centres eventually end up in prison. A term of imprisonment is only effective if it convinces the offender that it is the last place in the world he ever wants to return to. It is at this point that the two groups of extremists most fiercely differ. One faction says that prison should be so tough that no one in his right mind would ever want to go back; the other feels that life should be less regimented and more relaxed, with all efforts concentrated on rehabilitation.

The Howard League for Penal Reform seemed to hit on a good old fashioned compromise in its annual report published in September 1973. The nineteenth-century 'fortresses' should be pulled down and at the same time the prison building programme should be drastically cut. 'We do not want a large number of new prisons in remote places, with all the resultant difficulties for visiting, finding work for prisoners and staffing', they reported. Part of the money available should be spent instead on greatly increased non-custodial measures. And part should also go to help improve accommodation and employment opportunities for the homeless, the isolated and the others at risk, with varying degrees of support. For the significantly smaller number who need secure accommodation money should be spent on replacing the old prisons with purpose-built premises which could be converted to other uses when the prison population declined. The League also claimed that there was some evidence to show that 'attitude-changing regimes' could be most effective during eighteen months or less, although many courts were still imposing heavy sentences as 'punishment'.

Keeping a man on the 'straight and narrow' after he has been discharged from prison is a matter both the League and the National Association for the Care and Resettlement of Offenders view with increasing concern. They have accused the Home Office of being mean with the discharge grants given to prisoners, a factor which they feel helps a man to relapse into crime. Both organisations launched a campaign to pressure the Home Office to increase the £4 grant. Nine other similar bodies joined the campaign, significantly one was the National Association of Probation Officers, which provided evidence to show the grant was hopelessly inadequate. Despite the meteoric rise in the cost of living the grant had not been increased since the middle 1960s. Without help from friends or relatives outside, freedom was for many almost as miserable as prison itself.

With so little in their pockets they could not secure accommodation and without a proper address they could not qualify for other State benefits. The vicious circle, or the bureaucratic obstacle course, as the NACRO described it, often led straight back to prison, with only the very determined able to survive the temptation of petty crime to raise some quick cash. According to leaders of the campaign the absolute minimum required was £12 a week for at least the first fortnight, to give reasonable chance of finding a room. This would increase the Home Office's prison budget by about £1 million a year—hardly likely to bankrupt a Government Department which at that time, 1973, planned to spend £110 million of a five-year prison building programme.

Acceptance of a scheme at present operating in Denmark, might, however, raise more than a few eyebrows in Whitehall. There, some prisoners are given £60 a month pensions to help them keep out of trouble. Dr Georg K. Sturup, the medical superintendent at Herstdvester detention centre where some of the early work on the experiment was conducted, claimed that it was cheaper to pay a pension than for the community to lose property by theft. Over a period of about ten years 120 of his 'clients', as he called them, were monitored, and for five years 91 of them, high risk chronic criminals, were followed after receiving their 'disablement pension'. Only a fifth of them went back to prison. The normal rate in Denmark was about 50 per cent. Explaining his somewhat revolutionary approach to penal reform Dr Sturup said:

> It is necessary that we disregard our deep rooted moral prejudices. The result of the prejudices has, until recently, been that we would not allot a chronic criminal the same economic support as we, with good conscience, give to fellow citizens who are insufficient in their working abilities due to heart disease, rheumatism, as well as psychic diseases of different sorts. It is necessary to be realistic and give this group of fellow citizens the disablement pension, which can make it possible for them to become established in an independent little flat and—what may also be important—to re-evaluate their own situation and experience themselves as people on pension, not as ex-convicts.

It seems that such a Utopian situation will have to remain a dream for many years in Britain before such liberalism becomes a reality. There is no evidence that the British are any more hard-hearted than their contemporaries on the continent but there is plenty of statistical proof that the problem here could be said to match. For example: at the beginning of 1973 there were 888 people serving life sentences—682 of them for murder. It would take a very persuasive man to convince the Home Secretary, and the electorate as a whole, that some, if any, of these men, should be given a pension, especially at a time when there is a strong lobby for the return of hanging and corporal punishment.

In May 1972, one of those curious things that foreigners automatically associate with the 'Mad English' happened—the prisoners formed their own trade union. In an impressive document entitled 'Charter of Rights' the organisation PROP (Preservation of the Rights of Prisoners) laid down a twenty-five point 'New Deal'. It began:

> The following demands are made by PROP on behalf of all prisoners who are, or have been, or will be, inmates of penal institutions in England, Wales, Scotland and Northern Ireland. PROP calls upon the Crown, Parliament, Her Majesty's Government, the Home Secretary and the Prison Department to accede to those demands and to initiate such legislation and issue such directives as may be necessary to secure the early establishment and effective implementation of the following rights of prisoners.

Such a forthright, and many thought downright cheeky, approach deserved to be noticed, if nothing else. The charter demanded:

> The right to membership of PROP and the right to communicate with, consult with, and receive visits from representatives of PROP:
> The right to conduct elections within penal institutions on behalf of PROP with a view to the appointment of local representatives of that body and the

election of delegates to its national committees:

The right to stand for elections as a local representative of PROP and once elected to participate in the decision-making process, to attend all policy and staff meetings within the prison and to act as spokesman for his or her members in all matters relating to their pay, working and living conditions, leisure pursuits and general welfare.

The right to vote in National and Local Government elections:

The right to Trade Union membership and the right to have their pay and conditions determined by negotiations between the Home Office and the prisoner's elected representatives:

The right to institute legal proceedings of any kind, including actions against servants of the Crown, without first securing the consent of the Home Office:

The right to contact legal advisers in confidence without interference, intervention or censorship by the penal authorities:

The right to be legally represented and to call defence witnesses in internal disciplinary proceedings to which the Press should have free access:

The right to parole provided certain well-established and widely known criteria are met. This right to be supplemented by the right to receive expert and independent assistance in the preparation of parole applications, to be present and/or legally represented at the hearing of applications, to have access to all reports considered by the Board from whatever source and the opportunity to refute allegations of misconduct or unsuitability, the right to a reasoned judgement on the Board's decision and the right of appeal to the High Court against that decision:

The right to communicate freely with the Press and the Public:

The right to consult with a legal adviser before being subject to judicial proceeding, including hearings by Magistrates or applications by the Police for remands in custody:

The right to be given reasons for any refusal to grant bail:

The right to be allocated to penal institutions within their home region:

The right to adequate and humane visiting facilities within all penal institutions, including the ability to exercise their conjugal rights:

The right to embark upon educational or vocational training courses at the commencement of any custodial sentence, including the right to sit examinations and to be given adequate and appropriate facilities.

The right to demand an independent inspection of prison conditions, including hygiene, food, working conditions, living accommodation and the provision of adequate leisure facilities:

The right to adequate exercise periods and the provision of recreational activities:

The right to consult an independent medical adviser:

The right to enter into marriage:

The right to attend funerals of all near relatives:

The right to own and sell the product of their leisure-time activities, including hobbies, fine arts and writing:

The right to receive toilet articles for personal use as gifts from relatives, friends and organisations:

The right to adequate preparation for discharge, including:

(i) Programmes of pre release courses devised in conjunction with prisoners

and their families to assist them with problems of Housing,
Employment, Education, Marriage Counselling and Child Care related
to their special needs.
(ii) The right to Home Leave to be extended to all prisoners.
(iii)The right of allocation to an open prison and followed by allocation to
the pre-release hostel scheme.
(iv) The right to a fully franked insurance card on discharge and the
supplementary rights thereby to full State benefits.
(v) An equal right with all other applicants to employment in State concerns
whether they be run by central or local authority.
The right to have all criminal records destroyed within five years of discharge
irrespective of the last sentence served.

If only half of these demands were granted prisoners would have more rights
and privileges than members of the armed forces, who of course, volunteer to
serve their country. Prisoners' wives are a vociferous group, too, and not
wanting to appear to be letting their menfolk down they also formed their own
'trade union' in the autumn of 1973 in North London. One of the founder
members, whose husband was serving eighteen years, petitioned the Home
Office with several demands, including full conjugal rights. They also wanted
uncensored letters and full trade union rates of pay for the work done inside
prison. Viscount Colville, the then Minister of State at the Home Office, did not
exactly enthuse over the idea of providing 'love nests' inside prison. He said:

The problems are insuperable. The prison service is not equipped to provide,
without embarrassment and indignity, visits of this sort for wives and
prisoners. In any case it would be difficult to know who to allow in for the
purpose. It is one of the classical examples of the loss of freedom.

Several wives had expressed their fear that unless their men had regular
female company they would become homosexuals. Women detained in
Ribibbia Jail, Rome, were also attracting attention at about that time—they
climbed onto the prison roof demanding that they should receive regular visits
from men.

Attempts by Members of Parliament to persuade the Home Office to
establish an experimental scheme for conjugal visits, even on a limited basis,
were finally rejected, when Mr Mark Carlisle, for the department, told the House
of Commons: 'There are questions of the selection of prisoners, selection of the
relationship of the woman outside, and the place in which the visits could take
place—the practical arguments against are overwhelming.'

A series of experiments began at Wormwood Scrubs prison, London, early
in 1971, aimed at reducing the abnormal sexual urge which led many to terms of
imprisonment for sex offences. The experiment involved twenty-eight men, half
of them inmates and the rest either on parole or probation and attending a
psychiatric out-patients department. After a period of two years during which
they had received a new drug, Benperidol, all reported that the abnormal sexual

desires had been abolished. Although the trial will have to continue for several years it is significant that three years after the experiment began not one of the fourteen men living outside the prison had been charged with any sexual offence. Tests in Belgium and Holland show that the drug has only minimal side effects, none of which include physical changes.

Another experiment involving prisoners, conducted by the Home Office in the middle of 1974, caused considerable alarm among politicians and penal reformers when it was learned that hitherto 'hard cases' were being reduced to tears as a result of their treatment. The experiment began at Wakefield Prison where a new block was opened, known as a 'control unit', to house thirty-nine men who were considered to be persistent troublemakers, or in Whitehall jargon 'subverters of prison order'. A similar unit was established a little later at Wormwood Scrubs, London, for twenty-eight men.

The units were designed to provide a strict regime where facilities were 'deliberately austere' so that in time the trouble-makers would realise that the only way to return to normal prison life with privileges they formerly enjoyed would be to co-operate with the prison staff. Troublemakers in prisons anywhere in Britain were sent to the units after being recommended by their prison governors and the move agreed by the Board of Visitors. Where the Board disagreed with the recommendation the Home Secretary had the power to over-rule their decision.

Once at the unit the prisoner faces a course of 'treatment' divided into two phases. The first is ninety days in solitary confinement with just an hour a day for exercise. Conditions are such that not only do they see little or nothing of their fellow inmates, they rarely see the prison staff for long periods; in fact, contact is not encouraged. The prison authorities, however, do dangle a 'carrot' before the prisoners: be of good behaviour for three months and you will be moved to the second phase. Bad behaviour can include shouting or swearing at a prison officer, smashing cell furniture or refusing to work. When the scheme was first introduced it was laid down that the punishment for misbehaving would be to start the 'treatment' afresh from the first day which meant in effect that no matter how many days or weeks, or even months, the prisoner had been 'good' they were forfeit by a single act of bad behaviour.

So, theoretically, it would be possible for some prisoners never to get past the first phase stage. After pressure from within the House of Commons and from penal reform organisations, the Home Office decided that instead of wiping the slate clean completely because of one outburst the Board of Visitors should make a monthly review of conduct and where they felt it necessary that a prisoner should be punished they could order that he should lose a given number of days.

In the second phase, called the associative stage, the prisoner has certain privileges returned: he is able to mix with fellow inmates in the unit during working and leisure periods. During this spell, also of ninety days duration, the prisoner is encouraged to co-operate with the staff. It was this lack of co-operation which resulted in his being moved to the unit, he is told by the authorities. Again, just one simple act of bad behaviour is sufficient to undo all the good. It is possible for the Board of Visitors to order that the 'process' should be re-started with a return to the first phase. The experiment, therefore, even for a 'model' troublemaker, must last for a minimum of six months, and for many it is considerably longer. It is too early yet to see the results of the experiment although the effect it is having on some of the 'guinea pigs' has caused considerable concern to some of their families.

The sister of one of the first men to be sent to Wakefield returned home shocked. Her brother, until his 'treatment' a normally cheerful, well-built young man, she found had lost weight, was nervous, depressed and disorientated. He wept when she had to leave at the end of an hour's visit.

The wife of another who had to do an extra thirty-five days in solitary confinement because of misbehaviour said her husband was becoming more intractable instead of more amenable. After a meeting between representatives of the National Council for Civil Liberties, the National Association for the Care and Resettlement of Offenders, the Howard League for Penal Reform, Radical Alternatives to Prison, and others, a letter was sent to Mr Roy Jenkins, the Home Secretary, calling for an end to the control units. They contravened the European Convention on Human Rights which prohibits 'inhuman or degrading treatment or punishment', said the group, which added:

> The treatment provided for by the control unit regime—extended isolation and the fear that a fixed term will become endless—is, we believe, so dangerous to physical and mental health that it should never have been contemplated by the Home Office or your predecessor.

While many schemes and plans are tried in an attempt to make prison life more meaningful to those detained it often seems that the Prison Department overlook one vital section of the prison population—the staff. The 13,000 officers—they object to being called warders—in Britain's 120 jails are much misunderstood men and women who genuinely believe that they perform a worthwhile service for their fellow men and women. Few occupations could offer so little satisfaction, environmentally or financially, and so much boring routine and restriction. 'We are the lifers', they say when the uninformed make public statements about the hopelessness faced by those who receive long prison sentences. With very few exceptions the majority of the officers, or 'screws' as the inmates call them, join the prison service as a vocation.

Like their colleagues in the police force, however, they are often accused of being extremist right-wingers, even Fascists at times, and always they seem to be in the middle, sandwiched in their case, between the law makers and the law breakers. They walk an unenviable tightrope. If they have to resort to force to maintain order and discipline they are immediately dubbed as brutal sadists. And yet, a small act of kindness such as smuggling a letter from a worried prisoner to his wife, could lead to a carpeting or even dismissal. New recruits to the service quickly find that there are many more rules and regulations governing their daily lives than there are for their charges.

Men entering the service start at between £25-£30 a week, and married men eventually receive rent-free accommodation. With 2,000 men and women short of established strength the officers have long been pressing for higher salaries to help with recruiting and so reduce the twenty or thirty hours a week overtime many of them are expected to work. In the summer of 1973 the officers, many of whom were suffering from acute domestic problems due to their long hours of work, decided to ban all overtime over fourteen hours a week. Ironically their staunchest supporters were the prisoners, many of whom wrote to the Home Secretary asking him to see they got more pay. This was not as completely charitable and friendly as it appeared on the surface. While the officers were refusing to work, the prisoners had to be locked up in their cells for long periods during the day and leisure time was cancelled, including watching television, because of the lack of supervision.

Eventually a new salary structure was introduced which for the time being meant prison life returned to normal. During their struggle for a better deal the Prison Officers' Association, which represents most of the staff, conducted research among its members and discovered several significant facts. At least one in four, for example, was associated with organisations caring for and helping ex-prisoners; 40 per cent were engaged with other civic undertakings and at least a third of the men and women at present working in prison wanted at some stage before they joined to become probation officers. Probably the most startling fact they unearthed was that unless pay and conditions showed a rapid improvement more than 50 per cent would not be in the prison service at retirement age. Only the prisoners, and not by any means all of them, would take much comfort from that thought.

chapter twelve

Coroners

The 'perfect' murder   Death certificates for the living   Exhumation traps
wife-killer   The Bovingdon Bug

The perfect murder, so easily committed by the least expected in thrillers, is not in reality so difficult to get away with. In fact, the ease with which it is possible to commit 'undetected homicide', as lawyers and pathologists prefer to call it, has alarmed a growing section of the medico-legal profession for several years. There is a gap in the law through which a cunning criminal can escape, quite legally disposing of his victim, without a hint of suspicion. There is some evidence, meagre it is true, that perfect murders are being committed on a scale larger than the authorities are prepared to admit.

Under the law as it is at present, a doctor is not required to see the body before issuing a medical certificate of the cause of death if he has attended the diseased during his last illness. This loophole makes the law vulnerable in three areas. The first is that the fact of death is not always properly established. Cases have been known where death certificates have been issued by doctors for the living. The second unsatisfactory aspect of the present law is that, where a doctor does not see the body, he could in certain instances record an inaccurate cause of death. The third criticism is that violent or unnatural deaths could be passed off as natural.

One of the first to raise the alarm was Dr J.D.J. Harvard who in 1960 published a book entitled *The Detection of Secret Homicides*. In the introduction he wrote: 'A substantial proportion of cases of homicide are accompanied by an attempt to get the death certified and registered and to get the body disposed of through the normal channels as a natural death.' Four years later the British Medical Association repeated Dr Harvard's warning and in a report entitled 'Deaths in the Community' stated: 'The issue of a death certificate from "natural causes" is a fairly common finding in cases which are afterwards found to have been cases of homicide, e.g. on exhumation.'

In March 1965 Sir Frank Soskice, then the Home Secretary, set up a committee under Mr Norman Brodrick QC (now a judge) to take a close look at the fears which were then growing that people were literally getting away with murder. Its terms of reference were to (a) review the law and practice relating to the issue of medical certificates of the cause of death, and for the disposal for dead bodies and (b) to review the law and practice relating to coroners and coroners' courts and the reporting of deaths to the coroner; and to recommend what changes might be desirable. During the next six-and-a-half years the committee made a thorough investigation into unnatural death. A significant survey conducted by the staff of the Department of Forensic Medicine at the London Hospital Medical College was especially studied by the committee. This showed that of the 28,108 autopsies carried out between 1963 and 1967 on behalf of coroners, there were 5,038 findings of unnatural deaths. The survey singled out 263 of these for special attention because they had either suggested that death had been due to natural causes or did not indicate any contrary opinion.

Of these previously unsuspected unnatural deaths one was found to be homicide (an old man of seventy-seven years who had been smothered with a pillow) and seventeen other cases (all deaths of infants) in which violence appeared to play a part. The committee also investigated twenty exhumations conducted in England and Wales between 1959 and 1968. A case in Plymouth first caught their eye. In this a woman, aged fifty-nine, was buried after her husband had told a doctor that she had fallen from his shooting brake and had been run over by the rear wheels. The doctor recorded the cause of death as multiple head injuries including severe fracture of the skull. A pathologist was convinced that the injuries were not consistent with the husband's story. The exhumation in this case was granted after an application from the lawyers representing the husband who was subsequently charged with murder and sent to prison for life. Another interesting case involved another Devon woman, aged seventy-seven, who died, according to the certificate, from coronary thrombosis. She had been confined to her bed for some time and her doctor saw her body soon after death. She was buried in March 1962. Soon afterwards her son confessed to killing her by suffocation. In September her body was exhumed and a pathologist found no evidence of suffocation but he reported that it was unlikely that death was caused by coronary thrombosis. The state of the body was such that it was impossible to give positive evidence either way. A jury returned a verdict of death by natural causes and confirmed the death certificate.

These and other cases were minutely examined by the committee which found little concrete evidence to convince them that the reports which lead to their being formed were more than merely alarmist.

Our general conclusions are that the risk of secret homicide occurring and remaining undiscovered as a direct consequence of the state of the current law on the certification of death has been much exaggerated, and that it has not been a significant danger at any time in the last fifty years. We have reached these views after examining all the statistical evidence which might have been expected to give an indication as to the existence of a number of secret homicides and after taking evidence from doctors, lawyers, police officers and criminologists. We do not say that there is no possibility whatever of a homicide being concealed under the present procedure for certifying deaths. What we do say is that, balancing all the relevant factors and observable probabilities, there is no requirement to strengthen the present machinery of death certification simply in order more efficiently to prevent or detect secret homicide. So far as detection of homicide is a relevant objective, the present certification system has worked as satisfactorily as any modern community could reasonably expect. Advances in medical science (and forensic medicine) are likely to maintain that position. Our task, therefore, has been to make sure that, in the future system of death certification, an autopsy will be performed in all cases in which there is any doubt about the medical cause of death or suspicion about the circumstances in which the death occurred.

The committee did, however, recommend that the law should be amended so that before a doctor issues a certificate of the fact and cause of death he should have seen the body.

In April 1974, more than two-and-a-half years after the committee report had been published and handed to Parliament, it had still not been discussed in the Commons and doctors, lawyers, coroners and politicians were asking 'Whatever Happened to Brodrick?' They were referring to the report, of course, and not the committee chairman who had long since returned to the Bench. The Home Office said it needed more time to study the 418-page report. Dr Harvard, who sowed the original seeds of doubt in the minds of many, was convinced that the reason nothing had been heard of Brodrick was because it was 'full of tendentious reasoning and sadly lacking in scientific evidence for the more sweeping of its recommendations'. In a letter to the *British Medical Journal* he wrote:

As pointed out in your leading article the report discounted the 'alarming assertions' contained in my own book, one of which was that a number of cases of thallium poisoning must have been disposed of as natural deaths as a result of failure to distinguish such cases from polyneuritis. This 'alarming assertion' based on authenticated cases, was dismissed by Brodrick.

With a stinging swipe at the committee he added:

It may be that the Government's reluctance to act on the report may have something to do with the fact that a few months after it was published the details of the Graham Young case were made known, in which a number of victims had been murdered by thallium, at least one of whom had been certified dead from polyneuritis.

The case of Graham Young is one of the most extraordinary and astonishing of its kind since the Second World War. At twenty-four he was sent to prison for life for murdering two workmates by poisoning. One was given a lethal dose of thallium, the other, antimony. He also attempted to murder four others. At the age of fourteen he was at the Central Criminal Court charged with attempting to poison his sister with belladonna and his father and a friend with antimony. He was sent to Broadmoor under Section 60 of the Mental Health Act, the trial judge recommending that he should not be released for at least fifteen years without the permission of the Home Secretary. In fact, he was released on licence in under ten years. Throughout his detention he secretly pursued his morbid interest in poisons through the library services provided at Broadmoor. Young, a psychopath joined a firm of photographic instrument makers as an assistant storekeeper at their plant at Bovingdon, Hertfordshire. One by one he selected his victims, dosed their tea or coffee with thallium or antimony and then kept a daily record of their reactions as he continued slowly to poison them. Two died in agony and at least six others were showing similar symptoms before the horrible truth dawned. At first the spate of illnesses puzzled doctors who put it down to a virus nicknamed the Bovingdon 'bug'. It was not until the two men had died that a pathologist, having read the Agatha Christie novel, *The Pale Horse,* in which the use of thallium was described, passed his suspicions to the police. It was not the perfect murder but the implications of the Young case would have undoubtedly exercised the Brodrick Committee had it happened sooner.

Acknowledgments

Pictures are published by courtesy of the *Daily Express, The Times* and Scotland Yard.